The Changing Economic Geography of Globalization

I0885548

The Changing Economic Geography of Globalization examines the effects that recent developments in capitalism have had on shaping the global map as well as analysing the effect on people and places which occupy different positions in the global economic system.

An international team of scholars are brought together to assess, both theoretically and empirically, the effects of globalization over space and to critically examine the prevailing debates. Collectively the essays in this volume challenge the belief that globalization shrinks time and space and leads to a homogenized global economy.

This book explores the relationship between globalization, capitalist development, local competitiveness, regional innovation systems, European enlargement, inequalities and growth.

Giovanna Vertova is an Assistant Professor in Political Economy at the University of Bergamo, Italy.

Studies in Global Competition

A series of books edited by John Cantwell, The University of Reading, UK, and David Mowery, University of California, Berkeley, USA

Volume 1
Japanese Firms in Europe
Edited by Frédérique Sachwald

Volume 2
Technological Innovation, Multinational Corporations and New International Competitiveness
The case of intermediate countries
Edited by José Molero

Volume 3
Global Competition and the Labour Market
Nigel Driffield

Volume 4
The Source of Capital Goods Innovation
The role of user firms in Japan and Korea
Kong-Rae Lee

Volume 5
Climates of Global Competition
Maria Bengtsson

Volume 6
Multinational Enterprises and Technological Spillovers
Tommaso Perez

Volume 7
Governance of International Strategic Alliances
Technology and transaction costs
Joanne E. Oxley

Volume 8
Strategy in Emerging Markets
Telecommunications establishments in Europe
Anders Pehrsson

Volume 9
Going Multinational
The Korean experience of direct investment
Edited by Frédérique Sachwald

Volume 10
Multinational Firms and Impacts on Employment, Trade and Technology
New perspectives for a new century
Edited by Robert E. Lipsey and Jean-Louis Mucchielli

Volume 11
Multinational Firms
The global–local dilemma
Edited by John H. Dunning and Jean-Louis Mucchielli

Volume 12
MIT and the Rise of Entrepreneurial Science
Henry Etzkowitz

Volume 13
Technological Resources and the Logic of Corporate Diversification
Brian Silverman

Volume 14
The Economics of Innovation, New Technologies and Structural Change
Cristiano Antonelli

Volume 15
European Union Direct Investment in China
Characteristics, challenges and perspectives
Daniel Van Den Bulcke, Haiyan Zhang and Maria do Céu Esteves

Volume 16
Biotechnology in Comparative Perspective
Edited by Gerhard Fuchs

Volume 17
Technological Change and Economic Performance
Albert L. Link and Donald S. Siegel

Volume 18
Multinational Corporations and European Regional Systems of Innovation
John Cantwell and Simona Iammarino

Volume 19
Knowledge and Innovation in Regional Industry
An entrepreneurial coalition
Roel Rutten

Volume 20
Local Industrial Clusters
Existence, emergence and evolution
Thomas Brenner

Volume 21
The Emerging Industrial Structure of the Wider Europe
Edited by Francis McGowen, Slavo Radosevic and Nick Von Tunzelmann

Volume 22
Entrepreneurship
A new perspective
Thomas Grebel

Volume 23
Evaluating Public Research Institutions
The U.S. Advanced Technology Program's Intramural Research Initiative
Albert N. Link and John T. Scott

Volume 24
Location and Competition
Edited by Steven Brakman and Harry Garretsen

Volume 25
Entrepreneurship and Dynamics in the Knowledge Economy
Edited by Charlie Karlsson, Börje Johansson and Roger R. Stough

Volume 26
Evolution and Design of Institutions
Edited by Christian Schubert and Georg von Wangenheim

Volume 27
The Changing Economic Geography of Globalization
Reinventing space
Edited by Giovanna Vertova

The Changing Economic Geography of Globalization

Reinventing space

Edited by Giovanna Vertova

Routledge
Taylor & Francis Group
LONDON AND NEW YORK

First published 2006 by Routledge

Published 2017 by Routledge
2 Park Square, Milton Park, Abingdon, Oxon OX14 4RN
711 Third Avenue, New York, NY 10017, USA

Routledge is an imprint of the Taylor & Francis Group, an informa business

First issued in paperback 2012

Typeset in Times New Roman by Prepress Projects Ltd, Perth

British Library Cataloguing in Publication Data
A catalogue record for this book is available from the British Library

Library of Congress Cataloging in Publication Data
The changing economic geography of globalization: reinventing space / edited by Giovanna Vertova.
p. cm.
Includes bibliographical references and index.
1. International economic relations. 2. Globalization. 3. Capitalism. 4. Regional economic disparities. 5. Space in economics. I. Vertova, Giovanna, 1966-
HF1359.C446 2006
330.9′051′1–dc22
2005019374

ISBN 13: 978–0–415–35398–4 (hbk)
ISBN 13: 978–0–415–64648–2 (pbk)

Contents

Figures

Tables

Contributors

Bjørn T. Asheim is Professor of Economic Geography at the University of Lund, Sweden, and Professor at the Centre of Technology, Innovation, and Culture, University of Oslo, Norway. He is co-founder and Deputy Director of the new Centre for Innovation, Research and Competence in the Learning Economy (CIRCLE) at Lund University.

Riccardo Bellofiore is Professor of Political Economy at the University of Bergamo, as well as Research Associate in the History and Methodology of Economics Group at the University of Amsterdam. His current research interests include Marxian economics, endogenous theories of money and the economics of globalization.

Roberta Capello is Professor of Regional and Urban Economics at the Politecnico of Milan. She is a member of the Scientific Board of the Regional Science Association International and of the European Regional Science Association.

Lars Coenen is a PhD candidate at the multidisciplinary Centre for Innovation, Research and Competence in the Learning Economy (CIRCLE) and the Department of Social and Economic Geography at Lund University, Sweden. His research interest lies within comparative studies of regional systems of innovation.

Sergio Conti is Professor of Economic Geography at the University of Turin, where he was also the Dean from 2002 to 2005. His main fields of research have been the geographical organization of production in the Soviet Union and Eastern Europe and, more recently, the phenomena of technological transition to the urban and regional scale.

Paolo Giaccaria is Lecturer in Economic Geography at the University of Turin. His main interests are in the epistemology and methodology of geography in local development theories. He is currently working on the Mediterranean scale and on the Euro-Mediterranea Partnership.

Raffaele Paci is Professor of Economics at the University of Cagliari and Director of CRENoS (Center for North–South Economic Research). His main research interests are the growth process at the regional level and the diffusion of technological innovations.

Eric Sheppard is Professor of Geography and member of the Interdisciplinary Center for the Study of Global Change at the University of Minnesota. He is a former editor of *Antipode* and currently co-editor of *Environment and Planning A*. His current research interests include inter-urban policy and activist networks, the spatiality of globalization and geographies of the information society.

Alessia Spairani is a researcher at the Department of Management, Economics and Industrial Engineering at the Politecnico of Milan. Her main research area is regional and urban economics.

G. M. Peter Swann is Professor of Industrial Economics at the Nottingham University Business School. Most of his research addresses the economics of innovation, including the role of clusters, and he has held several advisory positions with government.

Marinella Terrasi is Associate Professor of Regional Economics in the Department of Economics at the University of Pisa. She has researched and written widely on regional development, regional convergence, and the location process of manufacturing industries during different phases of Italian post-war development.

Stefano Usai is Associate Professor of Economics at the University of Cagliari and a researcher of CRENoS (Center for North–South Economic Research). His main research interests are regional and development economics and the economics of technological change.

Giovanna Vertova is Assistant Professor at the University of Bergamo. Among the courses she has taught are economic geography, regional economics, and the economics of globalization. Her current research interests are the economics of globalization, space in the international division of labor, and national systems of innovation.

Richard A. Walker is Professor of Geography at the University of California, Berkeley. He is author, with Michael Storper, of *The Capitalist Imperative* (Blackwell Publishers, 1989) and, with Andrew Sayer, of *The New Social Economy* (Blackwell Publishers, 1992). His latest book is *The Conquest of Bread: 150 Years of California Agribusiness* (The New Press, 2004). A forthcoming publication is *The Country in the City: The Greening of the San Francisco Bay Area* (University of Washington Press, in press).

Acknowledgements

The chapters in this volume are revised versions of the papers presented at the conference Reinventing Space: the Geography of Globalization, held in Bergamo, Italy, on 19 and 20 December 2003. The conference was promoted and financially supported by the Department of Economics "Hyman P. Minsky" of the University of Bergamo. I would like to thank the head of the department, Giancarlo Graziola, for his welcome address at the start of the conference. I also wish to express my deep gratitude to Riccardo Bellofiore for the productive discussions we had about this initiative. A special thank-you goes to Giancarlo Beltrame for his friendly and constant support. Last but not least, the organizational work provided by Simona Locatelli before and during the conference and Laura Pedersoli's solutions to all bureaucratic problems were invaluable.

Introduction

"Reinventing space"

Giovanna Vertova

This book is an edited collection of papers gathered from an international conference held at the University of Bergamo, Italy,[1] which brought together regional economists, economic geographers, and international political scientists. The aim of the book is to assess the importance of space, by drawing together different related, although rarely integrated, strands of research. The main aim is to analyze the shaping and reshaping of the global map and to identify the major impacts on people and places which occupy different positions in the global economic system. Different approaches are grouped together here in order to understand the pressures and constraints put on space by the current phase of capitalist development. All the different streams of literature presented here have complementary arguments in both their theoretical and empirical composition, mainly in terms of the role of space in the global economy. Some consider space only in geometrical terms, others in relational terms, others in terms of power. These arguments feature throughout the book, which is structured in two parts. Part I is more theoretical and focuses on the different conceptualizations of space: space in political terms (Chapter 1), space in terms of power (Chapter 2), space as a system (Chapter 3), and space as an intellectual concept (Chapter 4). Part II is empirical and deals with the current role of space in this new phase of capitalist development.

The contributors to the present volume believe that a transformation of the world economy is taking place and that it has had a crucial impact on the way production is organized in space. The debate over the global economy was brought about by the political, economic, and social changes occurring since the mid-1970s, which affected all geographical scales – notably international, regional, national, and local. Since these geographical scales are interrelated in a complex way, and do not simply constitute a hierarchical structure from top (international) to bottom (local), the geography of contemporary capitalism can be viewed as a global jigsaw puzzle of organization of production.

At international level, a new division of labor has been brought about. Just after World War II, it was common to split the world into two great areas: the core, composed of the advanced capitalist economies producing mainly goods and services for international markets, and the periphery, formed by the developing countries, supplying mainly raw and natural materials (Myrdal 1957). Nowadays, the world is a more complex and kaleidoscopic structure, involving the fragmentation of many production processes and their geographical relocation. The emergence of new "newly industrialized countries" (i.e., the East Asian countries) as fresh centers for industrial production shows how difficult it is to understand contemporary global capitalism. The world economy can be represented as a system of prosperous polarized regional economies, surrounded by hinterland, ancillary communities, prosperous agricultural zones, and underdeveloped areas. Moreover, the current "financialization" has contributed to reshape the economic landscape. Financial flows of capital contribute, or even reinforce, rather than reduce, uneven geographical development (Martin 1999). Free movement of money and capital leads to spatial centralization of financial systems, concentrated in the big stock exchange markets, and to uneven development between different areas, due to outflow of capital from lower return zones to those with higher returns.

At a regional level, an increasing number of regional integration agreements has characterized the last decades.[2] Their main aim is a discriminatory trade liberalization: two or more countries can decide to lower trade barriers against one another vis-à-vis the rest of the world. Although regional agreements have been known since the end of World War II, this new phase of regionalism is quite different from the old one and presents several distinctive characteristics (Das 2004). While old regionalism was essentially confined to agreements between advanced countries or developing economies, the new regionalism is instead known for cross-alliances between developing, emerging, and advanced countries. Moreover, the new regionalism is not limited to neighboring economies, but creates bonds among economies far away from each other. Finally, the new regionalism is not exclusive, meaning that one country can simultaneously be a member of more than one regional agreement. This new regionalism helps to bring about changes to the landscape of contemporary capitalism, by creating spaces where the exchange of goods, services, and people is simplified, but also by raising barriers against the countries and/or areas excluded by this integration process.

At a national level, the most important issue related to the reshaping of the world economy is the role of the nation-state. The state has always had two main tasks – to contain distinctive institutions and practices and to regulate human interactions at all levels (social, political, economic, etc.) – which the literature about the nation-state has always acknowledged. Yet, nowadays, there are different positions regarding the role of the nation-state in the global economy. On the one side, some claim the "death of the nation-state" and exalt the "borderless economy", based on the conviction that the nation-state can no longer perform its two main tasks (Ohmae 1990). Those of this opinion contend that state borders are increasingly permeable and no longer contain those distinctive institutions and practices that used to characterize them. Moreover, international institutions increasingly regulate human interactions and, in this new international political system, the nation-state is just one level of a more complex system of overlapping hierarchical powers. Opponents of this argument affirm that, despite globalization processes, the role of the nation-state is still relevant and important, albeit altered (Jessop 1994, Weiss 1998). This group contends that there is still a national distinctiveness in all aspects of life and, consequently, the nation-state maintains its tasks, although they are performed differently.

At local level, the new information and communication technological paradigm has made possible the shift toward a more flexible form of production. The integration of electrical and electronic technology in the production processes has led to greater flexibility. With increasingly sophisticated automated processes and electronically controlled technology, great changes in production processes need not necessarily be associated with increasing scales of production. It has become possible to reduce the scale of production and maintain technological efficiency. Moreover, it is feasible to switch rapidly and to tailor production to meet customer requirements. All these changes in the organization of the production process could occur within the boundaries of the firm or outside them. Subcontracting and outsourcing are typical ways of breaking down the production process to a smaller scale in order to achieve increased flexibility. The "post-Fordist" era has begun. Today, the production chain of a single product has increasingly become an international linked sequence of functions in which each stage, usually geographically relocated, adds value to the process of the final goods or services. Nevertheless, the "post-Fordism" phenomenon as a new model of capitalist development is a highly controversial issue. On the one hand, this form of organization of production, based on smaller organizational units, is seen as a new characteristic of future capitalist development (Piore and Sabel 1984). On the other hand, less rigid and smaller-scale productions have always coexisted with mass production methods, because this is the way capitalism develops (Sayer and Walker 1992, Harrison 1997).

The aim of this book is to contribute to the debate about globalization and space, by bringing together a collection of original analyses, written by leading researchers in the field. The collection does not claim to be exhaustive in its coverage, nor does it seek to develop or impose any individual conceptual or methodological framework. However, the different studies and topics covered here do demonstrate persuasively the enduring role of space in the global economy. My task in the remainder of this introductory chapter is to sketch out some of the principal issues and themes which form the background to the rest of the book.

Globalization: a questionable phenomenon

In order to understand whether the global economy has undermined the role of space, it is crucial to remember that globalization is a highly controversial phenomenon. This section aims to quickly review the main opinions indicated in the literature, without laying any claim to being complete. The "globalization debate" refers to the views of two opposing camps: those who consider contemporary globalization as a real and significant phenomenon – "globalists" (Ohmae 1990, 1995, Reich 1991, Castells 1996, Dicken 2003) – and those who believe that globalization is just an ideological and mythical construction with marginal explanatory value – "skeptics" (Hirst and Thompson 1996, Held *et al.* 1999, Held and McGrew 2000, Went 2000). The disagreement starts from the very beginning: the definition.

There is no common and universally agreed definition of globalization, since the term has been vaguely defined and used with widely varying meanings. Giddens (1990) speaks about "action at a distance" to highlight the fact that the actions of one economic agent in one location can have an influence on economic agents located in other places. Harvey (1989) refers to "time–space compression" to show that new technologies have reduced time and space constraints on social organization. Modelski (1972) considers globalization as the "enlargement" of the geographical scope of human communities, thus stressing a more social aspect. Held *et al.* (1999) speak about the "global interconnectedness" in different historical periods. Castells (1996) talks about "network capitalism," based on global and structured social constructions, representing the new unit of analysis in the current phase of capitalism.

Important issues about globalization divide the social scientists. The first one is the novelty of the current phase of capitalist development. Globalists remark how this phase is completely new, and no comparison can be made with other historical phases of capitalist development (Ohmae 1990, Castells 1996, Dicken 2003). Flows of trade, capital, and people across the world have been facilitated by new infrastructures. The growing intensity of these flows enables states and societies to become increasingly interconnected with a worldwide system of networks and interactions. This speeding up and deepening impact of inter-regional flows should be seen as the emergence of an harmonious world society. We now live in a borderless world in which the "national" is no longer relevant. The contemporary world is a place where nation-states are no longer significant actors, and consumer tastes are homogenized and satisfied by standard global products created by global corporations. The fact that a significant segment of the world's population is either untouched or remains largely excluded from globalization does not seem to be an issue.

Skeptics believe that the "newness" of the current phase of capitalist development has been grossly exaggerated (Harvey 1989, Geyer and Bright 1995, Hirst and Thompson 1996, Held *et al.* 1999). We live not in a global economy but in a more international one, where national forces do still play a significant and meaningful role. Moreover, in order to understand the true novelty, this phase must be compared with past historical phases of capitalist development. Some authors believe that the originality of this latest phase has been to alter the distribution of global wealth in favor of Western economies (Modelski 1972) or to result directly in an increased Western expansionism (Geyer and Bright 1995). The different historical phases of globalization share not only the acceleration of European expansion but also, and above all, a new ordering of relations of domination and subordination. Both the Pax Britannica and the Pax Americana were attempts to establish global order. Hirst and Thompson (1996) compare this phase of capitalist development with the so-called *belle époque*. They conclude that we are far from a true global society, due to the lack of global institutions governing global economy, via a process of global democracy. By contrast, we live in a more internationalized world, with more flows of goods, services, and people around the world. The authors prefer to speak about "internationalization," "regionalization," and "triadization" of the world because of the growing links between essentially discrete national economies.

A second concern is about the role of the nation-state. Globalists believe that the global economy, dominated by stateless corporations and borderless finance, has rendered obsolete the concept of the nation-state as a unit of analysis (Ohmae 1990, 1995, Reich 1991). This state denial refers to a diminution or displacement of states as powerful actors in the national and international arena. Globalization seems to rapidly erode the power of the nation-state since capital, finance, and technology flow effortlessly across its borders. Therefore, the sovereignty itself of the nation-states is being undermined. According to this view, in this new era, transnational corporations stomp across the world randomly, and national governments are increasingly powerless to influence the economic welfare of their citizens. The "collapse of the welfare state," the "death of industrial policy," the "end of national diversity," and the "demise of the nation-state" are the key phrases of this new era of state denial.

By contrast, skeptics believe that the nation-state does still play a fundamental role in this phase of capitalist development. The nation-state is not disappearing but, instead, its role is changing. There is no doubt that the role of the nation-state has changed markedly since the Keynesian era. States are less autonomous, they have less exclusive control over the economic and social processes within their territories, and they are less able to maintain national distinctiveness and cultural homogeneity. Nevertheless, the state capacity, defined as general capabilities whether in the national or international arena, and whether in industrial, foreign, or social policy, is still crucial in the global economy (Weiss 1998). Evidence for this is the fact that some nations are notably more successful than others in anticipating and responding to economic change. In general, the highly coordinated market economies such as Japan and Germany have sustained a great capacity for growth with equity than have the least coordinated market economies (Weiss 1998). Moreover, state capacity is an important source of competitiveness for a variety of reasons. First, state coordination is vital to induce firms to engage in activities whose risk level is so high as to otherwise discourage them from doing so. Second, the state can resolve many important problems of coordination better than the market, by reducing transaction costs in the wider economy (Chang 1994). Finally, a quick look at world history shows that the state has grown together with the globalization process and has not, instead, been destroyed by it (Geyer and Bright 1995).

A third argument concerns transnational corporations (TNCs). Globalists have always considered TNCs as "the primary shaper of the contemporary global economy" (Dicken 2003: 198). The changing geography of the global economy is influenced by the TNCs' decisions to invest, or not invest, in particular geographical locations. The potential ability to take advantage of geographical differences in the distributions of factors of production and in state policy has some bearing on the TNCs' decisions to invest. Moreover, potential geographical flexibility, in other words the ability to switch resources and operations between locations on an international or even a global scale, plays a crucial role as well. TNCs' decisions to invest contribute to create an international production chain entangled in a spider's web of collaborative relationships. By contrast, skeptics quote the evidence that TNCs' investments do not extend all over the world but, on the contrary, are concentrated in certain specific geographical areas (Dunning 1997a,b). The reason is that production needs some physical and social infrastructures in order to work, and these are not available everywhere in the world. Therefore, TNCs' international production chains have a strong geographical connotation, reflecting the level of development reached by the different host countries.

A fourth issue of disagreement concerns the empirical evidence for globalization in the three key economic areas: trade, international finance, and foreign direct investments. Globalists argue that the post-war growth of international trade has led to the merging of distinctive national markets of goods and services into a global one. The underlying idea is that production and consumption in national economies have become separated, as consumers can now buy from around the globe. Therefore, international trade is one of the most important forces of globalization. By contrast, skeptics believe that the growth of international trade has been widely overestimated. They claim that world trade relative to output has only recently returned to the classical gold standard level. As far as international finance is concerned, globalists believe that the global financial flows achieved by the collapse of the Bretton Woods system and the removal of any barriers to capital mobility represent the ultimate perfect global market. Capital is now free to move where the rates of return are highest. Moreover, most of these transactions are speculative in nature, hence undermining and weakening the opportunity for countries to pursue independent monetary policy. By contrast, skeptics contend that almost all of these speculative financial transactions are concentrated in very few financial centers, the core of capitalism (Martin 1999). Finally, as far as foreign direct investments are concerned, globalists state that TNCs aim to shift production around the globe in order to respond to differences in economic conditions. TNCs tend to move productions to those locations where labor costs are lower and/or natural resources and input are cheaper and easily available. By contrast, skeptics point out that even in the case of the largest TNCs the majority of sales and assets are in the domestic country, along with their core operations. TNCs are seen as national companies with international operations, but subjected to national controls.

Space in the global economy

The common thread of this book, which gathers together authors adhering to different theoretical paradigms, is a shared dissatisfaction with the idea of globalization as a homogenizing force in space. Uneven development means that social and economic change in capitalist societies enhances the wealth of some places at the expense of others. Globalists believe that the resulting geographical differentiation into types and levels of development will disappear as soon as market forces are free to work or market imperfections are corrected. By contrast, skeptics believe that uneven development is the result of spatial expression of social differences, inequalities, and processes lying at the heart of the capitalist system of production. Despite theoretical differences among the contributors, this book aims to show that differentiation in space does still exist even in the so-called global economy. Global forces are not likely to reduce, or even eliminate, geographical differences. On the contrary, space still matters and an increasing differentiation between localities, territories, regional areas, or continents characterizes this phase of capitalist development.

The theoretical explanation of globalization as a flattening force finds its basis in the neoclassical growth theory (Solow 1956, 1957). With Solow's model, two different kinds of economic convergence can be analyzed. So-called absolute convergence occurs when poorer regions grow faster than richer ones, thus catching them up. Absolute convergence means that the further a region is from the common steady state in the initial year, the faster the growth rate turns out to be in the following period. This implies that there should be a negative relationship between the initial level of the economy and its average rate of growth. The negative relationship indicates that regions whose gross domestic product (GDP) is initially below average show an above average growth rate. Yet, this kind of convergence occurs only under two strict assumptions: (i) capital should show diminishing rates of return in the production function – meaning that poor economies, with a lower ratio of capital per worker and thus higher returns to capital, will experience a faster rate of capital accumulation and faster growth; and (ii) the economies should share the same economic fundamentals and differ only in terms of their initial level of income. This means that the economies should have the same production function and should converge toward the same steady state. Nevertheless, the steady state will be the same only if propensity to save, demographic growth, technological change, and the stock of human capital are the same in all the economies. In this case, the catching-up process will be inevitable and absolute convergence will then take place.

The assumptions required to hold for absolute convergence to take place are strict and very difficult to meet. Thus, a second type of convergence is taken into consideration, the so-called conditional convergence. In this case also, convergence exists when there is a negative relationship between the initial level of GDP and its average growth rate. Yet, convergence is conditioned by the controlling variables that measure differences in fundamentals and steady states across economies. This concept of convergence is more meaningful than absolute convergence because it predicts whether lagging regions would be able to grow quickly and catch up with leading regions if all the structural differences could be eliminated. In this case, growth rates can vary from region to region either because of differences in the parameters determining their steady states or because of differences in their initial positions. Thus, convergence occurs conditional to the set of variables controlling for structural differences of the regional economies. Differences in these variables are responsible for different processes of economic growth and, consequently, the chosen set of variables becomes crucial in marking the reasons why absolute convergence does not occur. Empirical evidence has not been conclusive, because some studies have confirmed the Solow model (Barro and Sala-I-Martin 1991,

Quah 1996, Sala-I-Martin 1996), whereas others have disproved it (Canova and Marcet 1995, Boldrin and Canova 2001, Canova 2004).

The new economic geography suggests that the existence of increasing returns and imperfect competition will lead to geographical divergence rather than convergence (Krugman 1991a,b, 1998, Krugman and Venables 1995, Ottaviano 2000, Neary 2001, Fujita and Krugman 2004). High fixed costs, widespread increasing returns, and externalities are the sources of geographical differentiation among space. In this case, a geographical concentration of economic activities would be the most frequent result. Increasing returns send the most productive factors flowing toward the advanced regions, where their returns are higher, leaving the disadvantaged areas further behind. The final result is a great geographical difference among territories, at whatever level, exacerbated by "market imperfections." Geographical concentration is the result of the relationship between centripetal and centrifugal forces (Krugman 1991b). On the one hand, firms want to locate close to the largest possible market and workers want to have access to a large number of goods. Both of these choices operate as centripetal forces and lead toward geographical concentration. On the other hand, firms need to serve the peripheral markets. This need acts as a centrifugal force, leading to geographical dispersion. Moreover, geographical concentration depends on the interaction among the share of manufacturing goods in total expenditure, the level of transport costs, and the extent of scale economies. If transport costs are high and/or the share of expenditure in manufactured goods is low, or scale economies are weak, no clustering will take place. However, when scale economies are high enough, firms will cluster and, because of transport costs, they will cluster where demand is great.

Both these traditions – Solow's growth theory and the new economic geography – consider "space" only in terms of metrical distance and give some suggestions for policy. The concentration of economic activities is either a short-term phenomenon or the result of market imperfections. In the first case, economic growth, and therefore wealth, will be broadened everywhere by the simple operations of market forces, which, in turn, will lead to homogenization of space, without any kind of state intervention. In the second case, intervention is limited to the removal of market imperfections, in order to permit market forces to spread wealth everywhere in the world.

In other traditions, space is seen in relational terms. Global space is characterized by strong and increasing differentiation between localities and territories, as a result of the relationships that firms form with local institutions. These approaches share the common view that a firm is not an isolated entity but is, instead, related to its territory by its relations and networks with other firms, institutions, and organizations clustered in the same geographical area. Social, economic, political, and institutional relations characterize the space where the firm operates.

Among these various approaches, the most notable is surely that of the industrial districts. The theoretical "pedigree" of the notion is quite well known, as it goes back to Alfred Marshall's (1990 [1890]) observation of the tendency of small specialized firms to concentrate in a limited geographical area. This phenomenon was explained by the opportunity for firms to reap external economies of scale. In Becattini's earlier revisitation (1979, 1987, 1990) of Marshall's tradition, the district gained a new impulse. Becattini (1990: 38) talks about the industrial district as "a socio-territorial entity which is characterized by the active presence of both a community of people and a population of firms in one naturally and historically bounded area." This definition marks a certain shift from the consideration of purely economic factors to the inclusion of social factors too: the "population of firms" must exist within a "community of people." Although the firm does not "melt" into the district, the collectivity of firms still captures more attention than their individuality. The "community of people" works in creating and maintaining a homogeneous system of values and the "population of firms" is specialized in one or a few phases of the production processes.

The *milieu innovateur* is another approach that stems from the Marshallian tradition, and investigates the relationship between technology and space (Aydalot 1986, Camagni 1991). The *milieu innovateur* is actually considered as the "incubator" of innovations and innovative firms, in which the firm is indeed a player, but just one of the many involved in the innovative process. In such an approach, firms are rooted in their territory and constrained by both their local industrial atmosphere and their social, institutional, and political condition. Interactions are given much more emphasis, to the point that they are considered more important than the availability of local factors and resources. Within the "milieu," non-market interactions, as well as interpersonal relations, create a local synergy that turns out to be a more powerful explanation of innovation and local growth (Maillat 1995). In this approach, the idea of space is evidently quite different from that of standard industrial economics – where industries come first and create the territory – or of economic geography – where it is, instead, space that comes first. In the "milieu" approach industry and space are ontological equals, as the territory has a twofold interrelated nature. On the one hand, it is the result of the innovation processes. On the other hand, it performs different collective tasks in order to foster innovation.

In addition, the regional innovation system and the learning region approaches consider space in relational terms (Braczyk *et al.* 1998, Howells 1999, Cooke 2001). A regional system becomes a crucial arena for localized learning and tacit know-how sharing, thanks to its institutional fabrics and informal links. The concept of a regional system of innovation or "learning region" is founded on five constituent elements: (i) the region as an administrative and political unit with some cultural and historical homogeneity and with some statutory power; (ii) innovation in the neo-Schumpeterian evolutionary approach; (iii) networks as relationships based on trust, reputation, custom, reciprocity, and reliability; (iv) learning processes in the sense of institutional learning; (v) interactions driven by formal and informal links and relationships. Whatever its exact composition, this conceptual framework is able to incorporate firms within specific regional contexts, but still keeps the former conceptually "independent" from the latter. This approach considers space as an administrative and cultural unit of analysis.

This brief review, which I do not claim to be exhaustive, shows a different concept of space. Space in geometrical terms (i.e., metrical distance) is irrelevant here. Space is considered in terms of the relationships and networks created among different economic agents, such as firms, institutions, organizations, local authorities, trade unions, etc. Moreover, all these different streams suggest that "localness" is an important source of competitiveness. The ability of a territory to succeed in a global economy is to stress and emphasize its local assets, based on local relationships. "Glocal" – think globally but act locally – has become the new keyword, suggesting that global competition can be won by relying more heavily on local capacity, expertise, and competence.

Finally, there is a stream of research that considers space from a class perspective. Marxist geographers believe that each mode of production creates distinct spatial arrangements, and that successions of modes of production alter landscape in any given space (Harvey 1982, Massey 1984, Storper and Walker 1989). The idea is not how economy is reflected in space but, on the contrary, how economy arranges the political, cultural, and social organization of space. The theoretical background is the Marxist theory of economic growth, which, under capitalism, puts capital accumulation at the center of a dynamic and inevitably expansionary mode of production. The capitalist system has a pathological expansionistic logic because capital needs to expand to new markets in order to maintain profits. Newly local patterns and improvements in transportation and communication technology are an inevitable and necessary part of capital accumulation. In fact, the increasing scale of production and the concentration and centralization of capital have been matched by urban agglomeration in a widening international capitalist space. Yet the collapse of spatial barriers does not imply a decreasing significance of space. On the contrary, the diminishing of spatial barriers gives capitalists the power to exploit spatial differentiation (Harvey 1989). Local availability of material resources, local variations of market taste, local difference in entrepreneurial ability, venture capital, scientific and technical know-how, local differences in social attitudes, and local labor markets consequently become sources of competitive advantage. Within this theoretical tradition, uneven development is the general rule rather than the exception, and it is intrinsic to capitalist development and not just a temporary out-of-equilibrium situation or the result of market failures. Uneven development is the spatial form taken by the geography of capital accumulation (Amin 1976). The source of uneven development is related to the division of labor, which is the product of competition between capitals and which perpetually divides places, as much as enterprises and people, on the basis on their ability to differentiate their systems of production from those of their neighbors and competitors. Therefore, uneven development is at the heart of capitalist development, thus enhancing the wealth of some places at the expense of others.

Outline of the book

The book is organized into two distinctive, but closely related, parts. Part I is concerned with different theoretical approaches to the space–globalization issue. Part II contains empirical evidence showing the enduring role of space even in the global economy. In Chapter 1, Bellofiore and Vertova focus on the relevance of space for uneven capitalist development as an intrinsically unbalanced process. The starting point is dissatisfaction with the ways space has been considered by neoclassical theory. The chapter surveys how space, agglomeration, and external economies have been theorized by both Walrasian tradition, extending to the new economic geography, and the Marshallian one, with the traditional district literature. The former neglects space as an element of differentiation in its basic model, and sees globalization as a homogenizing process. The latter praises local assets in global competition, but within what is substantially a "harmonic" social and economic view. In fact, in both perspectives conflict is abolished (i) at micro level, between individual capitalists; (ii) at macro level, between capital and labor; and (iii) at geographical level, between the center and the periphery. The authors then survey a different geographical paradigm in the Marxist tradition, that of David Harvey, as a promising alternative way to theorize space. However, some of his limits lead the authors to suggest a new heterodox approach based on (but also going beyond) an integration between Marx, Schumpeter, and Keynes as authors for whom the capitalist economy is a monetary economy characterized by endogenous development, instability, and crises. The critical point is the political as well as the spatial dialectic of the two "special" Marxian commodities: the "labor power" of the workers, from which living labor is extracted, and "money" as finance to production. In both cases, geographical specification and institutional (and state) regulation are fundamental. This is true also of the crucial role of "effective demand" in driving capitalist production. This analytical skeleton helps to focus on the general tendency toward the increasing "precariousness" or "casualization" of labor (whatever its skill or nature, manual or intellectual), on the "regionalization" of economies, on the free mobility of short-term capital, and on the aggressive competition between global players, as defining features of a contemporary "flexible" and "financial" capitalism. "Labor" and "space" are under stress nowadays because of the essential link between the primacy of finance and the instability of growth, on the one hand, and the fragmentation of work and territories, on the other. This new capitalism is built on a system of valorization whereby workers are automatically "controlled" by subordination to more stagnant and/or unstable commodity markets, subsumption to financial markets, and the consequent revolutions in the corporate governance, organization, and productive structure of firms.

In Chapter 2, Sheppard explores the question of how space still matters for the study of economic geography, by focusing on an aspect of space that has recently received diminishing attention in the field: the differential positionality of locations within the out-of-equilibrium dynamic capitalist space–economy. Positionality refers to how both social and geographical locations shape the conditions of possibility faced by economic agents. Starting from this definition, Sheppard develops a conceptualization of positionality as an emergent, socially constructed, and produced feature of complex economic systems that also shapes their evolution. Contrasting this view of positionality with the ways in which relative location is treated in the new economic geography in economics has significant theoretical implications. It challenges a number of standard propositions of non-spatial economic theory, neoclassical and Marxian alike. Sheppard argues that positionality also remains important to the evolution of contemporary spatial economic systems, notwithstanding the "shrinking world" thesis. While the world may be shrinking in absolute terms, and social distance is becoming more and more non-Euclidean, in relative terms, positionality differences matter as much as ever. The chapter ends by providing some empirical insights into the importance of positionality today in the global mobility of commodities, people, capital, and foreign aid. The world has become smaller and faster, in absolute terms, but it does not follow, however, that space is being annihilated by time. On the contrary, the space-transcending technologies and institutions of contemporary globalization are compounding the complexity of mapping social relationships in geographic space. Sheppard concludes the chapter with some suggestions. The same practices will not have the same consequences in differently positioned places. Instead, places need the freedom to pursue different political economic strategies. Yet local actions to improve the business climate have little chance of improving the positionality of disadvantaged places. What is needed is collective action across space.

In Chapter 3, Conti and Giaccaria analyze the local system as the basis to understand economic change in a world characterized by information flows, knowledge, competence and capabilities, and the community of practices. The aim is the rediscovery of external relations (and thus agglomeration) as a factor of cooperation and collective learning. The differentiation and specification of the territorial pattern of development and competitiveness pivots around the concept of identity, a term through which it will be possible to attribute to the local system an autonomy from the abstract laws of the economy. Given these premises, the capability of a local system might be defined as what a (territorial) organization is able to do better than others, including the ability to renew, augment, and adapt its "core competencies" over time. Spatial proximity is not, therefore, a sufficient condition. On the contrary, a territory, in given circumstances, must be seen as an entity that combines organizational proximity and institutional proximity. The authors assume that institutional proximity endows the system's actors with a common space of representation, roles, and models of learning and action, collectively internalized by the actors themselves. The evolutionary trajectory leads the system to give specific (local) responses to general (global) stimuli. According to Conti and Giaccaria, present local development is characterized by two main shifts: (i) from government to governance and (ii) from politics to policy. Starting from these assumptions, the question is posed explicitly of the point of view, i.e., the position from which one describes the system. A point of view external to the system leads to representing and interpreting the relationship of the system itself and its external environment in linear terms. In this way the territorial (local) system is seen as a mere subsystem of the global one, depriving it of its own conceptual autonomy. The idea of self-representation introduces, instead, the possibility of characterizing the system in terms of organization, of identity, inducing one to adopt a point of view internal to the system itself. Local policy as the mere expression of a development ethic that accepts the laws and dynamics of contemporary capitalism produces nothing other than a simple – local – specification of standardizing processes and forces. In this case, although attention to places modifies the vision of development process, it cannot change the concept of development itself. The thesis that now emerges is fundamentally different. The systemic perspective is the bearer of the idea of a place that reproduces its own identity, given by the organization of those social, cultural, and economic relations that make that place "unique." In this case, if the arbiter of development is no longer the market, but the local system, it follows that the benefits of local development are evaluated in terms of the maintenance of the system's identity. It follows that a development path is not valid at all scales and nor does there exist a temporal succession of hegemonic models of development. In conclusion, a local system is not a Pandora's box that encompasses all possible relations. In this sense, institutional biodiversity represents a fundamental condition for ensuring the availability to the local system of the greatest possible number of development paths.

In Chapter 4, Swann examines how, as geographical space loses one part of its economic meaning through globalization, it may acquire another economic meaning. According to Swann, competitive survival requires competitive distinction because, as the number of dimensions falls, the chance of a trader achieving competitive distinction within a given characteristics space tends to fall. Swann analyzes this "law" in what he calls the four ages of space: the medieval age, the industrial age, the age of global clusters, and, finally, the age of the new global village, which has yet to come. Before globalization, some traders would achieve competitive distinction simply through location. These traders might not perhaps offer a distinctive product or service, but what is distinctive is the location in which they trade. However, with the advent of space-shrinking technologies and the growth of globalization, place may no longer be the source of economic distinction that it was in the past. Traders may find new sources of competitive distinction from their spatial history, because traders seeking niches for themselves may have to invent new sources of competitive distinction. In an economy in which intellectual capital plays an increasingly important role in achieving competitive distinction, location may reappear as an indirect source of competitive distinction. If intellectual capital is the source of competitive distinction, and intellectual capital in turn is forged by the trader's history (including spatial history), then spatial history can shape competitive distinction. Spatial history shapes intellectual capital and, hence, place is still a source of competitive distinction. This will continue until all experiences are virtual – unconnected with place – if such a future will ever exist. In this apparently placeless world, distance may have died, but location – or, more specifically, the history of location – is not irrelevant, because place is still what we think with.

The second and empirical part starts with Walker's chapter, dealing with the transformation of the San Francisco Bay Area during and after the boom of the New Economy. According to the author, rarely do we get to witness anything like the collapse of the Twin Towers, yet the morphological changes in American cities are as inexorable in their destruction and alteration as acts of war. This relentless redevelopment of cities is driven by the logic of capital accumulation, which is capable of spectacular bouts of building that surpass anything in the past. In some cases, the economic forces are so compressed that they do their earth-moving right before our eyes. Such was the case in the San Francisco Bay Area in the late 1990s. An economic boom of unparalleled ferocity hit the place like a bomb. The city was picked up, shaken, and dropped into a new configuration. The author highlights several key aspects to this. First, the dot-com bubble in San Francisco was only the tip of the iceberg of a larger boom centered in Silicon Valley. Second, the Bay Area was tightly linked to volcanic movements of finance capital through Wall Street and gained – and lost – far more from the record-setting stock bubble than anywhere else. Third, this highly focused boom rested on the way in which the Bay Area became the paragon of the New Economy and the iconic space of the neoliberal 1990s. Fourth, the bubble economy drove local real estate markets insane, and prompted a massive makeover of the metropolis from SoMa (South of Market district) to San Jose, Santa Rosa to Tracy. Fifth, the collapse of the bubble and the New Economy ushered in the recall of Governor Davis and his replacement by the comic-book hero of California politics, Arnold Schwarzenegger. As usual, capital got off scot-free while others took the fall for the catastrophe. In short, the Bay Area of the 1990s provides a perfect case study for scholars of the geography of the capitalist economy, the dialectics of the local and the global, and the political economy of urban growth. This is a local story with a general lesson.

In Chapter 6, Asheim and Coenen show to what extent the analysis of the importance of different types of regional innovation systems must take place within a context of the actual knowledge base of various industries in the economy, as the innovation processes of firms are strongly shaped by their specific knowledge base. The authors distinguish between two types of knowledge base: analytical and synthetic. These types indicate different mixes of tacit and codified knowledge, codification possibilities and limits, qualifications and skills, required organizations and institutions involved, as well as specific competitive challenges from a globalizing economy. Moreover, Asheim and Coenen prove that the different knowledge bases of industries also have implications for the relations and analytical distinctions between clusters and regional innovation systems. They make a distinction between the existence of "pure" clusters, where regional innovation systems are built in order to support innovation and localized learning, and the coexistence of clusters and regional innovation systems as integral parts. The traditional constellation of industrial clusters surrounded by innovation-supporting organizations is nearly always to be found in the context of industries with a synthetic knowledge base (e.g., engineering-based industries). In contrast, the existence of regional innovation systems as an integral part of a cluster will normally be the case for industries based on an analytical knowledge base (e.g., science-based industries such as IT and biotechnology). The discussion of different types of clusters and regional innovation systems is put forward by empirical illustrations from a Nordic comparative project on small and medium-sized enterprises (SMEs) and regional innovation systems.

In Chapter 7, Paci and Usai tackle the issue of local economic performance in a scenario of an ongoing process of structural change, because they believe that it has meaningful implications for an analysis of the geography of economic activities, owing to the fact that several forces of agglomeration are at work. They assess the role of a large set of potential determinants of the process of local agglomeration of economic activity, distinguishing between manufacturing and service sectors. The authors also analyze the issue of spatial association of the local growth process. Paci and Usai acknowledge that, in the last decade, a vast body of literature has addressed the issue of the influence of local externalities on industry location and growth. Such literature has, however, paid little attention to the wider scenario in which such phenomena are rooted, that of an ongoing process of structural change that is transforming economies from manufacturing to service ones. This is the matter the authors intend to tackle with empirical evidence from the Italian case, by using a very ample database on socioeconomic indicators for 784 local labor systems and thirty-four sectors over the period 1991–96. The novelty in comparison with similar works is that their database covers both the manufacturing and the service sectors, so that the whole economic system is considered. The econometric results show that local growth in Italy is not a homogeneous process. On the contrary, it is characterized by significant differences across macro regions and especially across sectors. Moreover, the results confirm the existence of a very multifaceted picture when it comes to agglomeration forces operating in very small geographical units. Among the most important determinants of local industry growth it is worth mentioning the positive role of the diversity externalities. The authors also find robust evidence of the negative influence of specialization externalities on labor dynamics at a local industry level. Moreover, Paci and Usai assess the effects of other determinants of local growth such as human capital, social environment, and network externalities. Finally, the presence of spatial autocorrelation is detected for the aggregate economy and also in some sectors and therefore dynamic spatial models have been estimated.

In Chapter 8, Capello and Spairani assess the role of ICT policies for regional economic growth within Europe. The acknowledgment that national boundaries are no longer barriers to economic activity and trade, thanks to the institutional integration created by the European Union and advances in transport and communication technologies, leads to the concept of accessibility being increasingly important as a determinant of local and economic competitiveness. Accessibility defines the ability to overcome spatial distance at low transport cost, and gather strategic information before competitors. Therefore, in a worldwide economy, accessibility reinforces its role of strategic factors in regional competitiveness. However, Capello and Spairani believe that "virtual" rather than physical accessibility is the key factor. Virtual accessibility derives from information and communication technologies. The authors' empirical work uses descriptive and interpretative analyses to examine the impact of accessibility on regional growth, based on accessibility indicators covering both ICT endowment and ICT intensity of use. The main data source is a survey commissioned by the European Commission, covering 44,000 households in 130 regions of the fifteen member states. This overwhelming dataset is also used to assess economic growth in relation to varying policy options. Different impacts on regional performance are analyzed in relation to three policy actions: (i) a short-term policy of increasing ICT endowments; (ii) a medium-term policy of spreading the necessary skills and knowledge for strategic ICT use; and (iii) a long-term policy of influencing the efficiency of the whole productive system. Furthermore, the authors extend the results of the assessment model into the future by considering different accessibility policy options and their implications for future regional growth, by projecting the results in a twenty-year future scenario. Finally, Capello and Spairani highlight the differing impacts of accessibility policies on regions resulting from their different preconditions. ICT policies should take into account the different local preconditions relating to the level of ICT use, the level of ICT endowment, and the learning processes required to use these technologies. All these elements affect the impact of ICT policies in fostering regional development and cannot be ignored when policy actions are planned.

In Chapter 9, Terrasi is concerned with the effects that the new EU enlargement will have on regional inequalities and takes into account both the old and new member states. The effects of enlargement have been a frequent object of study in recent years, but they have mostly been analyzed at an aggregate level and from the point of view of the accession countries. At the spatial level, the main point of interest has been the problem of reforming European regional policy and reconciling the needs of the newcomers with those of the disadvantaged regions. In this chapter, the author turns her attention to the spatial effects of the enlargement by means of a more positive approach. First, Terrasi looks back at the experience of past enlargements in order to see whether it is possible to learn a lesson. In fact, the European Community has experienced other significant enlargements in its history even though in a different general economic context. The main tool of analysis is the Theil index of concentration and its disaggregation in different components, such as between and within country, productivity and employment, sectoral productivities. Subsequently, the author tries to understand whether some of the results obtained for the previous enlargements can be projected to understand the evolution of regional disparities after the next one. Terrasi uses a new dataset, provided by the regional database (REGIO) of Eurostat, for which the most recent data available are for the years 1995–2000 for the countries that were at that time the member states and eleven candidate countries. The Theil index is applied to the regional data of GDP per capita and gross value added (GVA) of different regions and sectors, in order to evaluate the change in regional inequalities and the contribution of different components at the enlarged EU level. These results, together with an examination of some crucial characteristics of the new globalized economy, make it possible to offer some hypotheses regarding the evolution of regional inequalities in the new EU and to evaluate their relevance for the reformulation of European regional policy strategies.

Notes

1 The international conference, Reinventing Space: The Geography of Globalization, was held on 19 and 20 December 2003.

2 The Economic and Monetary Union (EMU), the North American Free Trade Agreement (NAFTA), the Organization for Asia-Pacific Economic Cooperation (APEC), the Association of South East Asian Nations (ASEAN) and the Mercado Comun del Sur (MERCOSUR), to cite just some.

References

Amin, S. (1976) *Unequal Development*, New York: Monthly Review Press.

Aydalot, P. (ed.) (1986) *Milieux Innovateurs in Europe*, Paris: Gremi.

Barro, R.J. and Sala-I-Martin, X. (1991) 'Convergence across states and regions', *Brookings Papers on Economic Activity*, 1: 107–82.

Becattini, G. (1979) 'Dal "settore" industriale al "distretto" industriale. Alcune considerazioni sull'unità di indagine dell'economia industriale', *Rivista di Economia e Politica Industriale*, 5: 7–21.

Becattini, G. (ed.) (1987) *Mercato e Forze Locali: il Distretto Industriale*, Bologna: Il Mulino.

Becattini, G. (1990) 'The Marshallian industrial district as a socio-economic notion', in Pyke, F., Becattini, G. and Sengenberger, W. (eds.) *Industrial Districts and Inter-Firm Co-operation in Italy*, Geneva: International Labour Organization.

Boldrin, M. and Canova, F. (2001) 'Inequality and convergence in Europe's regions: reconsidering European regional policies', *Economic Policy*, 16: 205–45.

Braczyk, H.-J., Cooke, P. and Heidenreich, M. (1998) *Regional Innovation Systems*, London: UCL Press.

Camagni, R. (ed.) (1991) *Innovation Networks. Spatial Perspectives*, London: Belhaven Press.

Canova, F. (2004) 'Testing for convergence clubs in income per capita: a predictive density approach', *International Economic Review*, 45: 49–77.

Canova, F. and Marcet, A. (1995) *The Poor Stay Poor: Non-convergence Across Countries and Regions*. Discussion Paper no. 1265, London: Centre for Economic Policy Research.

Castells, M. (1996) *The Information Age*. Vol. I: *The Rise of the Network Society*, Oxford: Blackwell.

Chang, H.-J. (1994) *The Political Economy of Industrial Policy*, London: Macmillan.

Cooke, P. (2001) 'From technopoles to regional innovation systems: the evolution of localised technology development policy', *Canadian Journal of Regional Science*, 24: 21–39.

Das, D.K. (2004) *Regionalism in Global Trade*, Cheltenham: Edward Elgar.

Dicken, P. (2003) *Global Shift. Reshaping the Global Economic Map in the 21st Century*, London: Sage.

Dunning, J. (1997a) 'The European internal market programme and inbound foreign direct investment – Part I', *Journal of Common Market Studies*, 35: 1–30.

Dunning, J. (1997b) 'The European internal market programme and inbound foreign direct investment – Part II', *Journal of Common Market Studies*, 35: 189–223.

Fujita, M. and Krugman, P. (2004) 'The new economic geography: past, present and future', *Papers in Regional Science*, 83: 139–64.

Geyer, M. and Bright, C. (1995) 'World history in a global age', *American Historical Review*, 100: 1034–60.

Giddens, A. (1990) *The Consequences of Modernity*, Cambridge: Polity Press.

Harrison, B. (1997) *Lean and Mean: The Changing Landscape of Corporate Power in the Age of Flexibility*, New York: Guilford Press.

Harvey, D. (1982) *The Limits to Capital*, Oxford: Blackwell.

Harvey, D. (1989) *The Conditions of Postmodernity*, Oxford: Blackwell.

Held, D. and McGrew, A. (2000) 'The great globalisation debate: an introduction', in Held D. and McGrew, A. (eds.) *The Global Transformations Reader. An Introduction to the Globalization Debate*, Cambridge: Polity Press.

Held, D., McGrew, A., Goldblatt, D., and Perraton, J. (1999) *Global Transformations: Politics, Economics and Culture*, Cambridge: Polity Press.

Hirst, P. and Thompson, G. (1996) *Globalization in Question*, Cambridge: Polity Press.

Howells, J. (1999) 'Regional systems of innovation?', in Archibugi, D., Howells, J. and Michie, J. (eds.) *Innovation Policy in a Global Economy*, Cambridge: Cambridge University Press.

Jessop, B. (1994) 'Post-Fordism and the state', in Amin, A. (ed.) *Post-Fordism: A Reader*, Oxford: Blackwell.

Krugman, P. (1991a) 'Increasing returns and economic geography', *Journal of Political Economy*, 99: 483–99.

Krugman, P. (1991b) *Geography and Trade*, Cambridge, MA: MIT Press.

Krugman, P. (1998) 'What's new about the new economic geography?', *Oxford Review of Economic Policy*, 14: 7–17.

Krugman, P. and Venables, A. (1995) 'Globalisation and the inequality of nations', *Quarterly Journal of Economics*, 110: 857–80.

Maillat, D. (1995) 'Territorial dynamic, innovative milieus and regional policy', *Entrepreneurship and Regional Development*, 7: 157–65.

Marshall, A. (1990 [1890]) *Principles of Economics*, Basingstoke: Macmillan.

Martin, R. (1999) 'The new economic geography of money', in Martin, R. (ed.) *Money and the Space Economy*, New York: Wiley.

Massey, D. (1984) *Spatial Division of Labour*, London: Macmillan.

Modelski, G. (1972) *Principles of World Politics*, New York: Free Press.

Myrdal, G. (1957) *Economic Theory and Underdeveloped Regions*, London: Duckworth.

Neary, J.P. (2001) 'Of hype and hyperbolas: introducing the new economic geography', *Journal of Economic Literature*, 39: 536–61.

Ohmae, K. (1990) *The Borderless World: Power and Strategy in the Interlinked Economy*, London: Collins.

Ohmae, K. (1995) *The End of the Nation State. The Rise of Regional Economics*, London: HarperCollins.

Ottaviano, G. (2000) '*Ad usum delphini*: a primer in "new economic geography" ', *Giornale degli Economisti e Annali di Economia*, 59: 87–114.

Piore, M. and Sabel, C. (1984) *The Second Industrial Divide: Possibilities for Prosperity*, New York: Basic Books.

Quah, D.T. (1996) 'Regional convergence clusters across Europe', *European Economic Review*, 40: 951–8.

Reich, R.B. (1991) *The Work of Nations*, New York: Vintage.

Sala-I-Martin, X. (1996) 'The classical approach to convergence analysis', *Economic Journal*, 106: 1019–36.

Sayer, A. and Walker, R. (1992) *The New Social Economy*, Oxford: Blackwell.

Solow, R.M. (1956) 'A contribution to the theory of economic growth', *Quarterly Journal of Economics*, 70: 65–94.

Solow, R.M. (1957) 'Technical change and the aggregate production function', *Review of Economics and Statistics*, 39: 312–20.

Storper, M. and Walker, R. (1989) *The Capitalist Imperative. Territory, Technology, and Industrial Growth*, New York: Blackwell.

Weiss, L. (1998) *The Myth of the Powerless State*, Cambridge: Polity Press.

Went, R. (2000) *Globalization. Neoliberal Challenge, Radical Response*, London: Pluto Press.

Part I

Theoretical perspectives

1 Lost in space?

The geographical and political dimension of uneven capitalist development

Riccardo Bellofiore and Giovanna Vertova

Introduction

The recent debate about globalisation has been marked by a contraposition of the *continuity* and *discontinuity* points of view. Those favouring the former think that the globalisation at the end of the 1900s is nothing but the resumption of the long-standing well-known 'internationalisation' of the capitalist economy (Hirst and Thompson 1999). Those favouring the latter viewpoint believe, instead, in the radical novelty of the current phase, so that the term 'globalisation' pertains only to this new reality (Ohmae 1995). Such a polarity recurs in respect of the relevance of territories and space in the global economy.

In fact, two opposing positions reappear also for those accepting the globalisation paradigm. On the one hand, mainstream neoliberal theories argue that globalisation leads to a general tendency towards a *homogenisation* of firms, sectors and geographical areas that tends to cancel the role of 'place'. On the other hand, we find many authors stressing that, in the new context, local and regional dimension acquires a fresh role, leading to a *differentiation* of territories and thus to a renewed importance of the geographical embedding of the economy. These two positions are not to be considered as fixed or mutually exclusive, since it is possible to find many intermediate positions. This debate has also crossed arguments for or against the 'end of the nation-state' (Reich 1991, Weiss 1998) as well as for or against the 'end of work' (Rifkin 1995, Bellofiore 1999), which are supposed to be distinctive features of the new capitalism for the hyperglobalisation views. The discussion has also affected the 'radical' left interpretation of contemporary capitalism. Here, of course, we find again those asserting the tendency towards homogenisation or the tendency towards differentiation. What is interesting, however, is that for both groups labour seems to be 'lost in space' – so to speak. In other words, both those who stress the loss of 'local' advantages or its more intensive exploitation see a quantitative and/or qualitative 'collapse' of wage labour as being typical of the globalisation phase. Workers are no longer the 'central' subject of social progressive change within capitalism (Walker 1999).

This chapter starts with a discussion of the different basic paradigms in economic theory, in order to test how they are able to deal with the differentiation of the 'qualities' of productive resources, techniques, means of production and labour power as something structural and essential in capitalist accumulation. This internal drive to a differentiation of the methods of production is inevitably rooted in 'space' and deeply affects the 'local' dimension and its history, with the ascent and decline of entire economic regions. The second section illustrates how the two main neoclassical currents, stemming from Walras and Marshall, deal with (or elude) this topic. The third section describes the alternative Marxian approach, through a dialogue with David Harvey's re-reading and developments. The fourth section embarks on a more positive proposal on the terrain of economic theory, highlighting some problems in the Marxian system and suggesting the need for a confrontation of this tradition with the monetary heterodoxy of Schumpeter and Keynes. The fifth section applies this framework to the interpretation of contemporary capitalism. The final section shows how labour conditions are transformed in the new global economy. The concluding section clarifies in what sense these changes mark a historical watershed.

The dead ends of the neoclassical tradition

Since the beginning, neoclassical mainstream theory has been divided along two main lines: the general economic equilibrium (GEE), originating with Walras (1988 [1874]), and the partial economic equilibrium (PEE), originating with Marshall (1990 [1890]). At no time have these two paths converged although it is possible to discern a tendency of both theoretical and applied economics to oscillate between the two, with movement in one or the other direction at different times. This oscillation is based on the impossibility of making either one or the other of these two approaches a coherent and convincing framework for the inquiry of an intrinsically dynamic and monetary economy such as capitalism.

Sraffa's criticisms of marginalism

The internal logical soundness of marginalism in both its incarnations has been criticised on several occasions and with some justification. Piero Sraffa is the crucial actor in this story. In 1925–26, he attacked the Marshallian theory of perfect competition and the idea that limits to the size of output come from costs and the prevalence, after a certain point, of decreasing returns (Sraffa 1925, 1926). This critique challenges the idea that the competitive firm, necessarily small, works in a homogeneous market, in which it is indifferent whether to purchase from one firm rather than another. By contrast, there are many 'particular' markets and it is impossible to neglect market imperfections or product differentiation. In 1960, Sraffa destroyed the notion of 'capital' as a homogeneous factor of production and opened the way to the rebuttal of the aggregate production function. The view of profit as the remuneration of the marginal contributions to production of 'capital' as a factor of production was mortally wounded (Sraffa 1960). Sraffa denies the existence of a unique equilibrium distribution, and opens the economic system to conflicts in the distribution of the surplus. Social and political determinants may affect the 'productive configuration' and the methods of production of the system.

However, neither the Walrasian nor the Marshallian neoclassical traditions came out lethally injured by the attack against the laws of returns, or by the capital controversy, or by the revival of a Ricardian conflictual view of distribution. The way out from Sraffa's 1925–26 criticism was the Robinson–Chamberlin 'imperfect competition' literature. And the way out from Sraffa's 1960 critique of neoclassical GEE was along the lines of disaggregated intertemporal general equilibrium models without capital as an aggregate notion. But it is a paradoxical situation when economics fluctuates between a list of particular cases and the abolition of capital itself from economic discourse, since the object of analysis is precisely the study of a capitalist system.

This paradox is an indication of an unsettled situation, which deserves to be investigated more accurately, especially by looking at the way in which temporal and spatial dimensions can be integrated fully within neoclassical economics.

The general equilibrium and the theory of location

Walras's original general equilibrium model presents the relations of a one-point economy and the conditions for its equilibrium. The underlying assumptions – i.e. zero transport costs, perfect mobility of capital and labour, uniform technical conditions, neglect of local differences in supply and demand and the principle of 'pure' competition – are meaningful only when the economy is considered *abstracting from space as well as time*. The same is true for the later intertemporal version of general economic equilibrium (Debreu 1959). Here Walras's model is extended to a sequence of periods by assuming the existence of complete markets and perfect forecasting, thus introducing a false conception of 'time'. Commodities can be distinguished not only according to their product characteristics and the moment they are available, but also by the place where they are available and the states of nature. In this way, both time and space are considered but 'neutralised'. The same happens to money, which is inessential too. Not only, as in Walras, is there a central coordination mechanism, the 'auctioneer', but the model is also framed so that present and future coordination is guaranteed, and there is no uncertainty. In fact, in the initial period the destiny of the system is defined once and for all.

Neoclassical location analysis managed to introduce space in the general equilibrium framework, by considering the distance factor in terms of transport costs. Alfred Weber (1971 [1929]) was the first economist to undertake a systematic analysis of location in a neoclassical framework. Weber's main aim was to find the economic reason for the rapid urbanisation of the German economy by isolating three important explanatory forces: transport costs, labour costs and agglomeration forces. By taking into account these three determinants, an optimum location becomes the point of overall minimum transport costs, although both labour costs and agglomeration economies can shift the optimal location towards other points. Weber's work was indeed within the neoclassical tradition but limited to a partial equilibrium analysis. By contrast, Lösch (1954) developed a true general equilibrium analysis based on the definition of 'economic region' and its determinants. His main aim was to elaborate a model of location valid for independent producers and consumers, for agriculture as well as industry, hence a universal model. Each producer (or consumer) is represented by a set of coordinates and its boundaries are described in equation form. In this way, the regional economy is given by a system of mathematical equations, whose solution gives the optimum location for a firm.

Lösch shared with Christaller (1966 [1933]) the idea that a hexagon is the shape which the market takes by the expansion of producers (or consumers). The hexagon market principle enables both authors to define equations for the general equilibrium model for location. Predöhl (1928) believed that the location problem is a price problem, and that the principle of substitution enables firms to move from one location to another, according to the relative prices of the factors of production. Finally, Isard (1949, 1956), the post-war founder of the regional school, attempted to make the Weberian approach more dynamic, by introducing internal and external scale economies, and urbanisation economies. His equilibrium model of an idealised capitalist system was the result of the application of game theory to abstractly defined regions.

These theories of location all shared the same unrealistic assumptions, which were necessary to make the models work and give the equations a solution: a uniform–plain region with a uniform distribution of raw materials, a uniform transport surface, a uniform distribution of population, uniform tastes and preferences, uniform technical knowledge and uniform production opportunities. Almost all these authors were aware of the lack of realism of these assumptions. Weber breaks through the limitations of such artificial assumptions in a section entitled 'Reintroducing the Realities' (Weber 1971 [1929]: chapter V, section III). Lösch did the same in a small section entitled 'Economic Regions in Reality' (Lösch 1954: chapter II, section B15). Isard, commenting on his diagrams and figures, remarks that they 'pertain to a situation which abstracts from interest conflicts, undercutting and retaliation, advertising strategies, collusive action, market encroachment, and similar phenomena characteristic of firm behaviour' (Isard 1956: 264–5). Despite the acknowledgement of the unreality of their assumptions, the theory of location was the first attempt to include space in economic analysis.

Within the general equilibrium framework, geographical dimension can be related only to the choice of the optimum localisation of productive activities, and space can be considered only in terms of geographical distance (i.e. transport costs). Taking the technology as exogenous as well as the demand determined by voluntary households' choices, the problem is to identify the 'best' distribution of productive activities across space and the 'right' settlement to minimise costs. 'Consumer sovereignty' and exogeneity of techniques rule. The economic process is understood as a one-way avenue from resources to consumption. The only problem is, therefore, the 'efficient' and 'rational' allocation of resources, relative to the 'natural' aim of the satisfaction of needs.

All these neoclassical approaches to space are challenged by the same critiques to general equilibrium. First, asymmetric information and bounded rationality are not considered in the model, money is irrelevant, capital and labour are perfectly mobile and the production function is uniform throughout. Moreover, the conceptualisation of space, explicitly considered only in terms of transport costs, is inconsistent with the idea of perfect competition and, consequently, with the original neoclassical approach (Sheppard 2000). Indeed, if different places can be treated as single different markets, the necessary conditions of a large number of buyers and sellers for each commodity and for each factor of production cannot be fulfilled and there is no uniform price paid by everyone. Least but not last, supply, demand and price adjustments – the typical neoclassical tools – cannot explain the location of industries because they cannot be considered independent of space. On the contrary, they are produced by industries themselves over time through an ongoing interaction between the production system and the location behaviour of industry (Storper and Walker 1989).

The neoclassical general equilibrium approach to location is compatible with the neoliberal argument that a firm is free to choose any location, depending only upon production and transport costs. Capital is seen as 'footloose' with the power to move freely across space and set up plants and industries everywhere in the world. Yet, if this were true, nowadays all plants in industrialised countries would have moved to the Third World. This does not happen because there are some negative externalities in locating plants everywhere. Moreover, relocation is not always a costless option for firms. High sunk costs in terms of long-term fixed investments, which are bound to local markets or suppliers, and dependence on specific labour supply qualities or on local (physical and social) infrastructures, discourage the mobility of firms. Against all this, the neoclassical general equilibrium tradition enforces the idea of the global market as a homogeneous space, spontaneously created by market forces, where economic development occurs evenly. Nothing could be further from the truth.

Ways out inside the dominant theory: the new economic geography

The inessentiality of money, time and space has been considered as a serious limitation by the same authors working within the general equilibrium in more recent years. At the same time, other internal limitations of the basic foundations of neoclassical theory that appear to be even more damaging than the logical contradictions highlighted by Sraffa have been stressed. We refer to the discovery that the general equilibrium approach, even in its most abstract version – the intertemporal formulation *à la* Arrow-Debreu – is globally unstable, with multiple equilibria, and the very existence of equilibrium occurs only under specific and restrictive conditions. All these problems pushed forward a revision of the role of the general economic equilibrium model in neoclassical theory. The Walrasian world is no longer something that can be immediately applied to the analysis of 'real' economies (as, however, some neo-Walrasians still think). Instead, it is seen simply as a solution to an intellectual problem: what conditions are needed for 'coherence' in a social setting in which individual economic agents are 'dissociated' and 'opportunistic'; how a perfectly competitive market may give origin to 'order' and 'equilibrium', rather than chaos. The fact that the solution to this intellectual problem gives rise to a world where money, time and space are 'inessential' is not to be considered as a 'failure' of the theory. Instead, it asks researchers to define those minimal changes in the basic hypothesis of the model which has to be introduced so that money, time and space 'matter'.

Several attempts have been made along these lines. We can limit ourselves here to a reminder of some of them. The elimination of the auctioneer, so that the dichotomy between the phase of 'bargaining' and the phase of 'simultaneous exchanges' at equilibrium prices no longer holds and transactions at non-equilibrium prices are allowed. The non-existence of complete markets, so that markets must be thought of as reopening period after period, and the economy becomes sequential. The impossibility of economic agents foreseeing all future states of nature means that the presence of non-insurable risk or even of true uncertainty is the norm. Once 'imperfections' of this kind are taken into account, it becomes essential to consider that some commodities (first of all, labour and bank credit) do not possess the necessary characteristic of standardisation in order to be the object of buying and selling in auction markets. Transactions become 'individual', so to speak, with markets based on customer relationships between principal and agent. Not only must uncertainty be taken into consideration, but also the imperfect and asymmetric distribution of information becomes crucial. In contexts such as these, the local dimension is enhanced. Firms know the characteristics of their labour force better and can, therefore, control it better. Banks may better select entrepreneurs among their traditional borrowers. And so on.

In such a world, it is impossible to neglect exogenous shocks, increasing returns, market failures and asymmetric information. Here we are on the terrain of New Economic Geography, in which economies of scale, different local demands and externalities are taken into account. Standard location theory suggests that transport costs will limit geographical concentration. However, firms can benefit from geographical concentration when economies of scale are available. Therefore, transport costs must be assessed in relation to the gains from economies of scale. If the benefits of economies of scale outweigh transport costs, the incentive for firms to cluster will be high (Krugman 1991, 1995). It is often advantageous to locate to the region with the largest market when demand varies between geographical areas and when there are economies of scale (Krugman and Venables 1994, 1995). Moreover, in many cities where the existence of factors such as a natural harbour or navigable rivers leads to geographical concentration, firms discover, accidentally, the benefit of being located close to other firms engaging in similar types of operations and a process of clustering spontaneously emerges (Krugman 1996, Fujita *et al.* 1999).

What is crucial here is not the single event, sometimes considered as accidental, which starts the process of agglomeration of economic activities in space. Once the process has exogenously started, it is possible to assess its cumulative evolution over time, its mechanisms of adjustment and adaptation, the new equilibrium it will lead to. History, geography and even policy can definitely have a decisive role in the process, thus affecting not only the costs of production but also the transaction and the information costs. Yet, both the existence of multiple equilibria and the more complex representation of the rise and decline of industrial concentration do not modify what remains in substance a 'static' approach. Clusters of firms, technological poles and local production systems are evident signs of the presence of increasing returns to scale. The analytical framework is, however, still a mechanical one and, within it, imperfections are just what the name suggests: a mere 'deviation' from the ideal world where economic agents have the same power, the same position in the market, the same information. In other words, perfect equilibrium is again the reference point on which, ideally, the system is judged and to which it must tend. As a consequence, policy has the task to correct that deviation, accelerate the convergence and, if necessary, smooth likely social tensions.

We thus reach the current theoretical situation. Although it is theoretically weak on many fundamental grounds, and although it appears an individualistic and unhistorical method, the neoclassical paradigm of general equilibrium has shown itself to be so eclectic and greedy as to be able to deal with the very many 'complications' of reality, giving room also to the 'local' dimension. Here differentiation (among firms, sectors and also geographical areas) appears as something marginal and fortuitous in the basic theoretical abstraction. Yet, this random accident is what explains the structure of economic regions, organisations and territories in their actual and concrete history.

Ways out internal to the dominant theory: Marshall and the districts

This section deals with the stream of the common neoclassical body, the partial economic equilibrium tradition. For Marshall (1990 [1890]) the firm is a tree within the forest that is the industry. In the industry, the cluster of firms produces a sufficiently homogeneous commodity that it is possible to construct a demand curve for it. Industry is, therefore, the organisational precondition of 'perfect' competition, without which the formation and determination of price cannot be theoretically constructed.

Each tree has its own life, characterised by different moments such as birth, development, decay and death. Yet, the forest continues to exist near individual trees: it is not their simple sum, and it survives even when the single units of production, the small firms, disappear. The decay and death of firms is vital to the preservation of perfect competition, otherwise firms would grow bigger and bigger, and perfect competition would transform into monopoly. The ongoing life of the industry is even more essential because it avoids losing the advantages of the developments of firms. In the Walrasian system there is no intermediate agent between the firm and the economic system as a whole. In the Marshallian one, it does exist and it is the industry. The distinction between industry and firm enables Marshall to distinguish between the 'internal' economies – depending upon the scale of production of the single firm – and 'external' economies – relying on the development of the industry as a whole.

It is not a task of the present work to criticise the vagueness of Marshall's definition of industry, or to discuss the difficulties in separating internal from external economies. Instead, what we want to stress are two points. On the one hand, Marshall puts forward a detailed examination of those external economies due to the localisation of the industry. On the other hand, he also depicts the external economies as resulting from the fact that entire groups of intertwined industries develop in close proximity. Marshall's intuition becomes important when two aspects, missing in the Walrasian approach, are taken into consideration. The first is that industry sets itself as a systemic 'fact'. The second is that this element is intermediate between the micro level of the firm and the macro level of the economic system as a whole.

From here, the step towards the notion of the industrial district is a short one (Becattini 1979, 1987, 1990). Within the same cycle of production, small and medium-sized firms coexist thanks to a positive synergy of know-how and skills, technologies and labour power, a synergy that is also greatly facilitated by the fundamental homogeneity of culture, values and even of politics (Trigilia 1986). In the ensuing literature about industrial districts the focus is on cooperation among firms rather than on mere competition, on the network spread across the territory rather than on concentration and the increasing of scale, on the quality of labour rather than on its cost, on participation rather than on conflict. The belonging to a shared (not only industrial) history and to the same (not only productive) community becomes, at the same time, a competitive asset as well as a barrier to entry for outsiders. Similar characteristics are also found in other approaches to regional or local economics, such as the *milieu innovateur* (Aydalot 1986, Camagni 1991), the regional system of innovation (Braczyk *et al.* 1998), the flexible production system (Piore and Sabel 1984) and the new industrial space approach (Scott 1988). Complementarities among firms, spillovers and externalities are all at the core of the picture. Technology and firm dimension go hand in hand with other advantages that may generate a 'stratification' because of the concentration of professional skills, presence of specialised suppliers and ease of accessing information.

The merit of all these approaches is to reject the idea of the firm as an isolated entity with a maximising behaviour and, instead, consider it as 'embedded' in its territory. Firms are rooted in their territory through the industrial atmosphere created by relations and networks established with other firms, institutions and organisations placed in the same geographical area. Social aspects (Granovetter 1985) as well as institutions (Hodgson 1999) become crucial for the explanation of firms' behaviour. Social, institutional and territorial variables are the sources of external economies, explaining why firms tend to cluster together. Consequently, space is no longer considered in Euclidean terms, but in relational terms. The distance which matters is not only geographical but also, and fundamentally, economic, social, cultural and institutional.

The partial equilibrium literature, in its less orthodox and more interesting lines of inquiry, has led to a wealth of descriptions of particular situations (Rabellotti 1997, Bagella and Becchetti 2000, Guerrieri *et al.* 2001, Paniccia 2002, Becattini *et al.* 2003, Belussi *et al.* 2003, to cite just some of the many). But they have not produced a radical break with the mainstream and appear to suffer the same shortcomings as the traditional neoclassical literature. Market-driven capitalist competition is once again seen as economically and socially beneficial. The main difference is that there is now a richer (and less individualistic) sociological definition of the actors, which are now the territories with their own idiosyncratic assets making that particular place economically unique. 'Places' compete among themselves, and the best-endowed ones will survive. Moreover, the role of state and local authorities is very often limited to the correction of market imperfections, by creating proper 'factors' (i.e. education, infrastructures, etc.) that are believed to sustain local growth.

Some deeper perplexities cannot be passed over. To what extent can local systems of production be 'built' if history did not root them in a long-term evolutionary process? To what extent can they be considered a paradigm of industrial and territorial organisation able to become the 'whole', rather than just a partial element which can prosper only under particular conditions and macroeconomic policy? Is the cooperative and harmonic view of relationships between firms and other social agents not too idyllic? Is not technological change a phenomenon causing disequilibrium, whose causes are internal to a dynamic struggle between firms and, consequently, between social classes, a process that these approaches fail to appreciate enough? What is the role played by the monetary aspects of the capitalist process in all this?

The Marxian alternative

The Marxian economic geography works within a framework that puts 'space' at the core of a re-reading of the capitalist process as uneven development (see Swyngedouw 2000 for a survey). In contrast to the non-monetary general equilibrium of the neoclassical theorists, the basic model here is the *cycle of money capital* as described by Marx (1999 [1885]) in the second volume of *Capital*. In our interpretation, the capitalist process is illustrated by Marx mainly as a circular sequence sparked off by money capital, leading to the production of more money. Value and surplus value are nothing but the monetary expression of the abstract labour 'congealed' in commodities. The production of value and surplus value presupposes a social and physical 'infrastructure' that encompasses not only the legal system, the education system, the state administration, etc., but also a certain configuration of transport, environment and cities. The capitalist economy as a production of money by means of money can be reduced neither to a stationary economy, in which the surplus value is entirely consumed ('simple reproduction'), nor to a 'balanced' proportional growth of the system, with the different branches growing at the same rate. In both cases, techniques are given, and there is no room for structural and discontinuous qualitative change.

Following Marx, accumulation must rather be seen as an uneven process whereby:

1 the extraction of surplus value comes from a lengthening of the social working day beyond the point at which the living labour of wage workers reproduces the value represented in the wage bill;

2 technical progress is endogenously driven by the necessity to extract living labour from a potentially conflictual labour power;
3 capitalist competition is expressed not only by the 'homogenising' tendency among industries, resulting from the mobility of capital, which leads to an equalisation of the profit rate on the money capital advanced but also, and even more fundamentally, by the struggle among firms within industries for extra surplus value (and extra profits) that is the origin of an unending 'differentiation' and 'stratification' of units of production of different quality.

It is evident that such a vision of the capitalist system is opposite in each single element to the neoclassical theory. The capitalist process is characterised as an economic system in which access to money (as capital) is the privilege of one class (because money is not just a means of circulation that facilitates the exchange of goods). The relation of production is antagonistic, and the determination of wage is conflictual (because labour is not a factor of production among many, and the distribution of product is not cooperative). The introduction of innovations is internally forced by a permanent fight to obtain extra profit and ensure survival (competition is not just a simple adaptation to the already given optimum technique).

The Marxian starting point has significant consequences. The weaving of class struggle, technological dynamism and organisational change is prolonged into an analysis of structural instability and capitalist crises in which finance matters. The monetary and financial sector includes the banking system, which provides the initial finance to begin production, and the stock market, where firms can place securities among the savers. Thus, the accumulation of capital becomes independent from current surplus value or *ex ante* savings. Investments are less and less constrained from consumption. 'Dynamic' competition is empowered and makes the innovation–imitation sequence a process to which it is not possible to adapt gradually.

Capitalist development is thus a process inherently 'out of equilibrium', generating instability from within. This instability periodically breaks open in crises which at the same time express and solve the inner contradictions of the system. Investments and innovations become embodied in methods of production that use more elements of constant capital (means of production, raw materials, etc.) and expel living labour from production. This process may lead to a tendential fall in the rate of profit, if it is not countered by an adequate rise in the rate of surplus value. But a growing surplus value vis-à-vis the value of labour power exhibited in money by the wage bill leads to a fall in the relative wage, and thus a fall in workers' consumption and in aggregate consumption. This is the root of the possibility of realisation crises, which comes into being thanks to the interaction with 'disproportionalities' and the pathological explosion of 'fictitious' capital.

The alternation of capitalist development and crises depends upon the constant production and reproduction of capital and labour, within and outside the capitalist circulation of commodities. The financialisation of the capitalist economy can be interpreted as a means to overcome the overproduction of capital and commodities, either by lowering the turnover time of capital and increasing the potential rate of profit or by sustaining investment (by guaranteeing that the actual rate of profit is as close as possible to the potential one). This solution is temporary, shifts the contradictions to the future and requires a rise in indebtedness that sooner or later will prove to be unsustainable.

There is also a spatial dimension of the capitalist accumulation and its crises. It is here that a dialogue with Harvey (1975, 1982), the key author in the 'geopolitical' rewriting of Marxian historical materialism, becomes crucial. The transformation of space is not only an opportunity to invest. If the Marxian inquiry about capital accumulation mainly stresses the realm of the 'abstract' and the 'universal', a consideration of geographical dimension opens to the realm of the 'concrete' and the 'particular' through which valorisation necessarily must pass. In fact, the exploitation of labour power, technical change and production of commodities is not even possible without a coherent territorial structure (Harvey 1982). Labour power can be controlled and organised, and the subsistence level of wages can be defined, only within a 'region'. Moreover, within that 'region', infrastructures and fixed social capital are needed in order to enable and, when necessary, to limit the mobility of capital and labour power. The political dimension is crucial here, and it is also most visible in the control of money capital.

Along these lines, the capitalist contradiction becomes the dialectic between the spatial, concrete rootedness of capital, on the one hand, and the unlimited expansion of abstract wealth, on the other. At a given point in time, labour, production, innovation and finance can occur only within a particular and concrete space, and on the basis of infrastructures with a certain degree of 'fixity' resulting from political and state intervention. Through time, the continuous revolutionary changes resulting from capital accumulation put those spatial and regional configurations under pressure and create tensions. In this process, the creation of value shows its destructive face and its need to annihilate the concreteness of space to favour the growth of abstract wealth in a generic temporal dimension. With this approach, Harvey begins to include space within historical materialism in an essential and systematic way, going beyond the occasional remarks we find in Marx's work.

A geographical dimension can also be found in the way in which capitalism answers the recurrent tendency to crises. 'External' markets, capital 'exports', 'regional' alliances and competition among territories are all part of the history of the cyclical dynamics of capitalist accumulation. The state must intervene by enhancing the constitution, stability or dissolution of regional spaces. Nevertheless, it can never eliminate the tendency towards crises within the capitalist system of production.

The integration of Marx with Schumpeter and Keynes

Geographical dimension is not included in the foundational basic discourse of economic theory. Marx's critique of political economy is just a partial exception, which is why Harvey's connection between endogenous technological progress, uneven capitalist development, finance, instability and economic crisis is so important. In his interpretation, as in ours, the 'differentiation' of firms, industries and territories is not accidental and marginal but essential and central. Harvey's historical–geographical materialism also has the merit of being constructed outside a dogmatic approach to Marx. But we believe that Harvey follows the original formulation of Marx's *Capital* too much, without resolving some of the difficulties that have become more and more evident in recent times. We outline some of these briefly:

1 The monetary circuit is constructed in a framework where money is a commodity and the bank is a financial intermediary that is able to grant credit in a flexible amount but which is however, in the end, limited by the availability of the 'hard' metallic base.
2 Value as a monetary representation of abstract labour is grounded only in the eventual validation on the commodity market of the objective labour 'embodied' in the commodity.
3 The theory of crises in both of its versions (the tendency of the rate of profit to fall and the realisation crisis) underestimates the possibility of a capitalist way out.

To overcome these limits, we believe that Marxian critical political economy has to engage in a dialogue with the two great 'heretics' of the Walrasian and Marshallian traditions: Schumpeter and Keynes. Both authors share with Marx a vision of the capitalist economy as a system of production of money by means of money. In the case of Schumpeter, this is complementary to a dynamic vision of capitalist competition that is very similar to Marx's. In Keynes's case, the break with orthodoxy originates from a rebuttal of Say's law on which a continuity line with Marx may again be constructed. Indeed, both Schumpeter and Keynes break with the neoclassical tradition on points on which Marx distanced himself from Ricardo. What is novel in Schumpeter and Keynes is that they depicted the monetary sequence of the capitalist process following the lead of an author who was, in his 'real' analysis, a thoroughgoing neoclassical adherent, Knut Wicksell. From him, Schumpeter and Keynes took the idea that the nature of money is neither that of a commodity nor that of a bilateral credit instrument, but that of a three-party debt–credit relationship as in bank money. Both believed that money is a 'claim ticket' to real resources that precedes the production of commodities, and not only a 'receipt voucher' following it. The banking system, creating money *ex nihilo*, is a kind of centralised social system of accounts whereby the differential distribution of the claim tickets affects the command and distribution of real resources.

We want to stress two important aspects of this redefined cycle of money capital:

1 Since money circulates in a closed universe, a crisis resulting from lack of liquidity in the monetary system as a whole is impossible. Nevertheless, 'individual' national banking systems can find themselves in deficit or in surplus at the inter-bank clearing house. In this event, there are three ways out: a true world bank that produces the final means of payment to be utilised among national central banks; bilateral credits granted by national central banks to

each other; or the alienation of commodities. The third solution recalls the role of money as a commodity at the world level, which Marx refers to in *Capital*.

2 Since money is the necessary means to have access to real resources, the entrepreneur who wants to innovate needs bank credit first of all. This is the point stressed by Schumpeter. Dynamic competition among firms is made possible by the non-proportional distribution of the new purchasing power created by banks. Banks have the task of selecting potential entrepreneurs. Asymmetric information occurs here. On the one hand, entrepreneurs benefit from a 'micro' information advantage, related to a more realistic knowledge of their investment projects. On the other hand, banks benefit from a 'macro' information advantage, related to their better knowledge of the economic system at the different levels (local, national and global).

In this framework, bank money is two things at the same time. First of all, it is a centralised symbol of the social nexus, which can be politically managed at macro level in order to avoid excessive instability. Second, it is the monetary complement to innovation, essential for dynamic competition at micro level.

Within this analytical framework, relations among the macro subjects (the banking system, the firm sector, the working class) take priority over individual behaviour. Bank finance is essential to the firm sector as a whole, which has to advance the money wage bill to workers. In a closed economy without state intervention this is actually the only buying that takes place outside the sector; and this is, at the same time, the only way that workers can obtain money to buy the means of subsistence. Privileged access to money implies that firms have power over the allocation of the labour force among the production of commodities that will go back to workers and the production of those surplus goods that are appropriated by firms and banks. Despite the fact that these authors never admit it explicitly, the capitalist class autonomously defines the necessary labour (congealed in the commodities sold to workers) and the surplus value (the labour congealed in the surplus commodities sold for money). The surplus value commodities may be realised for an amount of money higher than that anticipated by firms thanks to 'external' markets (as in Luxemburg 2003 [1913]) or 'internal exports' (as in Kalecki 1991 [1967]) (i.e. budget deficits financed by a new inflow of money) or bank financing of firms' investment demand.

It is clear that Marx's two 'special commodities' – money and labour power – are the object of a political management with not only a 'state' but also a 'local' and 'regional' dimension. The Schumpeterian–Marxian dynamic view of competition fares better than the static neoclassical one because it necessarily implies a stratified differentiation of firms within industries from the very beginning. This 'pluralism' of firms is also different from the one we find in the Marshallian districts because of the stress on the destructive side of the competition among capitalists. This variety, so to speak, of qualities of firms has its counterpart in the attention that can be given to variations in the qualifications of workers. Indeed, in the perspective we propose, abstract labour is the living labour of the wage workers ante-validated by bank finance as labour tentatively producing surplus value. It is 'without quality' not because it is necessarily poor in skills or qualifications, but rather because the quality it has is imposed on workers by capitalist technological and organisational innovations. There may be phases in the capitalist accumulation in which valorisation requires partial reskilling and constrained autonomy of workers instead of the 'degradation of work'. Politics and economic policy may affect these various factors of the reproduction of capital.

A 'place' is defined by a certain coherent set of financial and real characteristics, but industrial dynamic competition can force a radical change in this spatial dimension. Also important is the balance between local, national, regional and global levels in banking. According to Minsky (1965: 101), the essential role of commercial banks in a local economy is the following:

> they supply 'loan' capital to (a) those local enterprises which must grow at least at the same rate as the local economy, and (b) those export enterprises which are too small, and perhaps too new, to be able to generate nationally-acceptable liabilities

Their essential role is thus not to intermediate local savings or to be instrumental for the import of capital, but to be a source of bank loans for those firms that are otherwise financially constrained. It becomes evident that a 'local' or 'regional' banking system, by contrast with a closed 'national' or 'world' one, can have its potential credit constrained by the availability of reserves.

Endogenous technical change, the essential role of bank money and intra-capitalist conflicts at all levels prevent a vision of globalisation as a tendency towards homogenisation.

Space and the end of Fordism

The crisis of the so-called Golden Age capitalism broke out in the middle of the 1970s, although the causes of the exhaustion of the Fordist–Keynesian model are probably a decade older. Since the end of Bretton Woods, with the introduction of flexible exchange rates and the oil crisis contributing to stagflation, a long series of destabilising events have been put in motion, marking the transition to a different kind of capitalism. The key turning points at the end of the 1970s and which defined the 1980s were the monetarist turn in economic policy by Volcker, the neoliberal governments of Thatcher and Reagan, the higher mobility of financial capital, the upward jump in nominal and real interest rates, the war against the welfare state and its transformation in workfare, the spread of market deregulation and the increasingly precarious nature of the labour market and labour process. This is a well-known story and we do not intend to tell it again in these pages.

According to some interpreters, at the beginning of the 1990s, a 'new capitalism' begins to make its appearance (Ohmae 1995, Castells 1996). It is anti-interventionist as far as economic policy is concerned. It is post-Fordist in the organisation of labour. It is global not only in relation to its financial aspects but also in production and markets. Manual labour is confined to the new industrialised countries, where labour costs are lower; in contrast, in the old industrialised countries, labour becomes more 'cognitive'. The advanced capitalist countries are said to live in a 'learning economy' (Lundvall and Johnson 1994). Higher quality at lower cost is required everywhere.

The Marxian prophecy about the globalisation of capitalism seems to have come true. Indeed, until the 1980s, the idea that spontaneous capitalist development would have resulted in the diffusion of prosperity everywhere appeared to be devoid of any sense of reality. According to the neoclassical theory, although it is true that growth is at first confined to particular areas, decreasing returns and external economies guarantee the extension of advantages to backward countries, and then result in territorial and geographical balance through the automatic working of the free market. Against all this, the Marxist theory of imperialism seemed more realistic. The periphery is seen as a land to be conquered in order to open new markets or guarantee new sources of raw materials, or as a place to invest capital in order to avoid the low profitability of the centre. The relationship between centre and periphery is in fact ruled by an 'unequal exchange' (Emmanuel 1972). These critical approaches also remained vital during the Golden Age. In that period, the Marxian collapse theory was proved wrong, but economic growth was occurring almost exclusively in the centre. The real challenge to this line of inquiry came later. The point was not that the distinction between developed and developing areas was going to disappear. The novel fact was that – certainly, because of active economic policies contrary to those suggested by neoliberalism – some peripheral countries managed to escape the poverty trap and became protagonists of the world economy. Here, a typical example is East Asia from the mid-1960s to the mid-1990s. Moreover, demand for commodities and capital movements were more and more concentrated in the centre of capitalism, something that falsifies Luxemburg's (2003 [1913]) and Lenin's (1948 [1916]) contrasting views on imperialism.

The end of Fordism also meant the crisis of a kind of 'third way' between the *laissez-faire* myth of the spontaneous diffusion of capitalist development and the Marxist theory of imperialism. We refer to authors such as Myrdal (1957), Nurkse (1953), Prebisch (1950) and Rosenstein-Rodan (1943, 1976). According to these authors, state economic direct action for infrastructures and investments is necessary in order to promote a balanced development. 'Planning' in public expenditures and/or incentives should be designed to guarantee, through the correct calibration of demand and supply interventions, a proportionate expansion of the structure of the economy, in order to make national growth independent from the international demand trend. Yet, what happened during the Golden Age was very different. After the end of the Second World War, public expenditure was not implemented according to some general interest, but instead followed a path partly imposed by some lobby groups (principally, the military and oil lobby). Moreover, state intervention went along with, but did not replace, the rapid growth of international trade, which was the prime mover of capitalist expansion. The primacy of foreign demand increasingly created imbalances rather than balanced development, and paved the way towards the globalisation that occurred at the end of the twentieth century.

Labour in curent globalisation

The literature on globalisation very often stresses its antinomies. The relationship with space is not an exception. It is common to read about globalisation as a process of diffusion of labour on a planetary scale. At the same time, the increasing polarisation in favour of more developed areas is well known. Financial globalisation has produced a huge concentration of money capital, so the flexibility made possible by the new technology in transport and communications does not cancel out but, instead, deepens the territorial anchorage of the big 'growth poles'. What is new is that the connection within networks of distant poles reinforces technological integration and communication among a few megalopolises, rather than between them and their hinterland. The dichotomy between centre and periphery, and the consequent increasing inequality, is no longer just between the north and south of the world, or between the advanced countries and many Third World countries. Now the periphery is within the centre, and the centre is partly within the periphery. The resulting urban and territorial structures have sometimes been depicted by the happy image of an 'archipelago' (Veltz 1996).

Labour is the more ticklish paradox among the many regarding global economy. On the one hand, there is no doubt that workers in the last few decades have lost their bargaining and conflictual power. On the other hand, slow growth, market uncertainty, replacement demand for consumer goods and new needs make the 'quality' of products – and therefore also the 'quality' of labour – a competitive asset.

Labour under pressure: the macro changes

The renewed importance of territory and the attention towards the district model also come from this peculiar context. With such an astonishing reduction in transport costs, quality and relational competences come to assume a strategic importance. There is, indeed, a great deal of ideology in all this, but there is also some truth. Within the labour process, partial requalification and some autonomy of labour are real requirements of the new capitalism. How to account for all this? We believe that the theoretical framework, developed in the previous sections, can cast some light on the debate.

Capitalist accumulation systematically causes a variety of productive conditions, that is a different 'quality' of the units of production. The degree of higher or lower 'quality' of labour depends upon a set of technical conditions together with social and market conditions. What happened between the mid-1960s and the mid-1970s was that the potential 'resistance' by wage labour was effective in controlling the extraction of living labour. All this led to a series of struggles on 'how' to produce (conflicts about the organisation of labour, health conditions in the workplace, etc.) and 'what' to produce (demand for a different composition of production, environmental issues, etc.). The crisis that followed the conflict in the social relationships of production, as well as the inter-imperialist conflicts between capitalist areas, and the conflict between manufacturing countries and raw materials-producing countries, determined a slowing down of real investments. The following financialisation of the capitalist economy further depressed aggregate demand, constrained public expenditures and made economies more unstable. What was at work was a tendency to stagnation that made the markets more competitive. Competition becomes ever more destructive because the global players in manufacturing and in service sectors carry out an aggressive strategy of investments, aiming to crowd out other producers. It is precisely when demand is low and unstable that productive capacity grows and thus the unused productive capacity increases further.

This tendency, however, has been opposed by a counter-tendency centred on the USA. Whereas Asia and Europe are mostly net export areas, the USA has consistently, for many decades, maintained a negative current account deficit in the balance of payments. The US domestic currency is still the pseudo-world money, and its financial centre is still the heart of global financial intermediation. It is mainly this country that has created effective demand for the whole world through an autonomous economic policy. Thus, the most visible paradox occurs: a unipolar world around a 'centre' experiencing a long crisis in its hegemony, and its nation-state gaining an almost absolute power while other nation-states are increasingly constrained by 'globalisation'. The leading position in the hierarchical order in the global economy has been kept through the active management of the privileged position in world monetary and financial markets. Global balance is then held together by a forced 'cooperation' around the USA, always at the risk of dissolving in the anarchy of inter-imperialistic conflict.

The same 'irrational exuberance' of the New Economy in the second half of the 1980s has been built around a kind of paradoxical financial Keynesianism. The boom of Wall Street was possible thanks to the expectation that the Federal Reserve would always act in such a way as to support it. The rise in financial wealth prompted an increase in consumption financed by household debt. The 'miracle' years of the New Economy are indebted more to this than to any technological factor – rather, it was the other way round, the rise in demand for some years permitted the exploitation of new possibilities, and the mechanism of expectation fuelled the expansion. The crisis did not occur because of exogenous events (i.e. September 11) or the constraint of a too-high deficit in the current account of the balance of payments. The terrorist attacks came when the crisis had already begun, and the USA has always escaped the rules it imposed on other countries, through the International Monetary Fund (IMF). The last world slump was mainly due to the internal unsustainability of both the US growth process as the pillar of globalisation and the New Economy. The crisis has been controlled and partly reversed thanks to the return of state expenditure in deficit, last but not least in the form of 'military Keynesianism', and to the consumer expenditure financed by banks.

Within this international setting – a reduced and unstable world growth rate, a composition of demand increasingly dependent upon an unequal distribution of income and an increasingly heightened financial instability – the partial reskilling of labour, the reduction of direct control, the flattening of hierarchical levels and the increased autonomy granted to workers went hand in hand with market uncertainty and with more flexibility in the labour market. The control of workers was guaranteed by the 'macro' mechanisms.

Labour under pressure: the micro changes

The 'casualisation' and 'precarisation' of labour within the labour process led to the same results exposed in the previous section. The radical uncertainty that became a structural characteristic of the system after the crisis of the Golden Age forced a radical change in firms' corporate governance and in the management of units of production and, consequently, in the forms of control of the workforce. There is a shift from procedures and norms which are defined 'a priori' in a stable organisational and technological context – production as a plan to be implemented – to a performance which is checked 'a posteriori'. Different fragments of the production cycle are considered as independent firms. In the 1980s, the main form taken by this process was outsourcing as externalisation; in the 1990s, the qualitative novelty was in-house outsourcing.

Thus, the market logic extends itself within the organisation of production. Even within wage labour, job performance becomes similar to formally independent labour, and formally independent labour is subjected to the same pressures as wage labour. Capital control over labour is now the control of workers over themselves. The high returns asked by financial capital constrain firms to reorganise their labour processes along this path.

We thus have two sequences leading to a heightening of control over labour: the increasing uncertainty and instability of the 'macro' markets and the internal destructuring of firms. Both present themselves as the automatic result of an increased power of market over production, when in fact the latter is a means to subject workers to the needs of the valorisation of capital within the labour process.

The real subsumption of labour to finance

Together with the two previous sequences, there is a third one, what may be dubbed the real subsumption of labour to finance. A new form of capitalism is taking shape, the 'pension fund capitalism', whereby workers' savings are channelled towards financial markets (Blackburn 2002). This is something already established in the USA, while it is still only a tendency in Europe and in most of the rest of the world. The premise is that a reduction in the real wage, together with an increased uncertainty of labour, typical of contemporary capitalism, can be compensated, in the present and in the future, by the financial returns of a pension fund. Moreover, in this way, developed countries, with an ageing population, can contribute to an acceleration in the growth of developing countries, with a relatively younger population. It is not our aim to criticise this suggestion here, which both the right and the 'third way' left have assumed during the 1990s. What is relevant here is that, once this institutional innovation is implemented, workers hold interests in exploiting other workers, and profit-making cannot but be dominated by short-term financial expectations. The working class is fragmented in separate households, which feel unified only as part of capital.

From this point of view, the processes of partial reskilling of labour and diffusion of networks and the vitality of districts cannot conceal increasing universal instability and uncertainty on the one hand and the disintegration of the working class on the other hand. It is typical of some literature about post-Fordism not to recognise the mutual links between the 'positive' and the 'obscure' sides of current globalisation. This literature is blind in the face of the unacceptability of the model, and wants to isolate some 'acceptable' parts which are, in any case, inseparable from the whole.

The remaking of the working class

The dynamics presented here contribute to explain both the relevance of space in globalisation and the irrelevance of workers in space. This may be the real epochal shift, the defining feature of a new globalisation. In a sense, we experience the synchronic presence of realities which belong to different past moments of capitalism. The financial globalisation of the end of the twentieth century determines a return to the cyclical instability of the nineteenth century. The resulting macro and micro changes in capital accumulation lead, in the long term, not to the end of labour or to the end of wage labour, but to a fragmentation and precariousness of any kind of labour which, from this point of view, takes capitalism back to the end of the eighteenth century. That was the time of the 'making of the English working class', to borrow the expression from E. P. Thompson (1963). Now is the time of the 'remaking' of the working class worldwide.

The fact that this tendency is powerful does not mean that it can be neither challenged nor defeated. The US hegemony is doomed to be crushed, the supremacy of finance leads to a succession of crises, labour flexibility ends up by undermining the same quality and productive power of labour. At the same time, this does not mean that social and economic contradictions will automatically lead to a collapse of capitalism in its new form. It is possible that the new mode of flexible accumulation and disintegrated labour may find some new form of regulation, making it sustainable in spite of its intrinsic instability. The fact that this world is not a necessary fate depends upon the subjective intervention of human beings once more. What is true is that this economic and social model cannot be made 'just' only with redistributive interventions. A radical reform must deal with both the 'macro' aspect of economic policy as well as the 'micro' aspect of the nature of labour.

References

Aydalot, P. (ed.) (1986) *Milieux Innovateurs in Europe*, Paris: Gremi.

Bagella, M. and Becchetti, L. (eds.) (2000) *The Competitive Advantage of Industrial Districts: Theoretical and Empirical Analysis*, Heidelberg: Physica.

Becattini, G. (1979) 'Dal "settore" industriale al "distretto" industriale. Alcune considerazioni sull'unità di indagine dell'economia industriale', *Rivista di Economia e Politica Industriale*, 5: 7–21.

Becattini, G. (ed.) (1987) *Mercato e Forze Locali: il Distretto Industriale*, Bologna: Il Mulino.

Becattini, G. (1990) 'The Marshallian industrial districts as a socio-economic notion', in Pyke, F., Becattini, G. and Sengenberger, W. (eds.) *Industrial Districts and Inter-firm Cooperation in Italy*, Geneva: International Labour Organization.

Becattini, G., Bellandi, M. Dei Ottati, G. and Sforzi, F. (2003) *From Industrial Districts to Local Development: An Itinerary of Research*, Cheltenham: Edward Elgar.

Bellofiore, R. (ed.) (1999) *Global Money, Capital Restructuring and the Changing Patterns of Labour*, Cheltenham: Edward Elgar.

Belussi, F., Gottardi, G. and Rullani, E. (2003) *The Technological Evolution of Industrial Districts*, Dordrecht: Kluwer.

Blackburn, R. (2002) *Banking on Death*, London: Verso.

Braczyk, H.-J., Cooke, P. and Heidenreich, M. (1998) *Regional Innovation Systems. The Role of Governances in a Globalized World*, London: UCL Press.

Camagni, R. (ed.) (1991) *Innovation Network. Spatial Perspectives*, London: Belhaven Press.

Castells, M. (1996) *The Rise of the Network Society*, Malden, MA: Blackwell Publishers.

Christaller, W. (1966 [1933]) *Central Places in Southern Germany*, New York: Prentice-Hall.

Debreu, G. (1959) *Theory of Value. An Axiomatic Analysis of Economic Equilibrium*, New Haven: Yale University Press.

Emmanuel, A. (1972) *Unequal Exchange: a Study of the Imperialism of Trade*, New York: Monthly Review Press.

Fujita, M., Krugman, P. and Mori, T. (1999) 'On the evolution of hierarchical urban system', *European Economic Review*, 43: 209–51.

Granovetter, M. (1985) 'Economic action and social structure: the problem of embeddedness', *American Journal of Sociology*, 91: 481–510.

Guerrieri, P., Iammarino, S. and Pietrobelli, C. (eds.) (2001) *The Global Challenge to Industrial Districts: Small and Medium-sized Enterprises in Italy and Taiwan*, Cheltenham: Edward Elgar.

Harvey, D. (1975) 'The geography of capitalist accumulation: a reconstruction of the Marxian theory', *Antipode*, 7: 9–21.

Harvey, D. (1982) *The Limits to Capital*, Oxford: Blackwell Publishers.

Hirst P. and Thompson, G. (1999) *Globalization in Question*, Cambridge: Polity Press.

Hodgson, G. (1999) *Evolution and Institutions: On Evolutionary Economics and the Evolution of Economics*, Cheltenham: Edward Elgar.

Isard, W. (1949) 'The general theory of location and space-economy', *Quarterly Journal of Economics*, 63: 476–506.

Isard, W. (1956) *Location and the Space Economy: a General Theory Relating to Industrial Location, Market Areas, Land Use, Trade, and Urban Structure*, Cambridge, MA: MIT Press.

Kalecki, M. (1991 [1967]) 'The problem of effective demand with Tugan-Baranovski and Rosa Luxemburg', in Osiatyński, J. (ed.) *Collected Works of Michal Kalecki,* Vol. II: *Capitalism: Economic Dynamics*, Oxford: Clarendon Press.

Krugman, P. (1991) *Geography and Trade*, Cambridge, MA: MIT Press.

Krugman, P. (1995) *Development, Geography and Economic Theory*, Cambridge, MA: MIT Press.

Krugman, P. (1996) *The Self-organizing Economy*, Oxford: Blackwell Publishers.

Krugman, P. and Venables, A. (1994) *The Location of Economic Activity: New Theory and Evidence*, London: Centre of Economic Policy Research.

Krugman, P. and Venables, A. (1995) 'Globalization and the inequality of nations', *Quarterly Journal of Economics*, 110: 857–80.

Lenin, V. (1948 [1916]) *Imperialism. The Highest Stage of Capitalism*, London: Lawrence & Wishart.

Lösch, A. (1954) *The Economics of Locations*, New Haven: Yale University Press.

Lundvall, B.-Å. and Johnson B. (1994) 'The learning economy', *Journal of Industry Studies*, 1: 23–42.

Luxemburg, R. (2003 [1913]) *The Accumulation of Capital*, London: Routledge.

Marshall, A. (1990 [1890]) *Principles of Economics*, Basingstoke: Macmillan.

Marx, K. (1999 [1885]) *Capital: a Critique of Political Economy,* Vol. 2, London: Penguin.

Minsky, H.P. (ed.) (1965) *California Banking in a Growing Economy: 1946–1975*. Berkeley, CA: Institute of Business and Economic Research.

Myrdal, G. (1957) *Economic Theory and Under-developed Regions*, London: Duckworth.

Nurkse, R. (1953) *Problems of Capital Formation in Underdeveloped Countries*, Oxford: Blackwell Publishers.

Ohmae, K. (1995) *The End of the Nation State. The Rise of Regional Economics*, London: HarperCollins.

Paniccia, I. (2002) *Industrial Districts: Evolution and Competitiveness in Italian Firms*, Cheltenham: Edward Elgar.

Piore, M. and Sabel, C. (1984) *The Second Industrial Divide*, New York: Basic Books.

Prebisch, R. (1950) *The Economic Development of Latin America and Its Principal Problems*, New York: United Nations Ecla.

Predöhl, A. (1928) 'The theory of location in its relation to general economics', *Journal of Political Economy*, 36: 371–90.

Rabellotti, R. (1997) *External Economies and Cooperation in Industrial Districts: A Comparison of Italy and Mexico*, Basingstoke: Macmillan.

Reich, R.B. (1991) *The Work of Nations*, New York: Vintage.

Rifkin, J. (1995) *The End of Work: The Decline of the Global Labour Force and the Dawn of the Post-market Era*, New York: Putnam's Sons.

Rosenstein-Rodan, P.N. (1943) 'Problems of industrialization of Eastern and South-Eastern Europe', *Economic Journal*, 53: 202–11.

Rosenstein-Rodan, P.N. (1976) 'The theory of the "Big Push" ', in Meier, G. (ed.) *Leading Issues in Economic Development*, Oxford: Oxford University Press.

Scott, A. (1988) *New Industrial Space: Flexible Production Organization and Regional Development in North America and Western Europe*, London: Pion.

Sheppard, E. (2000) 'Competition in space and between places', in Sheppard, E. and Barnes, T. (eds.) *A Companion to Economic Geography*, Oxford: Blackwell Publishers.

Sraffa, P. (1925) 'Sulle relazioni tra costo e quantità prodotta', *Annali di Economia*, 2: 277–328.

Sraffa, P. (1926) 'The laws of returns under competitive conditions', *Economic Journal*, 36: 535–50.

Sraffa, P. (1960) *Production of Commodities by Means of Commodities*, Cambridge: Cambridge University Press.

Storper, M. and Walker, R. (1989) *The Capitalist Imperative. Territory, Technology, and Industrial Growth*, Oxford: Blackwell.

Swyngedouw, E. (2000) 'The Marxian alternative: historical-geographical materialism and the political economy of capitalism', in Sheppard, E. and Barnes, T. (eds.) *A Companion to Economic Geography*, Oxford: Blackwell.

Thompson, E.P. (1963) *The Making of the English Working Class*, London: Gollancz.

Trigilia, C. (1986) *Grandi Partiti e Piccole Imprese*, Bologna: Il Mulino.

Veltz, P. (1996) *Mondalisation, villes et territories: l'économie d'archipel*, Paris: Presses Universitaires de France.

Walker, R. (1999) 'Putting capital in its place: globalization and the prospect for labor', *Geoforum*, 30: 263–84.

Walras, L. (1988 [1874]) *Éléments d'économie politique pure*, Paris: Economica.

Weber, A. (1971 [1929]) *Theory of the Location of Industry*, Chicago: University of Chicago Press.

Weiss, L. (1998) *The Myth of the Powerless State*, Cambridge: Polity Press.

2 Positionality and globalization in economic geography

Eric Sheppard

Introduction

Economic geographers have devoted much effort in recent years to contesting the idea that under globalization a ubiquitous neoliberal capitalism entails the death of distance and the end of geography (Cairncross 1997). They have argued that territory and scale still matter, albeit in novel ways, challenging the belief that globalization is overriding the distinctive characteristics of places. A dominant metaphor here is that of "glocalization," whereby transnational production systems require specific local place-based features (such as low wages), and seek to exploit differences between places in order to reduce the regulatory influence of territorial state institutions on capital mobility. Places with the right characteristics, such as the Third Italy, are seen as capable of "holding down the global" by creating attractive local conditions that are functional for the profitability of local and multilocational firms (Amin and Thrift 1994, 1995).

Others have critiqued the very terms of globalization, arguing that to equate globalization with the currently widespread neoliberal capitalist variant is to join its proponents in masking alternative, anti-capitalist forms of globalization – such as envisioned when Marx and Engels penned the immortal "workers of the world, unite!" (Marx and Engels 1952). In this view, the realization that other worlds are possible is necessary to deconstruct the argument that neoliberal globalization is inevitable. Some argue for the importance of non-capitalist modes of economic activity, occupying neglected spaces within those of capitalism (Gibson-Graham 1996), whereas others highlight the globalization of anti-globalization movements, such as the World Social Forum (Fisher and Ponniah 2003).

Yet, although critical of proponents of contemporary globalization, economic geographers tend to share one belief with their adversaries. They accept that a shrinking world implies that, if geography still matters, it is primarily because of place. David Harvey (1982), for example, notes the imperative under capitalism to speed up the circulation of commodities and capital. Globalization has accelerated time–space compression, making relative location within the global economy less vital to capital accumulation, and place characteristics more important. The result is a politics of place whereby cities and regions compete intensively to offer attractive local conditions to geographically mobile capital, making place-based inter-class alliances more important relative to class struggle (Harvey 1989a,b).

He has even argued that uneven development can now be conceptualized in terms of scale and place-based differentiation, rather than space- and place-based differentiation (Harvey 2000). In short, as Ron Martin (1999: 15–16) has written: "Globalisation may well have eliminated space …, but it has by no means undermined the significance of location, of place." Places are usually represented as territorial spaces, and debates about place and globalization have focused on whether and how territories still matter in a space of flows (Castells 1996).

In this chapter, elaborating on previous arguments, I contest the assumption that globalization has marginalized the significance of relative location (Sheppard 2002). I will suggest, instead, that positionality within the capitalist space economy matters – both theoretically and practically. The following section develops the idea of positionality, conceptualizing how both social and geographic location shape the conditions of possibility faced by economic agents.[1] I then analyze why close attention to positionality matters theoretically, calling into question some common presumptions in economic geography inherited from aspatial economic theory – such as those of the new geographical economics (Cairncross 1997, Fujita *et al.* 1999, Ottaviano and Thisse 2004). The third section suggests why positionality still matters in today's seemingly small and fast world, and sketches its shifting geography. The fourth section seeks to exemplify the persistence and significance of positionality through the example of international trade, and the conclusion draws out some implications for thinking about and responding to globalization.

Positionality and globalization

Geographers use a variety of terms to describe how places occupy different locations, the commonest of which are distance, relative location, accessibility, and situation. None of these is adequate for my purposes. Distance and relative location too often connote a Euclidean geometry, in which the connectedness of two places is approximated by a continuous mathematical transformation of their Cartesian coordinates. Accessibility and situation connote more complex ways of measuring connectivity or closeness, but tend to be envisioned as fairly static spatial attributes of a place, with less attention to time (but see Janelle and Hodge 2000). I propose the term "positionality" to describe how different economic agents are positioned with respect to one another in space–time.

In feminist theory, positionality describes the situated positions from which subjects come to know the world. The positionality of subjects is emphasized both to challenge the proposition that there is objective knowledge and to sensitize investigators to how analysis is shaped by their "social situatedness … in terms of gender, race, class, sexuality and other axes of social difference" (Nagar and Geiger 2006, forthcoming). Positionality is a relational construct: the conditions of possibility for an agent depend on its position with respect to others – as in network theory. Positionality also involves power relations, in the sense both that some positions tend to be more influential than others and that emphasizing the situated nature of knowledge challenges the power of all claims to objectivity. Third, positionality is dynamic; it is re-enacted in ways that simultaneously reproduce and challenge pre-existing configurations, a process that Judith Butler has termed "citation." Positionality is simultaneously durable, as re-enactments reproduce previous configurations, while also being vulnerable to unexpected change, because each repetition is imperfect (Rose 1997, Valentine 2002).

Geographic space has been missing from this area of feminist theory, an oversight that I seek to redress here by extending positionality to include how agents are situated in space–time. Space cannot be examined independently of the social aspects of positionality emphasized by feminists. It is now broadly accepted that space and time are social constructs, shaped by, but also influencing, social processes. This is best expressed through a dialectical conception of space–time (Soja 1980, Harvey 1996, Massey 1999a). As with any dialectical process, societies construct concrete places and spaces whose persistence makes them seem immutable or natural. The materiality of these places and spaces in turn has real and concrete influence over trajectories of economic change. Applying this conceptualization to positionality in space–time, it can be argued that the positionality of a place influences future possibilities there; core locations tend to be advantaged relative to peripheral ones in a space economy. At the same time, however, positionality can be reshaped through such spatial economic dynamics. While differences in positionality (e.g., cores and peripheries) are quite persistent, historical economic geography is littered with examples of long-standing patterns of uneven development, followed by key moments when those positional hierarchies are disrupted as peripheral regions find a way to join the core, or vice versa. These occasional but dramatic shifts in positionality exemplify the contradictions that characterize a dialectical analysis of space–time. As in feminist theory, the persistence of preexisting sociospatial inequalities in position and power is never immutable. Our understanding of the exact conditions under which this reshaping of positionality occurs is imperfect, but is key to better explanations of the out-of-equilibrium dynamics of uneven development.

Positionality cannot be separated from more territorial aspects of spatiality, such as place and scale. Place, as Massey (1991) argues, cannot be adequately understood without considering the complex positionalities that link people and the places they reside in with one another. The heterogeneity of any place reflects the different positionalities of its residents (Massey 1991). The construction of scale also inevitably involves shifts in positionality. For example, processes of globalization that more closely connect geographically distant places both reduce differences in their positionality and enhance the importance of more aggregate scales. Yet our understanding of the spatiality of globalization will be impoverished if our concern for place and scale leads us to neglect positionality. Positionality calls attention to how connections between places play a role in the emergence of geographical inequalities within the global economy. Positionality also implies that the conditions of possibility for a place to prosper depend not only on local initiative, as suggested in the industrial districts literature and structural adjustment policy, but just as much on its interdependencies with and dependence on other places.

Positionality and economic theory[2]

Detailed attention to positionality has led economic geographers to question some standard principles of non-spatial economic theory that have been taken as axiomatic by neoclassical and Marxian economic geographers and geographical economists.[3] I restrict my analysis here to mathematical economic theories, using the accepted basis of critique in this theoretical language of mathematical consistency (Longino 2002). I draw from the branch of economic geography that I have elsewhere called regional political economy: a research program extending mathematical analysis in the spirit of Marx, Kalecki, and Sraffa (Morishima 1973, Roemer 1981) to incorporate the space economy (Scott 1980, Marelli 1983, Clark *et al.* 1986, Dunford 1988, Liossatos 1988, Sheppard and Barnes 1990, Webber and Rigby 1999). Regional political economy entails different assumptions about space, time, economic structure, and social agency than those popularized in neoclassical economic geography (Table 2.1), differences that turn out to have substantial implications (Sheppard 2000a).

With respect to spatiality, in regional political economy not only is space treated as heterogeneous, thereby making positionality explicit, but, crucially, positionality is taken to be endogenous to the evolving space economy: accessibility is produced as a commodity in each region (Sheppard 1990). Geographical economists (Ottaviano and Thisse 2004: 34) also note that "one major step on the research agenda is the study of a multiregional system whose aim is to understand why some regions are more successful than others ... we need to account for the actual geographies of these regions."[4]

With respect to time, it is necessary to account for the time lag between when capital is advanced for production and when revenues are realized, because profitability depends not only on the difference between revenues and costs but also on how long capital has been in circulation. Furthermore, regional political economy emphasizes disequilibrium dynamics rather than spatial equilibria, since equi-

Table 2.1 Contrasting assumptions of neoclassical and political economic geography

Assumptions	*Neoclassical economic geography*	*Regional political economy*
Spatiality	Homogeneous "first nature" space Exogenous transportation costs	Heterogeneous constructed space Costs of communication are endogenous
Time	Instantaneous production Economic equilibrium	Production takes time Disequilibrium dynamics
Economic structure	Aggregate production functions Vertically integrated production	Interdependent multisectoral economy (input–output)
Agency	Fully informed individual rational choice	Individual actions based on imperfect information Class interests guide collective action

libria are typically destabilized by conflicts of interest between different groups of economic actors over the distribution of the economic surplus. Intersectoral interdependencies, detailing the input–output relations describing the flows of commodities between sectors and firms, describe the asymmetric mutual dependence of firms and sectors on one another. Attention to these has the important consequence that capital cannot be reduced to a homogeneous and exogenously given production factor, but is a heterogeneous bundle of interdependently produced capital goods. The destabilizing implications of this for aggregate neoclassical production functions and macroeconomic theory have been rehearsed at length elsewhere (Harcourt 1972).

With respect to agency, different kinds of economic actors occupy different positionalities within capitalism, particularly class positions, defined by the factors of production they own, their position in the hierarchy of economic decision-making, and their relative wealth. Positionality differentially conditions the possibilities available to social agents.[5] Shared economic interests within classes and conflicts between them create a potential for collective attempts to increase class share of the economic surplus. Thus, social structures condition action, making methodological individualism an inadequate conceptualization of human behavior.[6] Yet agents sharing the same general class position also differ in their positionality in other ways, in terms of geographic location, economic sector, resources, preferences, technologies, and so forth, implying a potential for intra-class conflicts that can undermine class-based alliances. Finally, agents possess only limited information about the current and future economic landscape.

To explore the implications of these more complex and realistic starting points, I briefly examine two cases.

Microeconomic spatial price competition

Consider the consequences of including positionality of the most basic sort; differences in the relative location of firms.[7] In the location theory pioneered by Lösch and Christaller and reinvigorated by Krugman, all firms competing in a spatially extensive market are generally assumed to be identical not only in their cost structure, but also in their relative location – they occupy identical positions at opposite ends of a line, or are equally spaced across an unbounded uniform plain. The challenge is then to explain agglomeration. Ottaviano and Thisse (2004) describe this as the principal goal of geographical economics: to account for the emergence of "second nature" (the geographical consequences of human action), assuming that "first nature" (exogenous geographical conditions) is undifferentiated. "Then, it asks what are the forces that can allow a *small* (possibly temporary) initial shock … to generate a *large* permanent imbalance in the distributions of economic activities" (ibid.: 2564, emphasis in original). In the absence of differences in positionality, agglomeration is explained by home market effects (place-based characteristics such as agglomeration economies or a larger local demand) or emergent core–periphery structures (accumulation of human capital in a place). Firms maximize total profits, and even after the emergence of agglomerations no-one makes excess profits; free entry means that profits net of fixed costs are zero (Fujita *et al.* 1999).

Introduction of exogenous differences in positionality can challenge such standard results in microeconomic theories of monopolistic spatial competition (Table 2.2). Consider identical firms competing for spatially distributed consumers with inelastic demand functions. Firms occupy fixed locations in a heterogeneous space, positioned differently with respect to consumers (i.e., differences in locational advantage exist). Consumers are incompletely informed, possessing limited choice sets, and stochastically choose to patronize a particular location based on its price relative to those of other locations in their choice set (Sheppard *et al.* 1992). In this case, profits, prices, and output differ between firms in spatial price equilibrium, as a consequence of differences in their positionality. Except for the geographically marginal producer, firms make excess profits reflecting their locational advantage.

Second, and in contradistinction to most mainstream economic theory (Dixit and Stiglitz 1977, Nell 1992, Krugman 1996), the Marxian goal of maximizing the rate of profit dominates the neoclassical microeconomic goal of maximizing total profits (Plummer *et al.* 1998, Sheppard *et al.* 1998). In heterogeneous space this results in distinctive equilibrium pricing, profit, and demand patterns (Haining *et al.* 1996). Third, competitive equilibria are only locally quasi-stable, with numerical simulations suggesting that small price deviations from equilibrium induce price wars (Plummer 1999). Instability is enhanced by more complex market structures, such as oligopolists seeking to serve spatially separated and differentiated markets (Plummer 1996a,b).[8]

Regional accumulation dynamics

When assumptions about distance, vertical integration, and agency are also relaxed further theoretical propositions are challenged (Sheppard and Barnes 1990). Consider the case of a spatially extensive multiregional economy in which commodity production is undertaken in interrelated economic sectors located in functional economic regions (metropolitan regions). Suppose we know the geography of production, with sectors employing different production technologies and real wage scales in different regions (Rigby and Essletzbichler 1997). Economic agents include capitalists, workers, and landlords, each with competing claims on the monetary surplus produced by the economy. Capitalists seek to increase rates of profit on capital advanced, workers to increase real wages, and landlords to increase rents per acre. Each class is also differentiated.

Table 2.2 Positionality and spatial price competition

Neoclassical monopolistic competition	*Variations in positionality*
No net profits; identical prices and outputs	Profits, prices, and outputs vary with positionality
Firms should maximize total profits	Firms should maximize the rate of profit
Stable Nash equilibria exist	Quasi-stable “knife-edge” equilibrium

For example, different firms in the same sector and region use different production technologies and mixes of differentially skilled workers.

Transportation produces a special commodity, accessibility, which is consumed whenever another commodity or person moves across space. It is produced in every region not as a direct input to production, but as an intermediate good necessary to bring products to market. Production technologies dictate the quantities of other goods required as inputs, but the amount of transportation needed will depend on the positionality of a firm with respect to suppliers. The price of transportation (freight rate), endogenously determined like the prices of other commodities (and unlike the iceberg model used in economics), shapes positionality and influences decisions about where to purchase inputs. Technological change in the communications sector is key to reducing the turnover time of capital and increasing the rate of capital accumulation, through a historical attempt to annihilate space by time that literally produces positionality as a by-product of the spatial dynamics of commodity production.

A self-reproducing dynamic equilibrium can be described for any such space economy, i.e., a distribution of relative production levels across regions, determined by wage levels, technologies, and transport costs, which entails an equal average profit and growth rate in all regions and sectors. Yet the existence of such equilibria is of little interest, since they are generally unstable. It is always in the interests of capitalists, workers, or landlords to destabilize them in their struggle for a greater share of the surplus. Thus, a major issue of contention is whether equilibrium conditions are of any relevance for understanding out-of-equilibrium dynamics. Webber and Rigby (1999) argue that equilibrium conditions are smuggled into many of the basic price and output equations used in economic geography. They reject price-based calculations in favor of labor values because the latter do not presume equilibrium.

Furthermore, standard neoclassical conclusions about regional specialization, trade, and growth cannot be assumed to hold (Sheppard and Barnes 1986) (Table 2.3). Individual entrepreneurs' rate-of-profit-maximizing choices of production technologies or specialization strategies may eventually reduce average rates of profit (a form of unintended consequences that, as Harvey (1982) notes, is equivalent to Marx's idea of the falling rate of profit). The free movement of capital and labor in response to wage and profit differentials may enhance, rather than reduce, uneven development. Finally, allocation of land through the land market need not maximize the efficiency of land use: the "highest" use need not be "best", because land rent need not equal the marginal productivity of land.

There are thus complex potential conflicts of economic interest between and within classes, conditioned by their positionality in social and geographic space. This is reinforced by the endogenous spatiality of the economy, making for such complexity that even fully informed rational agents cannot calculate the indirect consequences of their actions. Strategies that maximize landlords' rents or workers' real wages need not maximize capitalists' profits, and there is no distribution of income (between wages, profits, and wages) that is efficient in a Nash equilibrium sense.[9] Firm strategies include attempts to manipulate labor markets

Table 2.3 Positionality and regional accumulation dynamics

Neoclassical regional growth	*Endogenous regional growth theory*	*Regional political economy*
Cost-reducing technical change increases profit rates	When endogenous knowledge is ubiquitous, the equilibrium growth rate is independent of, but shapes, the geography of production. Under limited inter-regional knowledge spillover, the geography of production affects equilibrium growth rates. Enhanced spillover may enable peripheral regions to industrialize	Cost-reducing technical change may decrease average profit rates
Under free trade and/or factor flows, regional economies converge to a stable dynamic equilibrium	At least one stable equilibrium exists; other equilibria may be unstable. Regions grow at the same rate but may have unequal incomes and profits	Dynamic equilibria are unstable
Profit-maximizing production enables regions to gain from specialization and mutual trade on the basis of comparative advantage	Freer trade tends to increase the equilibrium growth rate but also to increase inter-regional inequality	There are no simple rules for defining comparative advantage
Free mobility of capital and labor reduces regional differences in growth rates	Free capital mobility equalizes regional profits and incomes	Free mobility of capital and labor may enhance regional differences in growth rates
In free markets, wages and profits represent the marginal social productivity of labor and capital		Factor prices need not reflect their marginal productivity; wages, profits, and rents reflect the political power of classes
Rent-maximizing land uses are socially optimal (maximizing the marginal productivity of land)		Rent-maximizing land uses reduce profits and wages

Source: Author's elaboration after Baldwin and Martin (2004).

to their advantage (Clark *et al.* 1986), labor organizes to enhance its share of the surplus (Herod 2001), and state regulation is continually necessary to negotiate these conflicts (Aglietta 1979). Strategies by one fraction of capitalists to enhance their mean profit rate may also reduce the mean profit rates of other fractions, locally or non-locally.

Unstable equilibria and unintended consequences, undermining rational expectations, mean that the space economy becomes an arena of constantly shifting competitive advantage, reflecting the economic and political strategies of differently situated actors. Firms' profits, a result of previous production decisions, current demand in different spatial markets, and competitive advantage in those markets, may be invested in higher output, technical change, relocation, or finance markets (from which money may also be borrowed). Finance markets smooth out the redistribution of funds, but interest rates must vary between regions of different sizes in order to maintain dynamic equilibrium (Webber 1987). Regional technological change depends on processes of innovation, imitation, and the entry and exit of firms using different technologies (Webber *et al.* 1992, Webber and Rigby 1996). Pricing strategies will depend on supply and demand (competitive advantage), sunk costs (Clark and Wrigley 1995), and planned technological and growth strategies ("strong competition"; Storper and Walker 1989). The resulting fluctuations in wage and unemployment rates affect labor costs and migration (Goodwin 1987, Plummer 1999).

The above arguments indicate a variety of ways in which consideration of positionality, along with other relaxations of the neoclassical framework, makes it possible for regional political economy to call many of the standard results of neoclassical economic geography into question. Yet Marxian political economy is also not immune to critique, once positionality is taken seriously (Sheppard and Barnes 1990, Sheppard 2004). Labor values cannot be taken as foundational for Marxian theory, because they are dialectically related to exchange values. Geographic differences in positionality imply that labor values generally vary across space (Sheppard and Barnes 1990, Webber 1996), profoundly complicating the plausibility that common class interests, let alone identity, can transcend spatial difference. As Harvey (1982) has also argued, workers in competitively advantaged regions may be motivated to increase their real wages by allying with local capitalists, as long as wages are low enough elsewhere to guarantee that local production remains profitable (Hudson and Sadler 1986). Fordism in Western Europe and North America benefited from such arrangements, in which unionized workers allied with corporate capital and the state to promote national development, until the increasing north–south wage gap exceeded the declining communications costs of global commodity chains, making it profitable to relocate production to Mexico, Thailand, and now India, China, and Vietnam.

Positionality and contemporary globalization

Notwithstanding the hype of globalization, the broad geographical contours of positionality within the global economy show a remarkably persistent path dependence. Enormous effort has been put into lowering communication costs, to deliver commodities to spatially separated markets and to recoup investments as quickly as possible, and into harmonizing state regulation and opening national markets worldwide. The last two decades of globalization can indeed be described as a period of accelerated, broader-ranging, and more intense and influential global interdependence (Held *et al.* 1999). The world is smaller, and faster, in absolute terms. It does not follow, however, that space is being annihilated by time. Whether one examines the global mobility of commodities, people, capital, or foreign aid, the geographical structure of international interdependencies still carries a strong post-colonial shadow (Figure 2.1). Even cyberspace, poster child for the death of distance thesis, shows a geography that still bears strong resemblance to the global geography of communications in the 1950s (Figure 2.2) (Graham 1998).

The general acceleration of space-transcending technologies and flows has always been unevenly applied geographically, enhancing the positionality of some places relative to others. The steamship, airplane, and telegraph enhanced transoceanic mobility, but the first to be transformed were the routes along which large shares of commodities and information already flowed – linking major markets. For example, the early efforts at intercontinental telegraphy were aimed at directly linking the New York and London stock markets very soon after the first successful transatlantic cable was laid in 1851. By 1890, British influence had placed London at the center of global telegraph and wireless networks, offering a decisive economic and geopolitical advantage shaping the outcome of World War I (Hugill 1999, Mattelart 2000). Today, direct telecommunication and air flights within the global south can still be difficult: New York and London remain

Figure 2.1 Largest foreign direct investment (FDI) affiliate partner, 1980 (Porter and Sheppard 1998).

Figure 2.2 Global internet traffic, 1993. Source: http://reid.org/brian.

positioned very close to one another in communications space, by comparison with Lagos and Cape Town. In the space of airline flight times, Los Angeles is much closer to Tokyo than is Guam (Figure 2.3). America's strategic position at the center of the production and organization of global telecommunications systems remains key to its military influence.

The altered experiences of and expectations about time associated with telecommunications also shape positionality. As time moves faster, small differences in timing matter more. The currency speculation that broke Barings Bank was based on small temporal differences in futures prices in Osaka and Singapore. Expectations about what constitutes an adequate time for financial information to be transmitted from New York to London have fallen dramatically over the last 200 years, from weeks to milliseconds. If the speed of communication linking two other places has only fallen from weeks to minutes during this time frame then, by comparison with New York and London, those places now would be relatively further away from one another than before. In this space, Frankfurt and Los Angeles are as close as Nairobi and Johannesburg. Thus, differences in positionality may increase even as time–space shrinks in an absolute sense.

Recognition of the durable importance of geographical positionality significantly affects our understanding of the complex spatial dynamics of capitalism. If we theorize on the presumption that geographical differences in positionality are not important, it is natural to conclude that the fate of territorial economies depends on local conditions. This is the basis for arguing that the prosperity of

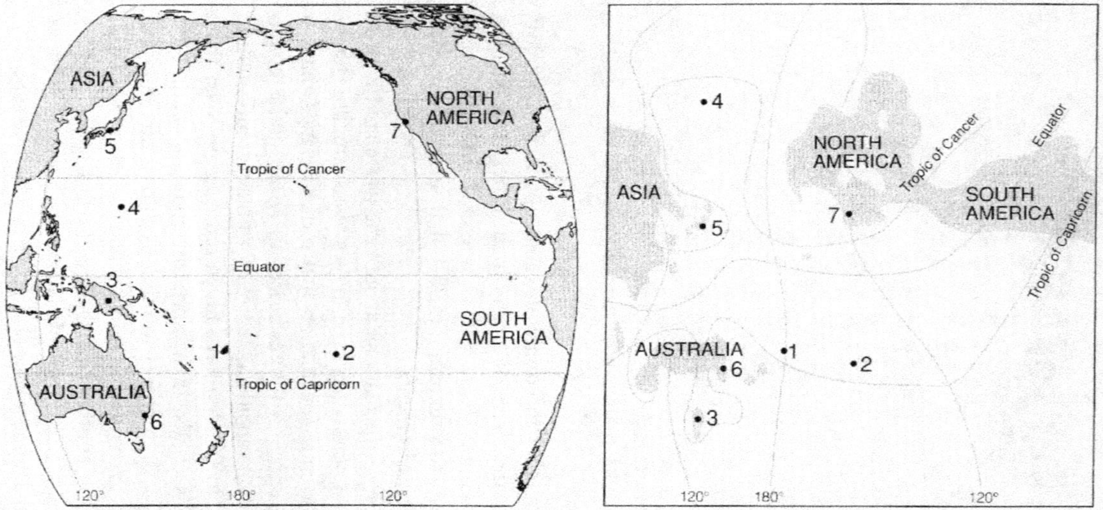

1 Fiji 2 French Polynesia 3 Papua New Guinea 4 Trust Territories of the Pacific 5 Tokyo 6 Sydney 7 San Francisco

(a) 'Conventional' projection of the Pacific basin

(b) Time–space map of the Pacific basin, based on relative time accessibility by scheduled airline in 1975

Figure 2.3 Differences in positionality with respect to airline flight. Note that, in the right-hand panel, distance is measured in scheduled airline flight time, 1975 (Haggett 1990).

industrial districts is a reflection of local conditions, perhaps shaped by larger-scale territorial processes such as national policies. Promoting the informal communications and learning associated with economic dynamism is then assumed to depend on getting the place right. At the national scale, structural adjustment policies are based on the parallel assumption that "good governance" (enhancing competitiveness, opening national economies to global markets, reducing the size and inefficiency of government, and promoting US-style democracy) is necessary and sufficient for national economic success.

Once we accept, however, that differences in positionality remain, such arguments become insufficient. Europe's positional proximity to the New World gave it a decisive advantage in the struggle over where capitalism agglomerated in the Old World after 1492, contra the popular accounts that explain this success in terms of such regional characteristics as climate or the protestant work ethic (Blaut 1993, Hausmann 2001). It follows that the now neglected arguments of dependency theory, that underdevelopment was a consequence of declining terms of trade between the Third and the First Worlds, rather than an original local condition, should be reassessed. The possibility of national economic growth in the former Third World, and indeed throughout much of the former Soviet Union, is surely still shaped by their dependence on and position within global networks of trade, finance, migration, and know-how. Similarly, as it has become more difficult to definitively pin down the local factors accounting for the success of industrial districts, researchers are beginning to re-examine the validity of the proposition that learning and trust are local, pointing instead to the many ways in which positionality within non-local networks may be as important to the success of a local economy as place-based factors (Amin and Cohendet 1999, Sheppard 2000b, Amin and Thrift 2002, Malmberg and Maskell 2002, Oinas 2002, Oinas and Malecki 2002, Simmie 2002, Bathelt *et al.* 2004).

Neglect of real geographical differences in positionality also has an important policy consequence. The assumption that both success and failure in a globalized world are in the hands of localities leads to a blaming of the victim. The economic stagnation of a territorial economy is explained as a failure of local capitalists and politicians to be sufficiently entrepreneurial. This, of course, was how colonialism was and structural adjustment still is legitimated: as a necessary intervention by external experts to overcome a failure of entrepreneurial ability. Orientalism, social Darwinism, and racism were also legitimated by this belief in the responsibility of the residents of a territory for their own prosperity. I do not wish to argue, of course, that local conditions are unimportant in a positionally differentiated world; economic geography has abundantly shown that they can be crucial. Yet it is necessary to critically re-examine the obsession with local factors in recent explanations of uneven development.

Social network theory has long stressed the relational nature of power, and the unequal conditions of possibility that this entails. Positionally advantaged agents are at the center of, and control, networks of relationships that simultaneously position others in a present and possibly future state of compliance or dependence (Van Tulder and Ruigrok 1997). It follows that unequal positionality can also be central to the reproduction of power hierarchies. As Johan Galtung (1971) has explained, positionally advantaged territories can shape the space economy to their advantage, reinforced by place-based alliances between local elites and other residents in such territories whose local inequalities and differences seemingly pale in comparison with their shared gains from uneven development. At the same time, differences within positionally disadvantaged territories may become enhanced, as local elites profit from the highly unequal geographical and social impact of dependent development (Marini 1973, Cardoso and Faletto 1979). A de facto alliance between peripheral elites and hegemonic territories may well reinforce the power of positionally advantaged territories. The willingness, since the 1980s, of positionally disadvantaged nation-states in the global south to adopt the Washington Consensus reflects their more marginal positionality. Elites (often trained, along with their advisors, in academic institutions of the global north) stand to gain from neoliberal open-border policies (Glassman 1999: 691).

Although this symbiotic relationship between positionality and power may suggest a global economy with persistent core–periphery relations, positionality demands a more nuanced account. Butler (1993) notes that all attempts at repetition of power–positionality relations are imperfect, creating the possibility of occasional dramatic and unexpected reworkings. Examples abound, from the emergence of Germany, Japan, and the USA to successfully challenge Britain during the twentieth century, to the more recent successes of a select few newly industrializing countries, and the rise to prominence of regions such as California, Seoul, and Shanghai. Local initiative was important in each case, but the transformation also required a reconfiguration of the positionality of that place within the global system. Too often, attempts at transformation founder on the difficulties of overcoming a disadvantaged positionality. Yet marginal positionality creates conditions for resistance and struggle, and it is sometimes remarkable to see seemingly unassailable power hierarchies collapse overnight.

The fact that positionality shapes the conditions of possibility for agents, at scales ranging from the body to the world region, requires close attention to its multiscalar nature. Positional differences within families are nested complexly within those differentiating neighborhoods, cities, regions, and countries. The Americanization of economic ideology, financial systems, music, and movies, worldwide, positions Boston and Washington (for neoliberal economics), New York (finance), Detroit (techno music), and Los Angeles (movies) at the center of globalization – or, more precisely, Cambridge, MA, the District of Columbia, downtown Manhattan, black Detroit, and Hollywood. These are not regarded as typically American places, and indeed are seen by many as places from which mainstream American values are being undermined. So when the USA successfully promotes its global positionality, the form that Americanization takes differs greatly from conventional constructions of the American way of life – small-town and suburban white America – as right-wing opponents of globalization are quick to emphasize. But the geography of positionality is more complicated than this (Mohanty 2003). The global north is constituted through a network of political and economic elites occupying privileged localities, networked together across the globe (Castells 1996). By contrast, the global south – whose population is disproportionately made up of "indigenous" communities, people of color, and women – is to be found everywhere: foraging the forests of South Asia, undertaking the double burden of housework and paid work, toiling in sweatshops within the USA, and living in urban quasi-ghettoes worldwide. These fractionated geographies of the global north and south, with poverty and disadvantage at times just across the street from wealth and privilege, mean that national boundaries do not even approximately separate development from underdevelopment. Indeed, it can be hypothesized that contemporary processes of globalization are making the geographies of global north and global south progressively fractal and geographically interleaved.

Geographies of positionality

Any abstract discussion of socially constructed space–time is fraught with a fundamental paradox for cartographic representations of the world. If space–time is a social construct, which coordinate system can be invoked to describe it? Coordinate systems are social constructs, and to invoke any particular such system as the basis for analysis contributes to its reification.[10] For the purposes of discussion, I will take the spherical coordinate system approximating the shape of the globe as my reference point. In doing this, I am asserting not that it is natural, but that it is commonplace. Maps are a commonly understood technique for depicting the geographical organization of society, notwithstanding the problematic nature of any cartographic representation of the world (Harley 1989).

As a relational characteristic, positionality is best represented by the intensity and nature of the interdependencies connecting economic agents through space–time (an insight from geography's spatial science tradition of gravity and hierarchical diffusion models – notwithstanding critiques of this tradition's spatial fetishism; see Sheppard 1995). It follows that similarity in terms of positionality correlates with the degree to which two agents are collocated within the social networks that these interdependencies create. It is reasonably straightforward to map positionality in social space using this principle (as in social network analysis), but mapping positionality onto the earth's surface is far more complex because there may be little relationship between positionality and geographic proximity. In addition, whereas geographic proximity is assumed to be symmetric, positionality generally entails asymmetric relationships: core agents exert more influence over peripherally positioned agents than vice versa.

The space-transcending technologies and institutions of contemporary globalization are compounding the complexity of mapping social relationships in geographic space. The telegraph first made it possible for information to move more rapidly than the body, severing the space–time movement of information from that of humans (Marvin 1988). Telecommunications technologies have taken this much further, allowing individuals both to communicate almost instantaneously with geographically remote people and places, and to be co-present in distant locations (by means of web-cams, television, and the cinema) (Virilio 1995). Such connections are unevenly developed, however, because the economic, political, and cultural forces creating and reinforcing presence-at-a-distance are highly selective geographically (Figure 2.3).

The multiscalar nature of positionality introduces a distinct challenge, as it creates difficulties for attempts to generalize from bodies to places. If the residents of a territory share a similar positionality, then this property can also be attributed to the place where they reside. Yet, as Massey (1991) insists, places are heterogeneous: their residents differ dramatically in their positionality, both within the place itself and through their distinct interactions stretching beyond the place (Amin and Thrift 2002). As feminist theory has shown, even households incorporate significant differences in positionality, reflecting gender, age, and power asymmetries amongst their members.

There is much anecdotal evidence that differences in access to the means of transportation and communication are increasing disparities in positionality among people and within the places where they live (Sheppard 2001, 2002, Aoyama and Sheppard 2003). Within any place, some residents have been able to exploit the fluidity of the global economy to dramatically improve livelihood possibilities, even as the majority has not, in ways that make noticeable differences to the trajectory of globalization. Differences in positionality from one household to the next may in fact be increasing, depending on who has access to telecommunications, as suggested by the digital divide thesis. Indeed, some have gone so far as to suggest that the internet is making place redundant, as well as space, whereas others vigorously contest this. At present, however, there is too little evidence to determine the validity of such generalizations.

Implications: geographies of trade

In this section, I will attempt to indicate how positionality both reflects and shapes the spatiotemporal networks of economic interdependencies, using the example of trade.[11] International trade has long been one of the principal interdependencies shaping and differentiating the positionality of places within the global economy, but has received relatively little attention from economic geographers. Trade is also a useful case through which to explore how positionality entails both discursive and material processes. Over the last 200 years, the free trade doctrine (i.e., that unrestricted commodity exchange between places is the best way to advance their mutual prosperity) has attained the status of "a scientific fact as indisputable as gravity" (Trentmann 1998: 226). At the same time, the material effects of trade frequently contradict this doctrine, with a history of more positionally powerful trading partners accumulating the lion's share of gains from trade.

Rhetorically, the free trade doctrine envisions a space–economy in which positionality does not matter, while place-based differences intensify. Places overcome unequal endowments of labor, capital, knowledge, and resources, by specializing in and exporting the commodities that exploit local comparative advantage. The distinctiveness of each place forms the basis of its comparative advantage, and is reinforced by specialization. In a fully globalized world, where transport costs are insignificant and trade barriers are eliminated, creating a level playing field with no geographic variation in positionality, the doctrine asserts that every comparative advantage offers the same possibilities for economic growth through specialization and trade. The principal obstacles to this are argued to be the high transportation cost burdens of geographical remoteness or unwise national trade barriers, although some economists have recently added tropicality to this list, in arguments reflective of environmental determinism (Hausmann 2001). In today's global world, the free trade doctrine has become so taken for granted that we have ceded its implementation to a bureaucracy (the World Trade Organization).[12]

The beginning of free trade as a global practice is conventionally assigned to a particular conjuncture in space–time: London on June 25, 1846, when Robert Peel repealed the British Corn Laws.[13] Agitation for Corn Law repeal was organized by the Anti-Corn Law League, a group of largely Manchester-based cotton textile capitalists led by Richard Cobden (Pickering and Tyrrell 2000). Manchester was a logical home for this social movement, as it had become the center of European textile manufacturing, at a time when textiles represented the major internationally tradable manufacture. Manchester's positional advantage was itself created by British mercantile trading policies during the eighteenth century, when the British government used its control over international shipping and a series of tariff policies to undermine, in turn, the competitiveness of continental European and Indian textile manufacturers.

Manchester boosterists and British trade officials each felt that they could take advantage of free trade to advance their positionality, advancing capitalists' class interests over those of landlords (and organized labor, the Chartists) in Britain, while relegating continental Europe and India to specializing in agriculture. They advanced and implemented a free trade doctrine that could be justified by influential contemporary texts in political economy: Adam Smith's arguments about how trade expands the market and David Ricardo's recently published principle of comparative advantage. These provided apparently rational grounds, rooted in the Lockean private property liberalism that currently was all the rage, for arguing that free trade is good for everyone (Sheppard 2005).

Britain practiced free trade as official policy until 1914, using its geopolitical clout as the pre-eminent global economic power to take the free trade doctrine to the supranational scale. Beginning in France in 1860, the doctrine diffused rapidly through Europe, where political and economic elites were either convinced by the rhetoric or used free trade to advance other partisan interests. France reversed course in 1875, however, initiating a counter-reformation. With the exception of the Netherlands, all European countries increased their tariffs. Germany was the last to do so, but eventually adopted Friedrich List's infant industry argument (now known as import-substituting industrialization). This return to protectionism was stimulated by distinct national economic experiences with trade. The grain invasion from Eastern Europe had undermined domestic agriculture, and import-substituting industrialization proved effective. German manufacturers prospered, and were competing successfully even in English markets by the first decades of the twentieth century. This also was a period when private property liberalism was being replaced by social liberalism, legitimating state intervention into the market (Polanyi 2001 [1944]). In this context, national sovereignty and freedom came to be associated with protectionism rather than with free trade.[14]

Free trade was not practiced outside Europe during this nineteenth-century boom. In Europe's white settler colonies and former colonies, notably the USA, protectionism to catalyze domestic manufacturing was practiced and preached from the 1840s to the 1940s. By contrast, other colonies were required to trade with their colonial mother countries, creating a group of trading cliques. In the British empire, the colonies signed "unequal treaties" stipulating that colonies' tariffs could not exceed 5 percent of the value of imports (Bairoch 1993).

It was only in the negotiations leading to Bretton Woods that the USA shifted its rhetorical position to support the free trade doctrine, using its power over Western Europe and Japan to break down pre-war colonial trading cliques.[15] This led to a second boom in the popularity of the free trade doctrine, which has proven more robust than the first phase a hundred years earlier. All major nations are now members of the World Trade Organization (WTO), to which, as signatories, they delegate the power to override territorial policies deemed inimical to the practice of free trade.

Falling transportation costs and the gradual elimination of barriers to international trade have not created a level playing field, however. Different nations continue to occupy unequal positions in global trading networks, with consequences for their conditions of possibility to prosper from specialization and trade. This can be seen particularly clearly for nations of the former Third World, for which the free trade doctrine, combined with political independence after colonialism, seemed to promise so much. First, in contradistinction to this doctrine (but consonant with the beliefs of British free traders in the 1840s), specialization in primary commodities has amounted to a positional disadvantage. Between 1950 and 2000, with the exception of members of the Organization of Petroleum Exporting Countries (OPEC) in the 1970s, the terms of trade have declined steadily for Third World countries specializing in primary commodity exports in order to finance manufactured imports (Figure 2.4). Even Third World manufacturing exports have been disadvantaged by comparison with First World manufacturing exports (Sarkar and Singer 1991). The import-substituting industrialization that worked for Germany and the USA was unsuccessful in many Third World nations, where the domestic production of consumer goods that emerged behind trade barriers generated unsustainable demand for other manufactured capital good inputs imported from the First World. Declining terms of trade pushed Third World nations to specialize further in primary commodities for export to finance their import bills, constituting a vicious cycle. This has been exacerbated by progressive First World tariff and non-tariff barriers, creating selective disincentives for Third World nations to move their specialization up the commodity chain from raw materials to manufacturing (Table 2.4). Between 1968 and 1988, the cost of manufactured imports for the Third World increased twelvefold, whereas Third World purchasing power only doubled, despite a threefold increase in primary product specialization and export (Figure 2.5).

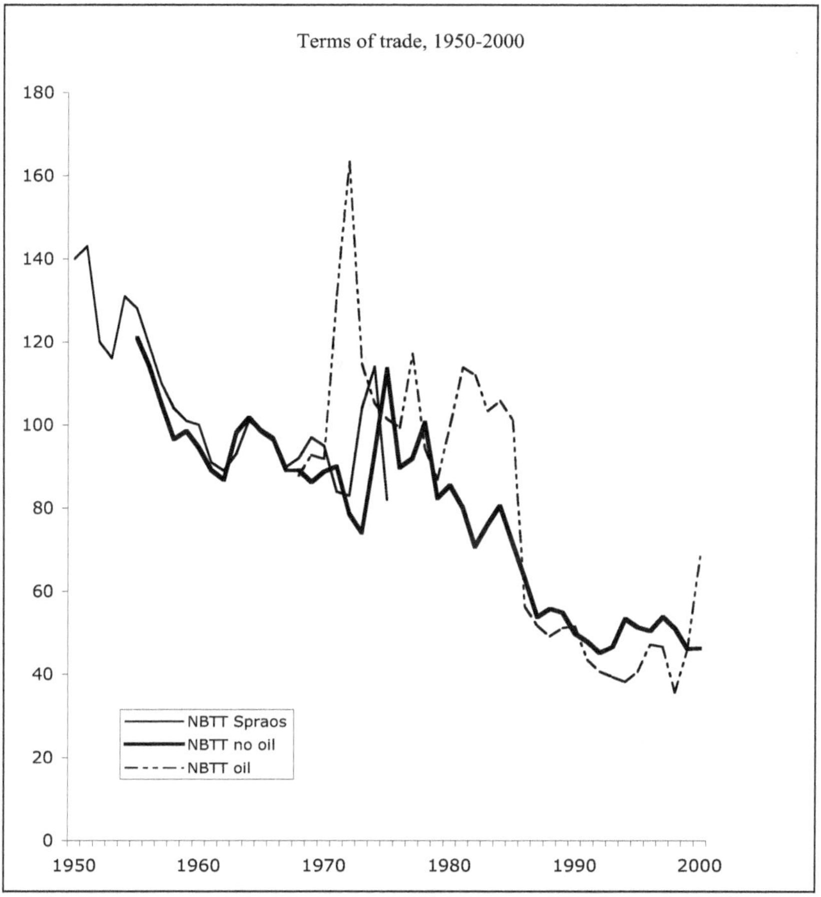

Figure 2.4 Net barter terms of trade for Third World primary commodity exports, 1950–2000. Source: author's calculation on Spraos (1983).

Table 2.4 Tariff protection on selected imports from the Third World, 1981

Commodity	*United States*	*European Community*	*Japan*
Cotton, raw	6.2	0.0	0.0
Cotton yarn	25.0	32.9	6.8
Cotton fabric	24.6	19.1	17.8
Cotton clothing	35.4	20.8	27.5
Bauxite	0.0	0.0	0.0
Alumina	0.0	11.1	0.0
Aluminum, unwrought	6.0	5.6	11.4
Aluminum, wrought	11.5	29.3	29.0

Sources: UNCTAD (1981), Colman and Nixson (1986).

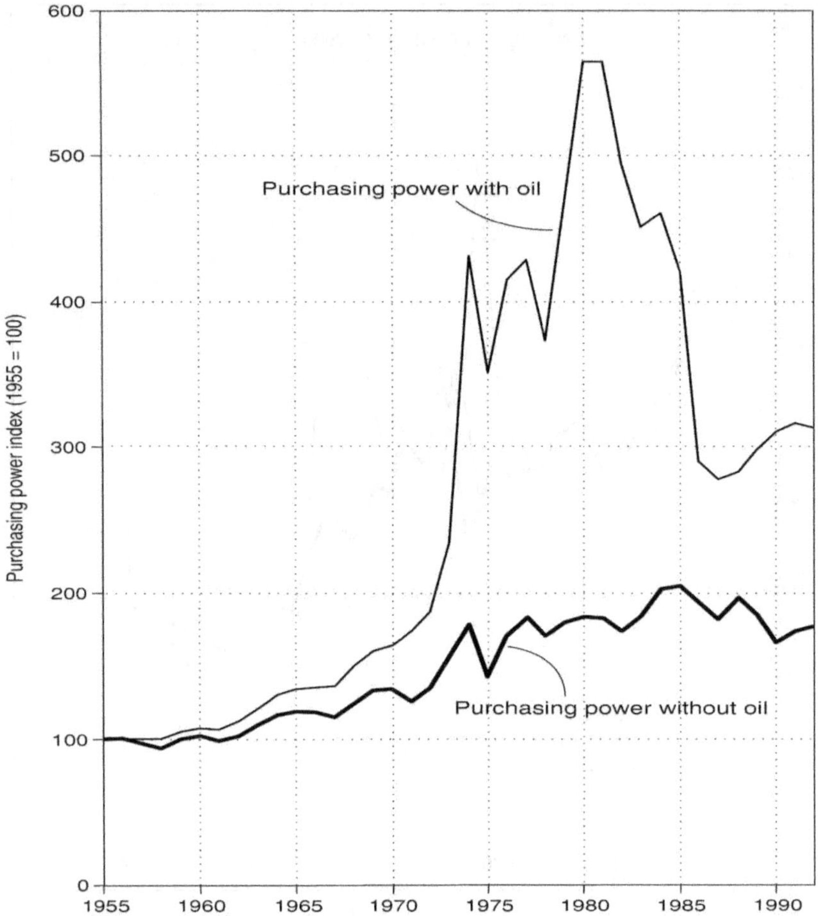

Figure 2.5 Third World purchasing power, 1955–93 (Porter and Sheppard 1998).

The geography of global trading networks both reflects and reproduces such differences in positionality. First, trade remains dominated by north–north trade, in specialized manufactures. By contrast, former Third World nations are minor and peripheral players, whose trade with the First World still reflects colonial connections; linking Western Europe with Africa and the Middle East, the USA with Latin America, and Japan with South-East and East Asia (Figure 2.6). This is reinforced by an asymmetric mutual dependence on trade between the First World and the Third World: Third World nations rely heavily on First World markets for their exports, but First World nations send less than 5 percent of their exports to the Third World. Second, nations of the former Third World rely more on specialization and trade, specialize in far fewer (and more easily substitutable) products, and export products with smaller shares of the world market. Under the hypothesis that market power increases with market share and diversifica-

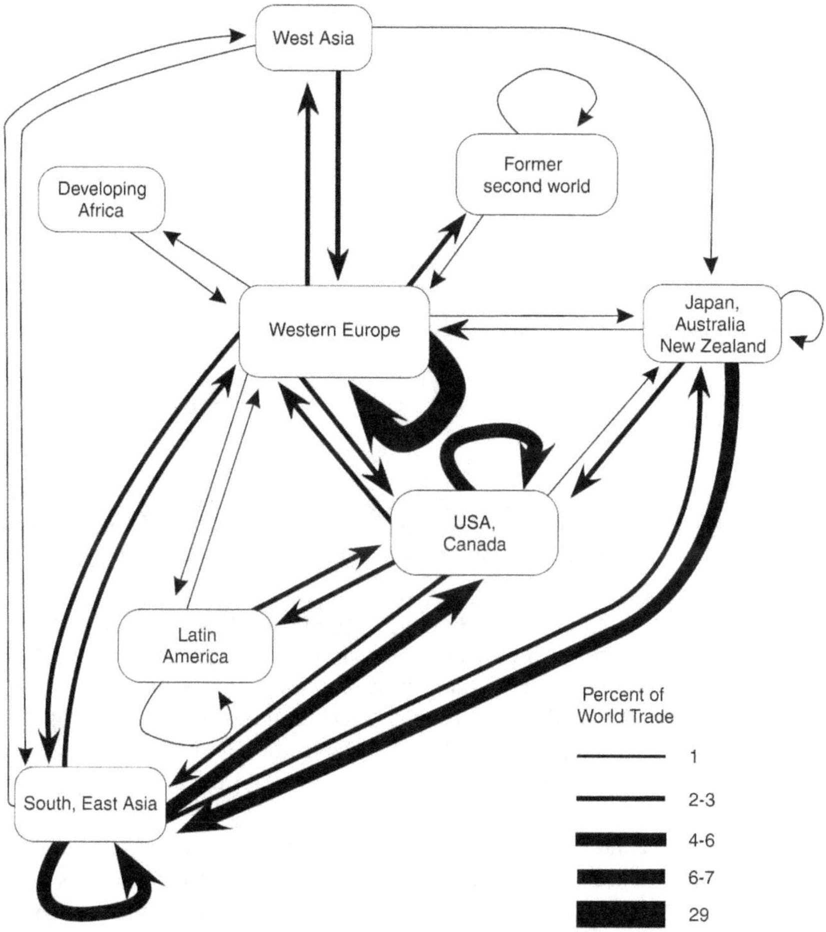

Figure 2.6 World regional trading networks, 1993 (Porter and Sheppard 1998).

tion (enhancing flexibility in the face of negative price trends on an exported commodity), the bargaining power of former Third World nations is tendentially lower (Figure 2.7). This reflects and reproduces the difficulty that Third World nations have faced in repeatedly trying to change global trading regimes in their favor, from the Group of 77 in 1964 to the Group of 21 at the October 2003 WTO meeting in Cancun.

In summary, the historical geography of international trade has been one in which the free trade doctrine promises equal opportunities for growth for all, particularly as transportation costs and institutional barriers fall and differences in positionality thereby supposedly dissipate. In practice, however, differences in positionality persist and are reproduced despite such developments. Positionally advantaged countries, initially Britain and more recently the USA, Japan, and the European Union, have taken advantage of their ability to both control discourse

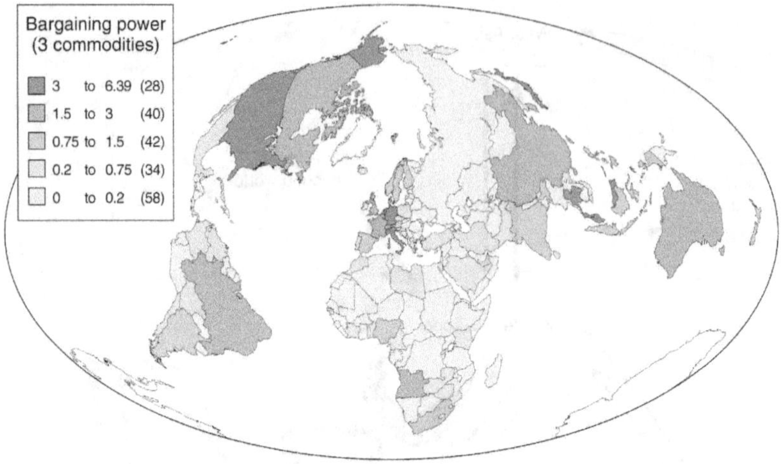

Figure 2.7 Trade bargaining power index, 1993. Note that the index equals the average world market share of the three largest exports, divided by the proportion of these three products in total exports (Porter and Sheppard 1998).

and shape material conditions of possibility to promote free trade, while violating its principles in practice whenever expedient (most notably, recently, refusing to eliminate the subsidies for agricultural production that undermine Third World agricultural exports). Positionally disadvantaged countries have been compelled to follow the logic of relying heavily on specialization and free trade, despite consistently receiving a disproportionately small share of the global surplus that trade has created.

These unequal conditions of possibility deriving from differences in positionality are persistent, and in some cases (notably sub-Saharan Africa) are increasing. Yet, as stressed above, positionality is not immutable. This has been shown by the experience of certain South-East and East Asian nations, such as South Korea and Taiwan, which drew on national state-led strategies mixing import substitution and export-oriented industrialization, combined with external support from the USA due to their strategic importance in struggles with the People's Republic of China, to embark on a successful strategy of industrialization. They have been able to improve their positionality in global trade networks (Figure 2.6), despite ongoing vulnerability in global financial markets. There is much evidence to suggest that China is now on a similar path, one that enables selected Third World nations to benefit from trade even as others are left behind. The mutability of positionality offers hope to each place, but the persistence of positional inequalities even under such mutations implies that capitalism thrives on geographically uneven development, not a level playing field.

Conclusion

Close attention to positionality challenges some current thinking in economic geography. For theoretical economic geography, it calls into question prevailing presuppositions about the efficiency, stability, and potential equity of unrestricted spatial competition. This suggests that the capitalist space economy is, instead, an out-of-equilibrium system of creative destruction, compounded by complex and overlapping conflicts of interest between economic agents. Even for those agents with the power to advance their self-interest, the complexity of spatiotemporal dynamics implies that their actions can have the unintended consequence of undermining their own interests.

Practically, recognition that differences in positionality persist despite powerful forces of globalization has important consequences for how we think about globalization and its consequences. First, unequal positionality implies that spatial competition is always plagued by a potential race to the bottom, in which positionally disadvantaged localities reduce wage levels and environmental and other regulatory standards for all, in their desperate attempt to attract capitalist investment. Second, the success or failure of different localities lies in the hands of political economic forces operating at scales beyond the control of those localities, raising questions about the degree to which local agency actually shapes local economic performance. Third, it no longer makes sense to theorize development as a series of stages that all places go through. Globalization's proponents operate within such an impoverished space–time imaginary (Massey 1999b), which eliminates spatial difference in favor of a universal narrative of change – a new modernization theory.

Recognition of the positionally differentiated nature of our world creates space to imagine other possibilities. The same practices will not have the same consequences in differently positioned places. Instead, places need the freedom to pursue different political economic strategies, in pursuit of their own visions of the good life. Attention to positionality suggests the importance also of translocal strategies for overcoming disadvantage. Local actions to improve the business climate have little chance of improving the positionality of disadvantaged places. Collective actions across space, such as south–south collaboration by states and civil society, are more likely to have the desired transformative effect. In this sense, civil society can also learn from corporate strategies, which have long prospered from translocal networking.

Notes

1 I use agent here in the broadest possible sense – to refer to any entity with causal power.
2 This section draws extensively from Sheppard (2000a).
3 This is not the only aspect of spatiality that can disrupt economic theory. Others have made similar arguments with respect to place and scale.
4 For a treatment of realistic geography in trade theory, showing how relative location affects gains from trade, see Eaton and Kortum (2002).
5 Gender, race, etc. are also important, particularly once the non-monetary spheres of capitalism, such as household labor, are recognized. I do not have space to treat these here, but they further complicate spatial economic dynamics.
6 In this context, methodological individualism is the position that economic agency can be reduced to the rational choices of individuals with given preference functions and resource endowments (Barnes and Sheppard 1992).

7 This is a minimalist version of positionality because it neglects difference in social location or power, and treats positionality as if it were exogenous to the economic system.

8 The neglect of "first nature" in geographical economics stems from a belief that pre-existing inequalities have entirely predictable, and thus not very interesting, consequences, i.e., favored locations perform better. Geographic research questions this. First, our research suggests that spatial price and profitability patterns are actually quite complex, even for simple non-isotropic geographies. Second, some of the truly interesting insights of economic geography address why some places prosper despite geographic disadvantage, moving from the periphery to the core. Third, "first nature" is not first in the sense that it is exogenous to and logically prior to uneven development. Rather, inequalities in relative location (and in the biophysical environment) are in part endogenous to spatial economic processes, an endogeneity that needs to be understood.

9 There are always agents who stand to gain by disrupting the equilibrium.

10 This paradox is common in social theory, such as debates in feminist theory about how any discussion of gender is in danger of reproducing the very social conventions about gender that theorists struggle against; or concerns in postcolonial theory that "postcolonial" reifies the historical categories it seeks to challenge (Butler 1990, McClintock 1992).

11 I artificially restrict discussion here to international trade. Similar arguments could be made with respect to geographical flows of capital, labor, knowledge, discourse, and power (notably, in economic geography, geographies of direct investment).

12 The doctrine also has an ethical dimension, that free trade entails the peaceful exchange of products, customs, and ideas between nations, a great improvement over the violence of interstate war and colonialism. This view dates back to Greek writings on trade, and was central to the arguments of the radical liberal Richard Cobden, who catalyzed the globalization of free trade.

13 The Corn Laws imposed a ban on wheat imports whenever the price fell below 80 shillings, offering a substantial state subsidy to large British landowners, and a penalty to British industrialists who had to pay higher cash wages. Parallels to today's agricultural subsidies in the European Union, North America, and Japan are very close.

14 Only in Britain were such arguments not extended to embrace trade protectionism, despite attempts to introduce an imperial preference system by Joseph Chamberlin, no doubt reflecting the belief that Britain was positioned to benefit most from free trade.

15 Note, however, that the US Senate refused to ratify the creation of the International Trading Organization to oversee freer trade, as it was not seen to be in the national interest.

References

Aglietta, M. (1979) *A Theory of Capitalist Regulation*, London: New Left Books.

Amin, A. and Cohendet, P. (1999) 'Learning and adaptation in decentralized business networks', *Environment and Planning D: Society and Space*, 17: 87–104.

Amin, A. and Thrift, N. (1994) 'Holding down the global', in Amin, A. and Thrift, N. (eds.) *Globalization, Institutions and Regional Development in Europe*, Oxford: Oxford University Press, pp. 257–60.

Amin, A. and Thrift, N. (1995) 'Institutional issues for the European regions: from markets and plans to socioeconomics and powers of association', *Economy and Society*, 24: 41–66.

Amin, A. and Thrift, N. (2002) *Cities: Reimagining the Urban*, Cambridge: Polity Press.

Aoyama, Y. and Sheppard, E. (2003) 'The dialectic of geographic and virtual space', *Environment and Planning A*, 35: 1151–6.

Bairoch, P. (1993) *Economics and World History*, Chicago: Chicago University Press.

Baldwin, R.E. and Martin, P. (2004) 'Agglomeration and regional growth', in Henderson, J.V. and Thisse, J.-F. (eds.) *Handbook of Urban and Regional Economics*, Amsterdam: Elsevier, pp. 2671–709.

Barnes, T. and Sheppard, E. (1992) 'Is there a place for the rational actor? A geographical critique of the rational choice paradigm', *Economic Geography*, 68: 1–21.

Bathelt, H., Malmberg, A. and Maskell, P. (2004) 'Clusters and knowledge: local buzz, global pipelines and the process of knowledge creation', *Progress in Human Geography*, 28: 31–56.

Blaut, J. (1993) *The Colonizer's Model of the World*, New York: Guilford Press.

Butler, J. (1990) *Gender Trouble: Feminism and the Subversion of Identity*, London: Routledge.

Butler, J. (1993) *Bodies that Matter: On the Discursive Limits of 'Sex'*, London: Routledge.

Cairncross, F. (1997) *The Death of Distance: How the Communications Revolution will Change our Lives*, London: Orion Business Books.

Cardoso, F. and Faletto, R. (1979) *Dependency and Development*, Berkeley, CA: University of California Press.

Castells, M. (1996) *The Information Age: Economy, Society and Culture,* Vol. 1: *The Rise of the Network Society*, Oxford: Blackwell Publishers.

Clark, G.L. and Wrigley, N. (1995) 'Sunk costs: a framework for economic geography', *Transactions of the Institute of British Geographers*, 20: 204–23.

Clark, G.L., Gertler, M. and Whiteman, J. (1986) *Regional Dynamics: Studies in Adjustment Theory*, London: Allen & Unwin.

Colman, D. and Nixson, F. (1986) *Economics of Change in Less Developed Countries*, New York: Barnes & Noble.

Dixit, A.K. and Stiglitz, J.E. (1977) 'Monopolistic competition and optimum product diversity', *American Economic Review*, 67: 297–308.

Dunford, M.F. (1988) *Capital, the State, and Regional Development*, London: Pion.

Eaton, J. and Kortum, S. (2002) 'Technology, geography, and trade', *Econometrica*, 70: 1741–79.

Fisher, W.F. and Ponniah, T. (eds.) (2003) *Another World is Possible: Popular Alternatives to Globalization at the World Social Forum*, London: Zed Books.

Fujita, M., Krugman, P. and Venables, A.J. (1999) *The Spatial Economy: Cities, Regions and International Trade*, Cambridge, MA: MIT Press.

Galtung, J. (1971) 'A structural theory of imperialism', *Journal of Peace Research*, 2: 81–116.

Gibson-Graham, J.K. (1996) *The End of Capitalism (as we know it)*, Oxford: Blackwell Publishers.

Glassman, J. (1999) 'State power beyond the "territorial trap": the internationalization of the state', *Political Geography*, 18: 669–96.

Goodwin, R.M. (1987) 'Macrodynamics', in Goodwin, R.M. and Puzo, L. (eds.) *The Dynamics of a Capitalist Economy*, Boulder, CO: Westview Press.

Graham, S. (1998) 'The end of geography or the explosion of place? Conceptualizing space, place and information technology', *Progress in Human Geography*, 22: 165–85.

Haggett, P. (1990) *The Geographer's Art*, Oxford: Basil Blackwell.

Haining, R., Plummer, P. and Sheppard, E. (1996) 'Spatial price equilibrium in interdependent markets: price and sales configurations', *Papers in Regional Science*, 75: 41–64.

Harcourt, G.C. (1972) *Some Cambridge Controversies in the Theory of Capital*, Cambridge: Cambridge University Press.

Harley, J.B. (1989) 'Deconstructing the map', *Cartographica*, 26: 1–20.

Harvey, D. (1982) *The Limits to Capital*, Oxford: Basil Blackwell.

Harvey, D. (1989a) *The Condition of Postmodernity*, Oxford: Basil Blackwell.

Harvey, D. (1989b) 'From managerialism to entrepreneurialism: the transformation of urban governance in late capitalism', *Geografisker Annaler*, 71: 3–17.

Harvey, D. (1996) *Justice, Nature and the Geography of Difference*, Oxford: Basil Blackwell.

Harvey, D. (2000) *Spaces of Hope*, Berkeley, CA: University of California Press.

Hausmann, R. (2001) 'Prisoners of geography', *Foreign Policy*, January/February: 45–53.

Held, D., McGrew, A., Goldblatt, D. and Perraton, J. (1999) *Global Transformations: Politics, Economics and Culture*, Stanford, CA: Stanford University Press.

Herod, A. (2001) *Labor Geographies: Workers and the Landscapes of Capitalism*, New York: Guilford Press.

Hudson, R. and Sadler, D. (1986) 'Contesting works closures in Western Europe's old industrial regions: defending place or betraying class?', in Scott, A.J. and Storper, M. (eds.) *Production, Work, Territory – The Geographical Anatomy of Industrial Capitalism*, London: Allen & Unwin, pp. 172–93.

Hugill, P. (1999) *Global Communications since 1844: Geopolitics and Technology*, Baltimore: Johns Hopkins University Press.

Janelle, D. and Hodge, D. (eds.) (2000) *Accessibility in the Information Age*, Berlin: Springer Verlag.

Krugman, P. (1996) *The Self-organizing Economy*, Oxford: Blackwell.

Liossatos, P. (1988) 'Value and competition in a spatial context: a Marxian model', *Papers of the Regional Science Association*, 45: 87–103.

Longino, H. (2002) *The Fate of* Knowledge, Princeton, NJ: Princeton University Press.

McClintock, A. (1992) 'The angel of progress: pitfalls of the term "post-colonialism"', *Social Text*, 31/32: 84–98.

Malmberg, A. and Maskell, P. (2002) 'The elusive concept of localization economies: towards a knowledge-based theory of spatial clustering', *Environment and Planning A*, 34: 429–49.

Marelli, E. (1983) 'Empirical estimation of intersectoral and interregional transfers of surplus value: the case of Italy', *Journal of Regional Science*, 23: 49–70.

Marini, R. (1973) *La Dialéctica de la Dependencia*, Mexico City: Ediciones Era.

Martin, R. (1999) 'The new economic geography of money', in Martin, R. (ed.) *Money and the Space Economy*, New York: John Wiley.

Marvin, C. (1988) *When Old Technologies were New*, New York: Oxford University Press.

Marx, K. and Engels, F. (1952) *Manifesto of the Communist Party*, Moscow: Progress Publishers.

Massey, D. (1991) 'A global sense of place', *Marxism Today*, June: 24–9.

Massey, D. (1999a) 'Space–time, "science" and the relationship between physical and human geography', *Transactions of the Institute of British Geographers*, 24: 261–76.

Massey, D. (1999b) 'Imagining globalization: power-geometries of time–space', in Brah, A., Hickman, M. and Mac an Ghaill, M. (eds.) *Global Futures: Migration, Environment and Globalization*, New York: St. Martin's Press, pp. 27–44.

Mattelart, A. (2000) *Networking the World, 1794–2000*, Minneapolis: University of Minnesota Press.

Mohanty, C.T. (2003) *Feminism without Borders: Decolonizing Theory, Practicing Solidarity*, Durham, NC: Duke University Press.

Morishima, M. (1973) *Marx's Economics: a Dual Theory of Value and Growth*, Cambridge: Cambridge University Press.

Nagar, R. and Geiger, S. (2006) 'Reflexivity, positionality and identity in feminist fieldwork: beyond the impasse', in Tickell, A., Barnes, T., Peck, J. and Sheppard, E. (eds.) *Politics and Practice in Economic Geography*, Beverley Hills, CA: Sage (forthcoming).

Nell, E. (1992) 'Demand, pricing and investment' in Nell, E. (ed.) *Transformational Growth and Effective Demand*, New York: New York University Press.

Oinas, P. (2002) 'Competition and collaboration in interconnected places: towards a research agenda', *Geografiska Annaler*, 84: 65–76.

Oinas, P. and Malecki, E. (2002) 'The evolution of technologies in time and space: from national and regional to spatial innovation systems', *International Regional Science Review*, 25: 102–31.

Ottaviano, G.I.P. and Thisse, J.-F. (2004) 'Agglomeration and economic geography', in Henderson, J.V. and Thisse, J.-F. (eds.) *Handbook of Urban and Regional Economics*, Amsterdam: Elsevier, pp. 2564–608.

Pickering, P.A. and Tyrrell, A. (2000) *The People's Bread: A History of the Anti-Corn Law League*, London: Leicester University Press.

Plummer, P. (1999) 'Capital accumulation, economic restructuring, and nonequilibrium regional growth dynamics', *Geographical Analysis*, 31: 267–87.

Plummer, P.S. (1996a) 'Competitive dynamics in hierarchically organized markets: spatial duopoly and demand asymmetries', *Environment and Planning A*, 28: 2021–40.

Plummer, P.S. (1996b) 'Spatial competition amongst hierarchically organized corporations: prices, profits, and shipment patterns', *Environment and Planning A*, 28: 199–222.

Plummer, P.S., Haining, R.P. and Sheppard, E. (1998) 'Spatial pricing in interdependent markets: testing assumptions and modeling price variation. A case study in St. Cloud, Minnesota', *Environment and Planning A*, 30: 67–84.

Polanyi, K. (2001 [1944]) *The Great Transformation: The Political and Economic Origins of our Time*, Boston: Beacon Press.

Porter, P.W. and Sheppard, E. (1998) *A World of Difference*, New York: Guilford Press.

Rigby, D. and Essletzbichler, J. (1997) 'Evolution, process variety, and regional trajectories of technical change in U.S. manufacturing', *Economic Geography*, 73: 269–85.

Roemer, J. (1981) *Analytical Foundations of Marxian Economic Theory*, Cambridge: Cambridge University Press.

Rose, G. (1997) 'Situating knowledges: positionality, reflexivities and other tactics', *Progress in Human Geography*, 21: 305–20.

Sarkar, P. and Singer, H.W. (1991) 'Manufactured exports of developing countries and their terms of trade since 1965', *World Development*, 19: 333–40.

Scott, A.J. (1980) *The Urban Land Nexus and the State*, London: Pion.

Sheppard, E. (1990) 'Transportation in a capitalist space economy: transportation demand, circulation time and transportation innovations', *Environment and Planning A*, 22: 1007–24.

Sheppard, E. (1995) 'Dissenting from spatial analysis', *Urban Geography*, 16: 283–303.

Sheppard, E. (2000a) 'Geography or economics? Contrasting theories of location, spatial pricing, trade and growth', in Clark, G., Gertler, M. and Feldman, M. (eds.) *Handbook of Economic Geography*, Oxford: Oxford University Press, pp. 199–219.

Sheppard, E. (2000b) 'Competition in space and between places', in Sheppard, E. and Barnes, T.J. (eds.) *Companion to Economic Geography*, Oxford: Blackwell Publishers, pp. 169–86.

Sheppard, E. (2001) 'Geographies of the information society', in Smelser, N. and Baltes, P. (eds.) *International Encyclopedia of the Social & Behavioral Sciences*, Oxford: Pergamon Press, pp. 7469–83.

Sheppard, E. (2002) 'The spaces and times of globalization: place, scale, networks, and positionality', *Economic Geography*, 78: 307–30.

Sheppard, E. (2004) 'The spatiality of *The Limits to Capital*', *Antipode*, 36: 470–9.

Sheppard, E. (2005) 'Free trade: the very idea! From Manchester boosterism to global management', *Transactions of the Institute of British Geographers*, 30: 151–72.

Sheppard, E. and Barnes, T.J. (1986) 'Instabilities in the geography of capitalist production: collective vs. individual profit maximization', *Annals of the Association of American Geographers*, 76: 493–507.

Sheppard, E. and Barnes, T.J. (1990) *The Capitalist Space Economy: Geographical Analysis After Ricardo, Marx and Sraffa*, London: Unwin Hyman.

Sheppard, E., Haining, R.P. and Plummer, P. (1992) 'Spatial pricing in interdependent markets', *Journal of Regional Science*, 32: 55–75.

Sheppard, E., Plummer, P. and Haining, R. (1998) 'Profit rate maximization in interdependent markets', *Journal of Regional Science*, 38: 659–67.

Simmie, J. (2002) 'Trading places: competitive cities in the global economy', *European Planning Studies*, 10: 202–15.

Soja, E. (1980) 'The socio-spatial dialectic', *Annals of the Association of American Geographers*, 70: 207–25.

Spraos, J. (1983) *Inequalising Trade?*, Oxford: Clarendon Press.

Storper, M. and Walker, R. (1989) *The Capitalist Imperative: Territory, Technology and Industrial Growth*, Oxford: Basil Blackwell.

Trentmann, F. (1998) 'Political culture and political economy: interest, ideology and free trade', *Review of International Political Economy*, 5: 217–51.

UNCTAD (1981) *Proceedings of the United Nations Conference on Trade and Development, Fifth Session, Manila,* Vol. III. *Basic Documents*, New York: United Nations.

Valentine, G. (2002) 'People like us: negotiating sameness and difference in the research process', in Moss, P. (ed.) *Feminist Geography in Practice*, Oxford: Blackwell.

Van Tulder, R. and Ruigrok, W. (1997) 'The nature of institutional change: managing rival dependencies', in Amin, A. and Hausner, J. (eds.) *Beyond Market and Hierarchy: Interactive Governance and Social Complexity*, Cheltenham: Edward Elgar.

Virilio, P. (1995) *The Art of the Motor*, Minneapolis: University of Minnesota Press.

Webber, M.J. (1987) 'Rates of profit and interregional flows of capital', *Annals of the Association of American Geographers*, 77: 63–75.

Webber, M.J. (1996) 'Profitability and growth in multiregional systems: theory and a model', *Economic Geography*, 72: 335–52.

Webber, M.J. and Rigby, D. (1996) *The Golden Age Illusion: Rethinking Postwar Capitalism*, New York: Guilford Press.

Webber, M.J. and Rigby, D. (1999) 'Accumulation and the rate of profit: regulating the macroeconomy', *Environment and Planning A*, 31: 141–64.

Webber, M.J., Sheppard, E. and Rigby, D. (1992) 'Forms of technical change', *Environment and Planning A*, 24: 1679–709.

3 A systemic approach to territorial studies

Deconstructing territorial competitiveness[1]

Sergio Conti and Paolo Giaccaria

A narrative about complexity

The profound changes in the world economy in the last few decades have deeply changed the way geographers think about the world, bringing "new" economic geographies to the forefront in the Third World, as a consequence of the displacement of considerable segments of production, as well as in the peripheries of North America and Western Europe. Alongside these significant shifts, the developed world has seen the emergence of numerous new industrial spaces, the expression of both the consolidation of high-tech areas (such as Silicon Valley or Route 128) and the revitalization of areas with a manufacturing tradition (Third Italy, Denmark, Baden-Württemberg). The rise of the "world cities," around which intense interdisciplinary debate has developed, is part of this process. These phenomena, accompanied by the weakening of the old industrial cores which had expressed and sustained the mass production system, cannot be isolated from a dual and dialectical process, which Markusen (1996) defines as the paradox of "sticky places within slippery spaces": on the one hand, the hypermobility of financial capital and technology; on the other hand, the strength of the clustering (agglomeration) of industries and companies. The duality between deterritorializing and territorializing forces is a question that the economic sciences and geography have examined at length: significant contributions have been made recently by geographers, and also by political economists, sociologists, and international business scholars (Granovetter and Swedberg 1992, Storper 1995, Veltz 1996, Enright 1998, Becattini 2000, Dunning 2000, Gilly and Torre 2000, Hudson 2001, to cite just a few).

The debate about the status of territory and its relationship with economic process has seen two main contrasting arguments that deal with the broader issue of globalization. According to the first, the processes in question are echoed in an increasingly placeless economy, in which the economic development process "is passing from territorial institutions such as states to deterritorialized institutions such as intra-firm international hierarchies"' that are said to be gaining on territorial barriers, specificity, and frictions (Storper 1997: 19). The second case, instead, stresses the fact that economic development is combined with continuing specificity in development patterns. Accordingly, faced with the liberalization of both internal and cross-border markets and the growing globalization of asset-exploiting activities by multinational enterprises, the further concentration of economic activities in dynamic agglomerative regions represents a fundamental feature of the new world economic map, against which regional authorities and practitioners must measure themselves (Saxenian 1994, Dunning 2000).

This new wave of geographical imagination about the links that connect space, places, and economic processes has brought to the forefront new concepts, which have rapidly increased their theoretical and empirical fortune. It is not by chance, in fact, that one of the fundamental terms in contemporary economic and social research is *local development*, a synthetic concept that underlies a multitude of other terms around which there has been heated debate, such as industrial districts (Sabel 1989, Pyke *et al.* 1990), industrial clusters (Porter 1990), learning regions (Florida 1995, Maskell 1998), innovative milieu (Aydalot 1986, Maillat and Perrin 1992), local production systems (Abdelmalki and Courlet 1996, Pecqueur 2000), "regional motors," and so on. The concept of local development implies something that is both truly complex and at the same time fuzzy: against a background of growing awareness of the incapacity of the traditional regional development models of analysis, the aim is to give meaning to the central role in contemporary development processes of an intermediate entity between the actor (the company, in particular) and the system as a whole, in respect of which the local system expresses both a space for cooperation between actors and their embeddedness in a given territorial context, from which they draw specific competitive and not easily reproducible resources and solutions.

Another concept that escalated to a large critical mass in contemporary debate is "territorial competitiveness," with its various scalar understandings – from local and urban to regional and up to the national scale. The idea that territories compete with each other has matched with the expectations of policy-makers and local administrators, establishing a broad body of arguments and praxis where territories are increasingly treated like economic agents, often outshining their social, cultural, and political dimensions. As a consequence, the debate about territorial competitiveness has been extremely varied in positions and perspectives; while some give a quite positive account of the process (Begg 1999), others vehemently deny that it is of any theoretical importance (Krugman 1996a), while yet others put forward a broad range of more cautious interpretations and caveats (Kresl 1995, Foss 1996, Cheshire and Gordon 1996, Budd 1998, Sharp 1998, Conti and Giaccaria 2001, Camagni 2002).

Nevertheless, despite the fact that these concepts were well received by policy-makers and practitioners, they grew up "too fast too furious," through a huge range of interpretations, perspectives, and judgments, which are quite difficult to bring together into a consistent framework. Moreover, concepts such as "territorial competitiveness" and "local development" show many ambiguities that cannot be solved without a comprehensive and systematic reflection on the conceptual basis they stand on. For instance, most of the contemporary arguments in economic geography draw on a sort of personalization and reification of territory and place, which are assumed to be person-like collective agents, able to express common representations and wishes and therefore to compete in some sort of market. Also, all the literature focusing on cognitive interpretation of territorial processes – such as the innovative milieu stream or the learning region approach – ends up by setting an holistic comprehension of territories that is highly problematic: What about dissonant voices in the milieu? Are they just noise?[2]

In our perspective, similar questions must be addressed in an epistemological way, looking for a comprehensive understanding of territories that re-establishes a balance between economic and territorial processes, without reducing the latter to the former. The arguments expressed here follow an explicitly systemic perspective (Morin 1977, Le Moigne 1992, 1994), within the broader realm of complexity studies (Wiener 1956, Atlan 1972, von Foerster 1982). One condition of complexity – and this needs to be recalled here, even if briefly – lies in the acknowledgment that reality cannot be reduced to the methods of simplification typical of orthodox modern economic and social science, in which reality is broken down into simple components that are easier to study and understand. With the theories of complexity, attention is now shifted to more complex mechanisms of interaction between elements. In particular, it is maintained that the unpredictability of the system stems from precisely the fact that the subsystems interact with each other through different types of relations and that they cannot therefore be analyzed separately.

In this chapter, we would like to focus on how territories can be conceptualized from a systemic perspective and to exemplify how systemic territorial theories can be applied to address some of the open issues of the contemporary debate in economic geography, specifically with reference to the concept of "territorial competition." The reference here is to the mechanism of *autopoiesis*, through which it is possible to characterize the organization of a system, as (it has been) elaborated by the Chilean scholars Maturana and Varela (1980, 1987). The starting point is the clear distinction between heteronymous and autonomous systems: while the former are characterized by an evolution according to the structure of the external world, autonomous systems are, instead, endowed with organizational closure, with the external world acting purely as a factor of disturbance. They thus appear to be independent from the forms of the outside world, with the exception of the flows that assume importance for the self-reproduction and survival of the system. In a system characterized by organizational closure, network interconnection between its components is the basis of the fundamental property of autonomy, which defines the closure and cohesion of the system with respect to the environment. The local system will thus be distinguished on the basis of its own rules of operation, which, instead of being dictated from the outside, represent invariants through which the system reproduces its own autonomy in its constant openness to the environment. These rules are dictated by the way in which the network of its constituent relations is represented internally, by a rather complex structuring of economic, political, cultural, social, etc., relations.

The key concepts are *organization* and *structure*. Although both concepts are of a relational nature, the sense is profoundly different. The organization is, in fact, given by the ensemble of relations between elements of the system that make the system what it is and not something else. The structure is, instead, given by the material and historic qualities of these relations. It is the structure that modifies itself more rapidly, following stimuli from both outside and inside the system. The organization instead maintains a greater degree of rigidity, in that a radical modification of the relations that compose it can lead to the disintegration of the system. Obviously, an organization evolves over time, according to its own laws (it is in this sense that the system is autonomous and autopoietic).

Territorial systemic interactions

Basically, there are two possible perspectives: the first one is to say that the territory is the environment where different systems evolve and interact, while the second is to model the territory itself as a system. For different reasons both these paths are impracticable. If the territory is just the environment of some systems (such as the firm, the class, the cluster, the state, a species, etc.), we are faced with two viewpoints, the choice of either of which would abruptly stop our reflection:

1. Either the territory has only an ancillary function with respect to the functioning of other systems, offering the material support for the (re)production of capitalism or representing just a rather uninfluential means of production. This is a *functionalist approach* to the territory, saying that it possesses some sort of function and that concepts such as identity and cohesion are unnecessary in order to understand and define the function. Or
2. It represents the environment in a truly systemic view, but in this case it is something that cannot be described and treated as a system. In fact, in systems theory environment is assumed to be something that is too complex to be consistently treated. Better put, a system increases its complexity in order to face and, somehow, reduce environmental complexity. Therefore, if systems are conceptualized because we cannot deal directly with environmental complexity, considering the territory as environment in a systemic meaning is equal to asserting that little or nothing can be said about it.

In both cases, there are no real advantages in adopting a systemic perspective to conceptualize territory as in the first case we can use simpler models to explain it, while in the second it is too complex even for autopoiesis theories.

On the other hand, representing the territory as an autopoietic system raises some theoretical and practical issues that cannot be addressed here. To cite only the main one, a system is an object that possesses a high degree of cohesion and organic oneness represented by its organization, while even the simpler territory has manifold facets that are not easy to draw back to a univocal interpretation. More specifically, the territory, unlike a generic autopoietic system, is not the outcome of a single internal process that creates a sort of organic harmony among its components: too many social, economic, and cultural groups act within a territory in order to drive its transformation according to their desires and strategies. Even if we can be influenced by the continuity in time of certain territories, to say that this continuity is prevailing over change and that it is produced solely by territory's organization is a strange statement to be defended.

Our position will somehow be intermediate. In generic terms, we shall consider territory as an environment where different elementary systems intermingle and we will represent it as the outcome of this systemic interaction. Secondly, and more importantly, we will consider the prospect that particular systems exist which can be considered good proxies for the territory. These systems – which we will term productive territorial local systems (PTLS) – must have the property of being more complex than the elementary systems that live in the territory but be less complex than the whole territory. In other terms, our aim is to build up an analytical object that is a non-exhaustive representation of the territory but which possesses some of the features that are related to the territory and cannot be found in the individual systems that are part of the territory.

Systems in the territory

Before describing the PTLS and their relationship with the territory, we must spend some time describing what we call elementary or individual systems. Our hypothesis is that the different collective actors (people, groups of people, associations, firms, clusters of firms, etc.) that play a role in the social game can be usefully described as systems. They can be either private (firms and businesses of various kinds) or public (e.g., the local administration), or a mix (like the education system or some development agencies). Some of them will be codified in organizations (e.g., trade unions, non-governmental organizations (NGOs), churches, or entrepreneurial associations), whereas others are based on more informal institutions, such as ethnic groups or sexual or social identities. The territory influences all of them and, vice versa, all of them play a role in the making of a territory.

In considering the nature of elementary systems, we must limit ourselves to setting a small number of systemic features that these systems seize. First of all, with respect to Maturana and Varela's framework (1980, 1987), we simply set as a fundamental the distinction between *organization* and *structure*.[3] In other terms, we just assume that every system is made up of some relationships between its components which are essential to define its *identity*, organization, whereas other relationships are merely the contingent expression of this identity. As to how these systems are built, we can think of them as "black boxes." This is not to say that how they are constructed is not important or cannot be investigated. It just means that:

1 how they are made is less important than how they interact;
2 a specific hypothesis about their internal processes can be designed according to the specific questions the observer is asking;
3 many of their characters are contingent and therefore related to their structure rather than to the organization.

For instance, how an ethnic group's culture is built or how trade unionism shapes the representations and the strategies of the working class are, no doubt, important issues, but they cannot take into consideration the model building, as these explanations would dramatically increase the complexity of the overall account. In other words, we do not have to define for each system what is inherent in its organization and what in its structure. This is because it is only an intermediate stage toward the construction of the real analytical object we are going to use, that is the PTLS.

The second hypothesis we make about these elementary systems is that their organization is defined in terms of *proximity*. Proximity is what gives each system its own cohesion and makes it distinct from other analogous systems and therefore recognizable. In this perspective, we can say that every system is a local system. This is equivalent to saying that, as a system must possess an "inside," it must be characterized by some form of proximity. Therefore, all systems are logically local. We have to note that this proximity can be institutional, geographical, or both. Subsequently, "local" is not a synonym for "geographical" or "territorial." Local is to be interpreted – closely to its mathematical meaning – as a property of a set which emerges from some sort of proximity which can be only institutional and not necessarily physical. Let us think about a transnational corporation (TNC): it is composed of a set of plants, sites, and people that share some features of institutional proximity, even in the absence of physical proximity. As a consequence of that proximity, we can also argue that the TNC possesses an identity that is not just juridical, but also cognitive and emotional – see for instance the broad literature about institutional learning (Gertler 2001) and the process of identification between a Japanese corporation and its workforce (Nakamura *et al.* 1997). Of course, there are some relationships with material territories, not least because the plants occupy a portion of land and can cause a huge crisis in the territories they are located in when they move away, but these links are not fundamental to that system's identity. To express it in autopoietic system terminology, we might say that for entities such as an archetypal TNC the relationships with a given territory are related to its structure rather than to its organization.

Therefore, there are some emergent properties in the systemic organization that depend solely on institutional proximity and others which rely on geographical proximity. Let us consider cohesion within a community or an association, which can be either geographical and local or just local, comparing rockers with freemasons. In fact, we can easily admit that cohesion is an emergent property of the system and not of the set of individuals belonging to it (Bunge 2004). Moreover, cohesion is a constitutive feature of the organization of a community as a system (what makes a community a system) and, second, particular forms of cohesion – based on different kinds of proximity – distinguish a community's organization from the others. In our specific example, both rockers and freemasons have a relationship with the territory, but for the latter – as freemasons – it is likely that geographical ties are just a matter of structure, while for a rockers' community the proximity relationship with their territory is organizative, that is, it is constitutive of their identity. This feature will affect the kind of cohesion that characterizes the organization of rockers versus freemasons: in the case of the former, organizative cohesion is both geographical and local, while for the latter it is only local.

A taxonomy of systemic interaction

The two properties of the systems that we have highlighted in the previous paragraph – the distinction between organization and structure and that between institutional and geographical proximity – can be used to analyze how systems interact and therefore how territory is produced. To this aim we can distinguish a taxonomy based on two variables:

1 The *kind of proximity* ruling interaction, which can be purely institutional – when interaction happens without strong reference to the territory – or territorial – when both institutional and geographical proximity play a role in the interaction.
2 The *nature of interaction*, which can be structural or organizative. Structural coupling, that is the "contamination" of part of the system's structure to maintain its own organization while adapting to some extent to other systems , is probably the typical way through which different systems interact. We can nevertheless hypothesize that, in some cases, interaction occurs at the level of organization, through what we might term "organizative synthesis," producing a new system whose components are the individual original systems.

By crossing the kind of proximity with the nature of the interaction, we can distinguish four possible types of systemic interaction: the first two give rise to aterritorial outcomes, while the last two express different types of territorialization (Table 3.1).

Let us start with the aspatial forms of interaction: the most interesting outcome is that what are often considered to be the fundamental institutions of capitalism – that is, market and hierarchy – can be explained and differentiated in terms of the nature of interactions among systems. In fact:

1 *Structural institutional interaction* refers to a situation that affords institutional proximity among systems but which does not cross the boundaries of the structure and does not affect the deeper organization of the systems involved. A typical example is the *market relationship* described in Williamson's (1985) account, in which economic agents exchange goods all at once in an instantaneous moment. Another good example is an international fair, where sellers and buyers converge for a short period in order to quickly update their knowledge about recent product and/or process innovation. In addition, the concept of a global commodity chain can be a meaningful example of this kind of interaction (Gereffi and Korzeniewicz 1994, Henderson *et al.* 2002).
2 When we are facing a deeper interaction at institutional level, one that involves not only the structures but also the systems' organization, we can talk about *organizative institutional interaction*. Many forms of economic hierarchies

Table 3.1 A taxonomy of systemic interaction

	Nature of interaction	
Kinds of proximity	*Structural*	*Organizative*
Only institutional	Markets	Hierarchies
Territorial (institutional and geographical)	Agglomeration	PTLS

can be interpreted in this perspective. The establishment of a transnational corporation (TNC), such as Ford, which is organized in three different bodies with a large degree of autonomy but which at the same time are closely tied to each other, is an example of this kind of interaction. In addition, the functioning of the contemporary global stock market can be assumed as an instance: different systems – that is, different national financial systems – have been so intensively tied in the last decades that the outcome is a global system of financial exchange, with its own organization and emergent properties – for instance, we might consider the contemporary speculative financial crisis as an emergent property of the global stock market.

If we move on to consider the interaction based on territorial proximity we find the last – but not least – two categories:

3 The third form of interaction is *structural territorial interaction*, in other words the fact that systems interact territorially – that is, according to both institutional and geographical proximity. When we are in the presence of a location process or simple geographical agglomeration, we can discern an ongoing process of structural coupling between various systems (one or more firms, the local labor force, the public administration, etc.) where they just share some part of their structure. Typically, a TNC's localization process reflects this kind of territorial interaction, searching for specific structural elements – resources – that are present in the territory and which the corporation wants to exploit. Also, most territorial competitiveness strategies fall into this category: policies to attract footloose foreign direct investment (FDI) – such as a call center or an assembly plant – are aimed solely at finding some sort of temporary structural coupling with international capital flows. This structural coupling will be described by the local administration as "low unemployment" and will be called by TNC managing board "low cost of labor."

4 The final type can be named *organizative territorial interaction* and it occurs when the interaction involves both structure and organization and with reference to both institutional and geographical proximity. It occurs when different systems mix their organization to such an extent that it becomes difficult to establish clear boundaries between them. In other words, a new system – what we will call a productive territorial local system (PTLS) – is territorially produced. Industrial districts and *milieux innovateurs*[4] are probably better-known examples of PTLS: in such territories, institutional and

geographical proximity are so tightly linked that there is a strong interconnection between the different systems. For instance, the network of firms' organization becomes closely related to the organization of the labor system: in that context, social mobility ceases to be an element of structural coupling between capital and labor and becomes an emergent property of a new system's organization. The network, rather than the market or the hierarchy, becomes the predominant arrangement among different systems (Grabher 1993).

Before outlining some consequences for our representation of the territory, we must introduce more precise statements about this taxonomy of systemic interaction:

1 In our opinion, the passage from structural to organizative interaction always implies the emergence of new properties. Therefore, the passage is not just quantitative – more relationships – but to a greater extent qualitative and ontological – the emergence of new relationships that define a new system's organization.
2 A system does not belong exclusively to one category. For instance, the existence of a PTLS does not exclude the possibility that in that territory there are ongoing processes of mere agglomeration or even simpler loose localization: a TNC might be interested in localizing in an industrial district merely to try to take advantage of some locally embedded resources. It is also possible for a PTLS to be part of a global commodity chain, or to buy raw materials or specialized services on the market, without engaging in an organizative interaction. In addition, we can conceive that some systems might undergo systemic interactions in all four realms simultaneously. Consider a global player such as Motorola: it can buy intermediate goods directly from the market – such as silicon, microchips, and software – or locate manufacturing plants in a developing country to take advantage of cheap labor, embedding some research facilities into Silicon Valley PTLS without losing its corporate identity.
3 Also, the same event can have different implications depending on the context in which it occurs. The closure of a Ford plant somewhere in Europe would most likely rupture a structural coupling with that territory, but the dismantling of the main plant in Detroit would probably trigger changes not only at the structural level, but also at an organizative one, causing a deeper identity crisis in the city.[5]
4 Finally, we have to point out that systemic interaction is a dynamic ongoing process and is therefore reversible. Consider any PTLS: a change in even a small process of structural coupling outside the boundaries of an industrial district – for instance the decision to relocate some low-quality part of the production process to Turkey or Romania – might have catastrophic effects on the strength of the territorial organizative interaction on which the very existence of the district is based. Consider, in contrast, the GM–Fiat agree-

ment: technically this is no more than a joint venture involving a minority share exchange and therefore it can be considered, for the time being, an institutional structural interaction with some effects on territorial structural interaction – such as rationalization of component production. However, if this agreement had been transformed into a full merger, something like an institutional organizative coupling, a new system would have been generated – physically a new corporation.

According to the aims of this work, our interest will necessarily be focused mainly on processes of territorial systemic interaction, that is, those interactions that occur in the presence of both geographical and institutional proximity and which consequently emphasize the ability to consider territory itself from a systemic perspective.

Toward productive territorial local systems: different kinds of territorialization

According to the taxonomy developed in the previous section, we can distinguish two different processes of interaction between systems and territories.

Structural territorialization: the territory as environment

The first process considers territory as the outcome of a structural coupling between different systems, some of which are manifestly geographical in their organization (for instance the labor system, the education system, or the public administration) while others are based on disembedded forms of institutional proximity (international agencies, world-class research centers, transnational corporations, sectors, etc.) (Figure 3.1). We can imagine having several systems – in our example {A, B, C, D} – all of which are "local" but not necessarily "geographical." Each of these four systems is based on a set of internal relationships that guarantee its organizative cohesion and by a set of both internal and external ties that represent its structure. In order to co-evolve with the other systems, each of them is involved in processes of structural coupling, that is, some of the structural features are shared with the other systems. For our purposes we can imagine territory as the outcome of many processes of structural coupling overlapping in time and space.

Figure 3.1 expresses only the spatial dimension of this process of multiple structural coupling, that is, the structure of structural couplings in a given moment *i*. To get the full picture of how territory emerges from intersystems interaction, we should add the temporal dimension of the process: structural change, in fact, occurs over time in order to match stimuli to change with organizative closure of the system. As a consequence, the processes of structural coupling will also be affected by the changes occurring in the single systems' structures and, therefore, that specific structural coupling that produces the territory will also be changing over time.[6]

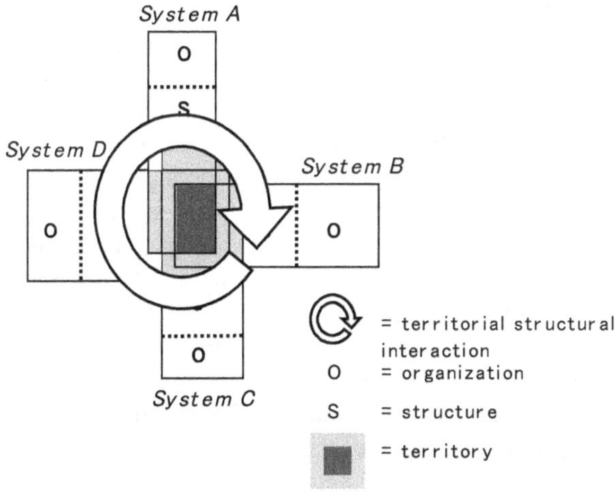

Figure 3.1 Territory as the outcome of multiple structural couplings.

If we accept this broad interpretation of territory as an environment in which different systems live and evolve, there is room for different theoretical and methodological approaches, which will be in charge of opening and dismantling the systemic black boxes. For instance, the new industrial geography (NIG) explanation of embeddedness and flexible specialization (Storper 1995) as well as the new economic geography (NEG) models on agglomeration and urban economy (Storper and Venables 2004) will offer useful insight about the structural coupling between economic activities and the other systems that are present in a given territory. The former focus more on the relational institutions while the latter draw attention to the role of market- and hierarchy-related institutional proximity. At the same time, this notion of territory as the outcome of structural coupling between different systems can offer a useful framework for more cultural approaches to territorialization and territorial transformation, analyzing, for instance, how different social or cultural groups – systems – shape their identity – organization – with reference to a given territory and to other systems interacting in that environment.

Organizative territorialization: the territory as productive territorial local system

As we have seen, in certain cases, besides the geographical structural interaction, there is a second process of systemic coupling where organization – and not only structure – is somehow mixed together leading to a new system, that we have named PTLS. If we think about our initial set of systems {A, B, C, D}, we can imagine that among a subset of them {B, C, D} there is a process of organizative synthesis, that is, the three systems become involved in some sort of organizative interaction. A is still part of the population of the territory but it does not share any feature of its organization with the newborn PTLS.

For instance, by looking at Figure 3.2, we can suppose that (i) "A" is a TNC, (ii) "B" is a cluster of small and medium-sized enterprises (SMEs) $\{b_1, b_2 \ldots b_n\}$, (iii) "C" is the local pool of labor, and (iv) "D" is the local higher education system (secondary schools and university). When we say that the subset of systems {B, C, D} is organized into a PTLS we mean that a synthesis occurred among the single systems' organizations and it produced the organization of a new system, the PTLS. What it is important to notice is that we do not have to think that the single systems {B, C, D} ceased to exist or that they lost their autonomy; nor can we say that the PTLS's organization is determined by its components. In both cases we would not be looking at systems. We can therefore imagine that a given PTLS can survive as a system even in the presence of changes in its elements. For instance, a given PTLS might continue to exist even if part of the system of SME "B" delocalizes part of the production. What is more important is that we do not have any a priori guarantee that the PTLS will survive a dramatic change in the interaction between the composing systems. At the same time we have to consider that the single elements {B, C, D} maintain their systemic autonomy and are therefore involved in other processes of systemic interaction, for instance in some structural coupling with system "A": the cluster of SMEs could be suppliers of the TNC localized in the territory, the labor system will supply the workforce, and the education system will contribute to train the workers of both the PTLS and the TNC.

What is more important here is the relationship between PTLS and territory. The PTLS is not, of course, the whole territory, as there are other systems in the territory that are autonomous from the PTLS. At the same time, the PTLS's organization can be assumed to be a good proxy of the territory as it is characterized by emerging properties, which are territorial, defined in terms of both geographical and institutional proximity. In other words, the PTLS is not *the* territory but it behaves like *a* territory. We have to remember that there is *not a bi-univocal*

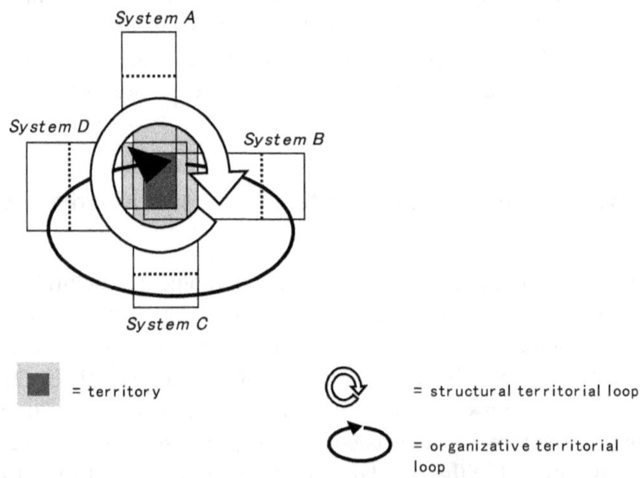

Figure 3.2 From structural to organizative territorial interaction.

relationship between a given territory and a PTLS: every PTLS identifies a territory, but a territory can host a number of PTLS, which either coexist or are in competition with each other. As we have argued above, there is no feasible way to rigorously theorize something like a "territory" as an autopoietic system, because it is in fact too complex. Take, for instance, Prato and London. As the former is small and relatively non-complex, we might assume that just considering one PTLS (the industrial district) would be a good proxy for the whole territory, that is, we might accept the simplification that by comprehending Prato's industrial district we also grasp the wholeness of Prato itself. In the case of London, it is evident that its complexity is so great that we cannot *reduce* its "identity" to particular processes ongoing, for instance, in the City or in Brixton. Better put, the City, which is just one of London's various PTLS, is not an exhaustive proxy for the whole city. Moreover, there are changes and challenges even in smaller localities like Prato, questioning that such an identification between PTLS and the whole territory is sustainable and can be taken for granted in the long run.

Consider, as an example, the consequences of huge immigration flows from China into all the major Italian industrial districts. In the beginning, the immigrant communities were integrated in the "basement" of the PTLS's structure, being functional to the price competitiveness of the industrial district but without substantially altering its systemic organization. Subsequently, these expatriate communities seemed to constitute autonomous PTLS, with their own organization and structure, coming to represent a competitive challenge from within the industrial district. Thus, it might now be the case that a bag and leather wholesaler in east London will buy low-quality, low-cost bags and wallets from Chinese communities near Florence, without making any connection with the original PTLS hosting this enclave. Therefore, it is likely that in Prato or Valenza[7] there are now at least two PTLS, each with its own specific organization and structural coupling with that particular territory. If we go on accepting acritically the full identification between the PTLS and the territory in industrial districts, we will never understand what is going on. For instance, we will be unable to grasp why, despite many claims that the tacit dimension of knowledge was the basis of their competitiveness, in many districts the focus has now shifted toward forms of codification – for instance establishing brands and trademarks that secure the originality, the recognizability, and the uniqueness of local production. The fact is that the challenge is not just from overseas imitator rival firms, but it is internal, from embedded vanguards.

The opposite can also be true: not every territory has one or more PTLS. One of the main weaknesses of territorial competitiveness and, more generally, of local development literature is to infer from the experience of highly cohesive and successful territories – such as Baden-Württemberg, the Italian industrial districts, or Silicon Valley – that each locality can be the protagonist of a local development path, based on trust, shared values, untraded relationships, and creative entrepreneurship. In fact, such a risky inference is barely sustainable on scientific grounds. Therefore, by distinguishing PTLS from territories we explicitly admit that not all territories can be interpreted through the lens of PTLS. Nor does this mean that, from an elitist perspective, local development and territorial competitiveness are exclusively a matter of luck. It simply implies that:

1. some territories are better viewed as the outcome of territorial structural interaction;
2. there are no policies that can automatically guarantee the success of local development as, in a genuinely complex situation, the emergence of a PTLS is largely unpredictable.

Distinguishing organization and structure: an institutional approach

Introducing our interpretation of territorial systems as an autopoietic system we made a clear statement about the internal differentiation between organization and structure and we said that both of them are characterized by "productive" processes: organization produces itself through the production of a structure. Producing a structure implies, in turn, the production of both goods and meanings that allows the structural coupling with the environment and/or with other systems. Here it is necessary to develop a brief but effective description of how an organization works out its autopoietic process and how this interacts with structural change.

An institutional approach to organization and structure

From the introduction of the autopoietic systems theory in the previous section, we have seen that a system is made up of components and relationships. In particular, the organization is made up only of relationships, whereas the structure is composed of both relationships and components. As a consequence, the specific features of the components are just contingent and not necessary to the definition of that particular systemic organization. It is clear that such a position is antithetic to methodological individualism, in which all the individual features are sufficient to explain the properties of the whole.

In translating the systemic approach to social and territorial phenomena, we must therefore clarify how to emphasize the ontological differences between PTLS' organization and structure. In the following pages, we will try to do so by adopting an old economic institutionalism[8] approach. First of all, we establish two simple equations:

Relationships = Institutions

Components = Organizations

Let us start with institutions. As many commentators have noted, the word "Institutions" is not univocal. We therefore adopt a simple definition of "Institution" as "a stable and shared way of organizing relationships."[9] Thus, "Institution" denotes a broad set of laws, habits, rules, praxis, routines, and values through which a social system tries to reduce the complexity of human relationality in order to make decisions more easily and quickly. In the process of institutional production, some *institutional fixes* also arise, which are usually named Organizations: the church, the family, the market, the firm, the rugby club are all forms of "institutionalized Institutions," which are mainly based on a set of Institutions that are crystallized in a formal set of relationships. This confers on the Organizations a sort of collective agency or, even more explicitly, a juridical personality. Of course, even if they rely on a limited set of formal Institutions, organizations get involved in a broader set of formal and informal Institutions, exactly as individuals do.

From (3.1) and (3.2) we can establish a further step in our comprehension of PTLS:

$$\text{organization} = \{\text{Institutions}\} \tag{3.1}$$

$$\text{structure} = \{\text{Institutions; Organizations}\} \tag{3.2}$$

By merging systemic and institutional approaches we can say, in a first approximation, that the PTLS's organization is made up of Institutions, whereas the structure is composed of both Institutions and Organizations. This distinction has two important consequences. First, we must be able to distinguish between organizative Institutions and structural ones. Second, the presence of a specific set of Organizations in a PTLS must be considered as contingent to a particular stage of the structural change. This is because the PTLS must be able to reproduce its organization even in the presence of a dramatic change in its components. This principle is also applicable to the need to distinguish between Institutions: which are the organizative and which the structural ones? We can think of organizative Institutions as a set of fundamental Institutions that are characterized by a *longue durée*, quite apart from the fact that they are crystallized in formal organizations. The Braudelian idea of *longue durée* is central (Braudel 1974): organizative Institutions have a longer duration than contingent structural ones, but they do not possess the characteristics of universality, necessity, and eternity that are proper to reductionist sciences such as Newtonian physics and neoclassical economics.[10] The spatial interpretation of *longue durée*, we believe, echoes the concept of *institutional thickness* introduced by Amin and Thrift (2003). In this framework, new industrial geography (Bathelt and Glückler 2003) has now produced a broad account of institutions that are territorially thick: trust, untraded interdependencies, producer–supplier relationships, shared values, quality of life, and familism are just some examples of institutional arrangements which, when territorially concentrated, enhance the success of clusters, industrial districts, *milieux innovateurs*. Nevertheless, these institutional approaches are biased by an excess of optimism and are good narratives only for certain kinds of PTLS: what about systems in which mistrust, competition, and hierarchy supply the adhesive? And what about the mafia, where familiar relations and reciprocal trust are fundamental and opportunistic behavior is so damaging that it is punished by the death penalty?

The role of knowledge and learning

In order to generalize the application of systemic theories and to identify the specific relationships that make up organizations, our position is that the organization of a PTLS is given by its specific knowledge and that its autopoietic activity can be thought of as a specific process of learning. This process is elaborated through a particular set of structural institutions and organizations in what we might name institutional learning. This solution mirrors Luhmann's (1995) approach to social systems, but with a fundamental difference: whereas in Luhmann the main content of social systems was information, and the autopoiesis therefore consists in a *communication* process, in the case of PTLS the organizative substance is knowledge and the autopoietic process is therefore *learning*. The point now is "which kind of knowledge are we talking about?" The answer depends essentially on the kind of PTLS we have constructed, that is, on the questions the observer is asking a territory. If we are investigating the premodern Siberian shaman community, the knowledge in question will likely be a sort of magic gnosis about the relationship between mundane and supermundane realities. In contrast, if the object of the analysis is a manufacturing system such as an Italian industrial district, the knowledge in question might be some technical know-how combined with esthetic values inherited from the past. If, instead, we are dealing with a *milieu innovateur*, we will probably be interested in identifying a scientific high-tech knowledge.

Moreover, we do not need to push our reasoning too far to hypothesize that a PTLS, by producing knowledge, also produces meanings. Meanings are produced by psychic systems, like individuals, eventually interacting with other individuals within a group: PTLS do not necessarily have to possess psychic properties in order to process knowledge – in fact, they are not minds. In a cybernetic perspective PTLS are like computers, which possess only syntax and not a mind. In other words, the process of organizative synthesis is simply syntactic and computational: individual systems – such as the education system or an ethnic group – produce cultural meanings, PTLS do not.

At the same time, we must recognize that the knowledge we are talking about is not inside component systems but is an emergent property of the PTLS itself.[11] In other words, the knowledge we are talking about is never fully possessed either by individuals or by particular organizations. As a consequence, organizative knowledge is always characterized by a strong component of tacit knowledge, which is implicit in routines and habits and therefore not fully expressed in codes and texts (Polanyi 1966). As has been largely recognized by NIG, it is the tacit dimension that keeps this knowledge rooted in territories and impedes the direct and exclusive appropriation by individuals and organizations (Maskell and Malmberg 1999, Amin and Cohendet 2004). As a consequence, the learning process is also affected by the tacit dimension of organizative knowledge: institutional learning is different from the account of learning organizations,[12] a concept that became widespread in management studies following the seminal work by Nonaka and Takeuchi (1995). There are, of course, many assonances and a conceptual similitude between the two, but the perspective is quite different:

most learning in Organizations is about appropriation of tacit knowledge from the PTLS, whereas organizative learning is about embedding tacit knowledge. In addition, in the learning Organization approach increasing emphasis is placed on forgetting obsolete knowledge (Noteboom 2000), whereas organizative learning is primarily concerned with maintaining continuity with the inherited knowledge changing the structure: for PTLS forgetting is broadly equal to disintegration.

Thus, we can summarize the content of our analysis in a set of five new propositions:

$$\text{organization} = \{\text{Knowledge}\} \tag{3.3}$$

$$\text{structure} = \{\text{Institutions; Organizations}\} \tag{3.4}$$

$$\text{organization} = f(\text{organization} \mid \text{structure}) \tag{3.5}$$

$$\text{organization} = f(\{\text{Knowledge}\} \mid \{\text{Institutions; Organizations}\}) \tag{3.6}$$

$$f = \text{institutional learning} \tag{3.7}$$

This set of propositions can summarize the whole argument we have developed about PTLS. First of all, we have identified the core of organization as knowledge (3.3), whereas the structure is given by a set of institutions that bond together a number of Organizations (3.4). Proposition 3.5 expresses the autopoietic principle that organization results in the production of a structure. Given (3.3) and (3.4), therefore, the autopoietic process can be declared by saying that a core knowledge is reproduced through the establishment of a contingent asset of both Institutions and Organization (3.6). This autopoietic process is what we called "institutional learning" (3.7).

From the ongoing argumentation, the relationship between *knowledge* and *specialization* and why the former refers to a PTLS's organization whereas the latter is inherent in structure should be clear. In particular, the establishment of a specialization can be interpreted as the outcome of a structural coupling between the PTLS and the environment – which from time to time can be represented as the sector, the international division of labor, the global economy, etc. In different periods, therefore, the same organizative knowledge[13] can be "structurally applied" in different sectors: when dealing with a former Fordist system, let us say Turin engineering PTLS,[14] a specific knowledge focused on mechanical engineering, which goes back to the presence of Savoia's arsenal in the eighteenth century, has been reproduced through an endless process of learning and applied subsequently to different production and specialization, from weapons to stagecoaches, from car bodywork to automotive components, from machine tools to robots.

Analogously similar knowledge in different territories can lead to different specializations because of unpredictable divergences in the learning process through which organization reproduces itself. Consider, for example, Turin's and the Swiss Jura's engineering PTLS: both have their roots in preindustrial techniques and know-how, but, whereas Turin's PTLS evolved through specializing mainly – but not exclusively[15] – in mass production and developed a Fordist regulation system, the Jura is historically specialized in micro-engineering workmanship performed in small workshops. With a simplification, it is possible that these divergent structures are the outcomes of deep differences in the process of institutional learning: whereas Turin witnessed the emergence of just one large car producer adopting the Fordist division of labor (out of more than 100 independent competitors existing at the end of the nineteenth century) and therefore a strong class conflictuality hegemonized by the Communist Party, the Swiss Jura's institutional learning has probably been influenced by the presence of an outstanding anarchist self-reflexivity, embodied in the Proudhonian watchmakers (Vuilleumier 1988).

Some epistemological and theoretical implications for economic geography: the case of territorial competitiveness

When it comes to the issue of territorial competitiveness – that is the realm where we would like to offer some evidence of the consequences of the framework we have adopted – it should be clear that the systemic approach we developed has major implications. The first consequence is extremely important: we are questioning not whether a territory as whole can be assumed to be competitive, but how specific PTLS are competitive. Second, a PTLS is productive at both the organizative and structural level:

1 The organization produces itself: in this perspective, productive means autopoietic.
2 In producing itself, the organization also produces a structure.

Therefore, when talking about territorial competitiveness, we must distinguish between the ability of the system to reproduce its organization (*organizative territorial competitiveness*) and the success of contingent competitive phenomena that occur at the level of the structure, such as selling manufactured goods or attracting FDI or new inhabitants (*structural territorial competitiveness*). Moreover, such a systemic standpoint can help us to clarify some of the ambiguous features of the competitiveness debate.

Identity and personality

One of the first and mainly unsolved issues that has arisen from the growing debate on territorial competitiveness is the question of whether talking about territorial competitiveness necessarily implies that territories possess a *clearly identifiable identity* that bestows on them some form of collective agency. This problem has been summarized by questioning whether or not territories hold something like a *personality*, like firms, which are said to have a juridical personality. Following what has been said in the previous sections, we can try to briefly address the question consistently with the systemic approach we have adopted.

The first point, here, is to recall the distinction between territory and PTLS. The first, in fact, has been conceptualized as the outcome of reiterated processes of structural coupling among different local systems – both territorial and aterritorial. In other words, we have adopted a skeptical position with reference to the possibility of speaking about territories' systemic organization: the process of territorialization – that is attributing a meaning to territories – is so complex that there is no feasible way of assessing whether territories do have a clear and univocal organization, that is, an identity, that is, a personality. The first conclusion is therefore that the concepts of identity and personality are such controversial monolithic concepts that they cannot be applied easily to the territory as a whole.

The second step is to consider how the concept of PTLS can be characterized through the metaphor of personality. At first glance, because of the conceptual proximity between systemic organization and identity, we might infer from the existence of PTLS' organization that PTLS possess a full personality. Nevertheless, if we consider the real implications of our approach we have to consider several issues:

1 The first and probably most important issue is about the nature of the PTLS's organization itself: as we have seen from the beginning, the organization, and therefore the identity, of the PTLS should be interpreted, in a cybernetic framework, as a syntactic process, rather than a semantic one. Thus, the PTLS lacks one of the main features that would allow us to speak about a full personality: it does not produce emergent meanings, but it holds only computational processes of a combination of meanings produced at other levels in order to produce a specific form of knowledge. More radically, when considering systemic organization, we are interested not in the set of contingent meanings, but in the cognitive process of learning. Contingent meanings are important to evaluate the processes of structural coupling and structural change, but with respect to the systemic organization these are just signs processed in a computational procedure.
2 Moreover, unlike individual firms or associations, the PTLS is a system whose components are other systems rather than individuals. This implies that there is a higher level of both organizational and reflexive complexity, which, in the absence of a linear and univocal causation chain, makes it impossible to move from the individuals to the PTLS maintaining the personality's properties, which we can find at the individual level and eventually at the associational one.
3 Autopoietic systems are not teleological in their functioning, whereas following determined scopes and strategies is one of the main features of being a person. Strategies and scopes can be present, but they are always secondary in that they are attributed by an observer, which can be external (a scholar, a consultant, or a national policy-maker, just to give a few examples) or internal (an association, a trade union, or a Schumpeterian entrepreneur).
4 Finally, even in the presence of an organization that seems to be legitimized to speak and act on behalf of the PTLS (for instance a local development

agency or an export-oriented consortium as in many industrial districts), we must bear in mind that the existence of such actors is simply a structural feature of the PTLS and not an organizative one: they are instrumental to the organizative closure and therefore they are not part of the organization. In designing policies for local development, it should therefore be clear that this kind of collective agency is just interpreting, and not standing in for, the organization of the system.

As a consequence, it seems inappropriate to talk about the juridical personality of territories: for sure, they must possess an identity, but, for the reasons pointed out, this identity must be conceived in cognitive, computational, and syntactic terms rather than in vitalistic, semantic, and idealistic ones. Recognizing that territories are important for the human spirit does not necessarily imply that they have a spirit (Buttimer 1993). Even more importantly, the way we address the issue of territorial competitiveness seems to allow us to reduce the importance of the personality issue: as autopoietic systems are characterized by organizative closure, the competitive issue is related to maintaining the organization, that is, to reproducing the fundamental knowledge that distinguishes the PTLS from other systems. Competitiveness toward other territorial systems becomes secondary when considering the contingent processes of structural coupling and change, through which the organization closure is maintained.

Path dependence and emergence

The second issue we have to address relating to territorial competitiveness concerns the character of path dependence, which is traditionally associated with agglomeration and competitiveness, and how it interacts with the ideas of emergence and novelty, which are central in complexity and systemic epistemologies. We will argue that the shortcut to explain the coexistence of both *continuity* (that is, path dependence) and *emergence* (that is, invention of new paths) is given, once more, by the distinction that Maturana and Varela (1980, 1987) introduced between organization and structure. There are, in fact, some similarities between how we defined the operationality of the autopoietic system and the emphasis that both NEG (Krugman 1996b) and NIG (Malmberg 1997) put on path dependence. More precisely, the application of autopoiesis to social systems and territories allows us to distinguish two kinds of path dependence, a structural one and an organizative one:

1 *Structural path dependence* refers to the concept of structural determined change, that is, the fact that the changes in a system are changes in the structure, which depend on the previous states of the structure itself.
2 *Organizative path dependence*, that is, the fact that the PTLS maintains continuity in the basic set of relationships that define its identity. In other words, organizative path dependence can be assumed to be a synonym for organizative closure.

At the same time, both structure and organization can change over time, but in different ways. More precisely, the structure has a broader range of possible variation, as long as the organization remains relatively still and maintains its internal consistency. From a theoretical perspective, we might admit also that the organization changes over time without substantial alterations. Nevertheless, in practical terms, it is very difficult to set a boundary beyond which the PTLS has changed its organization so much that it becomes something different. Therefore, we can hypothesize that the organization either changes dramatically and catastrophically – and therefore that the PTLS becomes something completely different – or stays mainly unchanged over time.

This systemic account of emergence and path dependence allows us to address some of the open questions we have inherited from the literature. We can briefly consider three of them here: Krugman's account of history and path dependence; the emergence of innovation within a PTLS; and the problems of lock-in, inertia, and creative destruction:

1 Krugman's account of path agglomeration and path dependence refers mainly to the structure of a PTLS, in that he focuses his explanation on the two concepts of *increasing returns* and *monopolistic competition*, which are actually features of the contingent structure, rather than the immanent organization. As a consequence, NEG seems to fail in addressing long-term continuity, which is (un)explained using the concepts of QWERTY or pure chance. In a systemic perspective, what Krugman sees as "chance" is instead a specific learning process with a relatively clear beginning and development. Of course, at the very beginning, we agree that a random fortuitous event might be the spark that leads to the birth of a PTLS, but focusing on the learning organizative core, rather than just on structural mechanisms, might help us to shift the boundaries of our interpretation and comprehension.
2 The second issue is about the emergence of innovation. In a systemic perspective, given that the organization will preserve PTLS closure, innovation will occur in the structure, either internally as a result of the process of autopoiesis or internalized from the environment, through the process of structural coupling. Even in the presence of a "catastrophic" account of innovation, such as the Schumpeterian reworking of Kondrat'ev's innovation-led economic cycles, we can maintain that even scientific revolutions affect only a PTLS's structure and not its organization: organization can still be imagined as a sort of Braudelian *longue durée* that lies beneath such epochal and epic transformations, just finding some form of structural coupling with them.[16]
3 NEG and management scholars involved with the knowledge-based and institutional learning approach share some worries about the *lock-in trap*. Path dependence and continuity, as well as tacit forms of knowledge, imply, in fact, a certain degree of inertia, which might prevent the adaptation of the economic system to changing times.[17] In fact, in an autopoietic perspective, this is largely a fake problem: as far as structural change is concerned, the troubles of lock-in can be avoided without sacrificing the organizative continuity.[18]

As a consequence, we do not have to face a trade-off between path dependence and emergence, as the systemic distinction between organization and structure implies that both dependence and emergence vary in amplitude and scope and therefore that they can coexist in different layers of the PTLS.

Cohesion and power

In considering the implication of systems theory for understanding territorial competitiveness, the third and last issue we would like to address relates to cohesion and power. The territorial competitiveness literature often emphasizes internal cohesion among groups and classes within the territory, whereas conflicts are seen as favoring competitors, making the territory unattractive for FDI and wealthy inhabitants and decreasing productivity. On the other hand, its critics have stressed that territorial competitiveness policies often hide neoliberalist shifts in the national power balance (Brenner 2004) or, at least, that there are specific shareholders who benefit more than others (Cheshire and Gordon 1996). This issue is particularly sensitive within the theoretical framework we have adopted. Since Menemio Agrippa's (in)famous apologue in Ancient Rome, organicism – and, broadly speaking, the use of biological metaphors in social science – has been seen as teleological and therefore aimed at maintaining existing power relationships among social groups and classes. More recently, Luhmann's social systems theory has been repeatedly accused of being intrinsically conservative, if not reactionary (Zolo 1986, 1990). The misunderstanding is also possible when considering the "political" implications of PTLS. Saying that the variety of meanings refers to the structure and not to the organization – and that therefore they are contingent – might be interpreted as a neglect of power relationships and conflicts. The criticism of the application of a systems theory in social studies is also partially substantiated because of its apparently strong anti-individualist inspiration. Nevertheless, we claim that this judgment depends on the confusion that is often made between organization and structure.[19]

The idea that power and struggle are fundamental in shaping important systemic processes – such as structural coupling – is, in fact, quite self-evident. Moreover, our point is that power and conflict are important not only in regulating the external relationships between different systems,[20] but also in defining territorial and local assets. In fact, power relationships and conflictuality are central to defining both the territory and the PTLS:

1 Territory has been conceptualized, in fact, as the outcome of iterated structural coupling processes and therefore is, by antonomasia, produced by different systems that are not necessarily harmoniously committed to each other.
2 PTLS itself is produced by a process of organizative synthesis that is not necessarily and intrinsically peaceful: the interaction between the systems that form the PTLS entails an emergent order, and thus some form of cohesion, but there is no specific need to make this synthetic process easier.

A corollary to this is the fact that a PTLS's organization must be stable in order to keep the system itself in existence, but we cannot take it for granted that the system will last for ever and ever: conflicts can increase and produce an irreversible crisis (deterritorialization) that will lead to a new organization and therefore to a new PTLS (reterritorialization). Moreover, we have insisted that the process of organizative synthesis is a syntactic procedure that processes different meanings and knowledge in a unique knowledge, which represents the core of the systemic organization. In this process, new knowledge is computed but no new meaning is necessarily produced, so that there is no automatic moral judgment about the goodness of what is produced: the Italian mafia might also be described as a PTLS that reproduces itself by producing institutional knowledge.

Conclusions: needs for rethinking local development

Taken together, these argumentations emerge from the conceptual framework that we have constructed so far: if reality is complex and multidimensional, every interpretation of it will be a point of view in a single process of understanding phenomena which, to be comprehended, must be observed in their many facets. It follows that knowledge is no longer conceived to be predetermined, but can be developed only through interaction between the subject-observer and the object of knowledge.

Local policy as the mere expression of a development ethic that accepts the laws and dynamics of contemporary capitalism produces nothing other than a simple – local – specification of standardizing processes and forces. In this case, although turning attention to places modifies our vision of the development process, it cannot change the concept of development itself. To state that places (whether they are defined as clusters, industrial districts, *milieu innovateur*, or by any other metaphors) play a fundamental role in the contemporary economy does not mean to state that they are central.

The thesis that now emerges is fundamentally different. The systemic perspective is the bearer of the idea of a PTLS that reproduces its own identity, given by the organization of those social, cultural, and economic relations that make up its "uniqueness." In this case, if the arbiter of development is no longer the market but the local system, it follows that the benefits of local development are evaluated in terms of the maintenance of the system's organization. It follows that the political solutions possible are those compatible with the identity of the local systems, i.e., with their capacity for self-reproduction. Otherwise, as we have seen, there would be a shift from a logic of local development to one of mere valorization, and thus of possible destruction of the system.

In conclusion, the relationship between the local scale and possible development paths and policies appears fundamentally dialectic. A development path is not valid on all scales, nor does there exist a temporal succession of hegemonic models of development, each of which dominates a given historical period. On the contrary, they coexist at the same time and in the same place. This *depends on the position one takes in order to decide*, i.e., on specific institutional assets. It is these, in fact, that define the way in which local actors organize socioeconomic relations internally, the exploitation of local resources, and the relationship with other scales.

Notes

1 Although this chapter is the product of joint reflection and mutual confrontation of ideas and methods, the sections "A narrative about complexity" and "Conclusions: needs for rethinking local development" are mainly Sergio Conti's work, while the others ("Territorial systemic interactions," "Toward productive territorial local systems: different kinds of territorialization," "Distinguishing organization and structure: an institutional approach," and "Some epistemological and theoretical implications for economic geography: the case of territorial competitiveness") can be attributed to Paolo Giaccaria.

2 The application of the concept of "noise" from cybernetics and complexity theories to social theories is actually quite a disturbing metaphor, even if there is something in a positive evaluation of noise itself: noise is necessary, but still powerless and functional to the reproduction of dominant relationships.

3 The focus on the distinction between organization and structure is more important, from our perspective, than the emphasis usually placed by systemic social theorists – such as Luhmann – on autopoiesis. Autopoiesis is, to some extent, implied by the organization/structure dialogic, but stating that all the systems considered are fully autopoietic is an arguable hypothesis.

4 More generically, the reference here is to the so-called "social networks," in which different realms are intertwined and therefore we are facing something more than mere geographical proximity.

5 Of course, the closing down of a satellite factory can also be painful in terms of unemployment and therefore induce strikes and protests. For instance, the Fiat restructuring produced more vigorous street riots in the south of Italy than in Turin. The fact is that here we are considering wider long-term effects than simple "structural adjustment."

6 This account of territory might show some superficial similarities with localities studies and specifically with Massey's geomorphological metaphor of territory as a stratification of different layers left as "tangible" residues of subsequent stages of capitalistic development (Massey 1995). Nevertheless, the differences are deeper and more important than the assonances. The most important dissonance is that in the localities explanation external influence predominates – specifically, successive stages of capitalism determine territorial structures, by processes that are neither local nor territorial, at least in their consequences. In contrast, in our opinion, even if territories are not systems, they are nevertheless defined through the interaction of local and supralocal, territorial and aterritorial systems. Moreover, the proposed systemic account is also more dynamic, in that there is a continuous change in the boundaries and in the outcomes of territorialization, with a process of reciprocal cross-fertilization between the territory and the systems that live in it.

7 Valenza, in Piedmont, is probably the most important industrial district worldwide for jewelry making. Recently, many producers and associations have reported a growing Chinese community progressively becoming autonomous from the original district and competing by design imitation as well as cheap prices.

8 This is not the place to discuss the history of economic institutionalism. We simply accept the distinction between old and new economic institutionalism in order to distinguish between Veblenian revival among evolutionary economists and neoclassical institutionalists *à la* Williamson. For an account of the debate see Amin (1999).

9 This definition echoes the one by Lawson: "I suggest that the term 'institution' be used to designate those systems, or structured processes of interaction (collecting together rules, relations and positions as well as habits and other practices), that are relatively enduring and identified as such" (Lawson 1997: 318n). Nevertheless we have opted for a simpler definition in order to avoid the use of concepts such as "system" and "structure" with a different meaning from the systemic one.

10 In his latest book, Wallerstain (2004: Ch. 5) praises a marriage between Braudel's *longue durée* and Prigogine's arrow of time. He also preaches for a convergence between the two main opponents to Newtonian physics – complexity theorists and post-structuralist ones – under the Braudelian – and his own as well – systemic flag: nevertheless, we think that world-system theory will continue to be disregarded by post-structuralist scholars as hidden structuralism and general system organicism.

11 There is a strong intellectual proximity between this cybernetic account of diffused knowledge and von Hayek's latest reflections on the nature of knowledge (von Hayek, 1983). It is therefore no surprise to note that Hodgson (1999: Ch. 6) introduces the "second Hayek" among the precursors of NEAR (novelty-embracing anti-reductionist) evolutionary economics.

12 For a complete review of the learning organization framework see the *Handbook of Organizational Learning and Knowledge* (Dierkes *et al.* 2001), in which learning organization is presented almost as a new paradigm investing not only management studies, but also economics, sociology, anthropology, and other social sciences.

13 By organizative knowledge we simply mean the knowledge that represents a given PTLS's organization.

14 For a general account of Turin production in a systemic perspective see Giaccaria (1999) and Conti and Giaccaria (2001).

15 In Turin there are still some small workshops where the shells of cars are worked by hand, with heavy hammers and wooden shapes, in order to produce tailor-made Rolls Royces for Arab sheiks.

16 For a theoretical account of the contemporary implications of Braudel's systemization, with particular reference to the concept of "*longue durée*," see Wallerstain's most recent work (Wallerstain 2004), in which Braudel's account of duration is reinterpreted in the light of complexity theorist Ilya Prigogine's thought. For some empirical evidence, see Porter's narration of how competitive advantage changed in Sassuolo's industrial district (Porter 1990): tiles production, in fact, started in premodern times and evolved mixing local knowledge produced within the PTLS with epochal innovations such as engines and electronics. Not only has the traditional knowledge been preserved, but it also has been used to create a competitive advantage in emergent sectors, such as the production of machine tools related to tiles production.

17 Hence, the revival of the Schumpeterian emphasis on "creative destruction" as part of the innovation process which keeps capitalism alive.

18 We cannot in any case exclude a priori the possibility that a PTLS can face such a deep crisis that even its organization risks becoming obsolete – that is, in systemic terms, there is no possible structural coupling with the fast-changing environment and therefore that particular organization will implode. Nevertheless, this represents the last *ratio*.

19 Luhmann himself fostered the ambiguity of his interpretation, misrepresenting the distinction between organization and structure – which is seminal in Maturana and Varela's (1980, 1987) original theory – and focusing only on the process of autopoiesis.

20 Considering purely external conflictuality – implicit in the notion itself of territorial competitiveness – would, in fact, be consistent with the alleged accusation of excessive emphasis on internal consistency.

References

Abdelmalki, L. and Courlet, C. (eds.) (1996) *Les nouvelles logiques du développement*, Paris: L'Harmattan.

Amin, A. (1999) 'An institutionalist perspective on regional economic development', *International Journal of Urban and Regional Research*, 23: 365–78.

Amin, A. and Cohendet, P. (2004) *Architectures of Knowledge. Firms, Capabilities and Communities*, New York: Oxford University Press.

Amin, A. and Thrift, N. (2003) 'Globalization, institutional thickness and local prospects', *Revue d'Economie Regionale et Urbaine*, 3: 405–27.

Atlan, H. (1972) *L'organisation biologique et la théorie de l'information*, Paris: Herman.

Aydalot, Ph. (1986) *Les technologies nouvelles et les formes actuelles de la division spatiale du travail*, Paris: Dossier du Centre Economie Espace Environment, no. 47.

Bathelt, H. and Glückler, J. (2003) 'Toward a relational economic geography', *Journal of Economic Geography*, 3: 117–44.

Becattini, G. (2000) *Il Distretto Industriale*, Turin: Rosenberg & Sellier.

Begg, I. (1999) 'Cities and competitiveness', *Urban Studies*, 36: 795–809.

Braudel, F. (1974) *Capitalism and Material Life, 1400–1800*, London: Fontana and Collins.

Brenner, N. (2004) *New State Spaces. Urban Governance and the Rescaling of Statehood*, New York: Oxford University Press.

Budd, L. (1998) 'Territorial competition and globalisation. Scylla and Charybdis of European cities', *Urban Studies*, 35: 663–85.

Bunge, M. (2004) *Emergence and Convergence: Qualitative Novelty and the Unity of Knowledge*, Toronto: University of Toronto Press.

Buttimer, A. (1993) *Geography and the Human Spirit*, Baltimore: Johns Hopkins University Press.

Camagni, R. (2002) 'On the concept of territorial competitiveness. Sound or misleading?', *Urban Studies*, 39: 2395–411.

Cheshire, P. and Gordon, I. (1996) 'Territorial competition and the predictability of collective (in)action', *International Journal of Urban and Regional Studies*, 20: 383–99.

Conti, S. and Giaccaria, P. (2001) *Local Development and Competitiveness*, Dordrecht: Kluwer.

Dierkes, M. Antal, A.B., Child, J. and Nonaka, I. (2001) *Handbook of Organizational Learning and Knowledge*, New York: Oxford University Press.

Dunning, J.H. (2000) 'Regions, globalization, and the knowledge economy: the issue stated', in Dunning, J.H. (ed.) *Regions, Globalization and the Knowledge-based Economy*, Oxford: Oxford University Press.

Enright, M.J. (1998) 'The globalization of competition and the localization of competitive advantage: policies towards regional clustering', Paper presented at a workshop on the *Globalization of Economic Activity and Economic Development*, University of Strathclyde, Glasgow, 15–16 May.

Florida, R. (1995) 'Towards the learning region', *Futures*, 27: 527–36.

von Foerster, H. (1982) *Observing Systems*, Brighton: Harvester.

Foss, H.J. (1996) 'Higher order industrial capabilities and competitive advantage', *Journal of Industry Studies*, 3: 1–20.

Gereffi, G. and Korzeniewicz, M. (eds.) (1994) *Commodity Chains and Global Capitalism*, Westport, CT: Praeger.

Gertler, M.S. (2001) 'Best practice? Geography, learning and the institutional limits to strong convergence', *Journal of Economic Geography*, 1: 5–26.

Giaccaria, P. (1999) 'Learning and local competitiveness. The case of Turin', *GeoJournal*, 49: 401–10.

Gilly, J.-P. and Torre, A. (2000) *Dynamiques de proximité*, Paris: L'Harmattan.

Grabher, G. (ed.) (1993) *The Embedded Firm. On the Socioeconomics of Industrial Networks*, London: Routledge.

Granovetter, N. and Swedberg, R. (1992) *The Sociology of Economic Life*, Boulder, CO: Westview.

von Hayek, F.A. (1983) *Knowledge, Evolution, and Society*, London: ASI.

Henderson, J., Dicken, P., Hess, M., Coe, N. and Wai-Chung Yeung, H. (2002) 'Global production networks and the analysis of economic development', *Review of International Political Economy*, 9: 436–64.

Hodgson, G.M. (1999) *Evolution and Institutions. On Evolutionary Economics and the Evolution of Economics*, Northampton: Edward Elgar.

Hudson, R. (2001) *Producing Places*, New York: Guilford Press.

Kresl, P.K. (1995) 'The determinants of urban competitiveness: a survey', in Kresl, P.K. and Gappert, G. (eds.) *North American Cities and the Global Economy*, Thousand Oaks, CA: Sage.

Krugman, P.R. (1996a) 'Making sense of the competitiveness debate', *Oxford Review of Economic Policy*, 12: 17–25.

Krugman, P.R. (1996b) 'How the economy organizes itself in space. A survey of the new economic geography', Santa Fe, CA: SFI working paper 96-04-021.

Lawson, T. (1997) *Economics and Reality*, London: Routledge.

Le Moigne, J.-L. (1992) *La modélisation des systèmes complexes*, Paris: Dunot.

Le Moigne, J.-L. (1994) *Le constructivisme*, Paris: ESF.

Luhmann, N. (1995) *Social System*, Stanford, CA: Stanford University Press.

Maillat, D. and Perrin, J.-C. (eds.) (1992) *Entreprises innovatrices et développement territorial*, Neuchatel: EDES.

Malmberg, A. (1997) 'Industrial geography. Location and learning', *Progress in Human Geography*, 21: 573–82.

Markusen, A. (1996) 'Sticky places in slippery space: a typology of industrial districts', *Economic Geography*, 72: 293–313.

Maskell, P. (1998) 'Sustainable patterns of specialisation in a globalised economy', in Maskell, P., Eskelinen, H., Hannibalsson, I., Malmberg, A. and Vatne, E. (eds.) *Competitiveness, Localised Learning and Regional Development. Specialisation and Prosperity in Small Open Economies*, London: Routledge.

Maskell, P. and Malmberg, A. (1999) 'Localised learning and industrial competitiveness', *Cambridge Journal of Economics*, 23: 167–85.

Massey, D. (1995) *The Spatial Division of Labor. Social Structures and the Geography of Production*, London: Routledge.

Maturana, H. and Varela, F. (1980) *Autopoiesis and Cognition. The Realization of the Living*, Dordrecht: Reidel Publishing Co.

Maturana, H. and Varela, F. (1987) *The Tree of Knowledge. The Biological Roots of Human Understanding*, Boston: Shambhala.

Morin, E. (1977) *La méthode. 1: La nature de la nature*, Paris: Seuil.

Nakamura, M., Vertisnky, I. and Zietsma, C. (1997) 'Does culture matter in inter-firm cooperation? Research consortia in Japan and the USA', *Managerial and Decision Economics*, 18: 153–75.

Nonaka, I. and Takeuchi, H. (1995) *The Knowledge Creating Company. How Japanese Companies Create the Dynamics of Innovation*, New York: Oxford University Press.

Noteboom, B. (2000) *Learning and Innovation in Organizations and Economies*, Oxford: Oxford University Press.

Pecqueur, B. (2000) *Le développement local*, Paris: La Découverte & Syrios.

Polanyi, M. (1966) *The Tacit Dimension*, New York: Doubleday.

Porter, M.E. (1990) *The Competitive Advantage of Nations*, New York: The Free Press.

Pyke, F., Becattini, G. and Sengenberger, W. (eds.) (1990) *Industrial Districts and Local Economic Regeneration*, Geneva: International Institute for Labour Studies.

Sabel, C. (1989) 'Flexible specialization and the re-emergence of regional economies', in Hirst, P. and Zaitlin, J. (eds.) *Reversing Industrial Decline? Industrial Structure and Policy in Britain and Her Competitors*, London: Routledge.

Saxenian, A. (1994) *Regional Advantage. Culture and Competition in Silicon Valley and Route 128*, Cambridge, MA: Harvard University Press.

Sharp, M. (1998) 'Competitiveness and cohesion. Are the two compatible?', *Research Policy*, 27: 569–88.

Storper, M. (1995) 'The resurgence of regional economies: ten years later. The region as a nexus of untraded interdependencies', *European Urban and Regional Studies*, 2: 191–221.

Storper, M. (1997) 'Territories, flows, and hierarchies in the global economy', in Cox, K.R. (ed.) *Spaces of Globalization. Reasserting the Power of the Local*, New York: Guilford Press.

Storper, M. and Venables, A.J. (2004) 'Buzz: face-to-face contact and the urban economy', *Journal of Economic Geography*, 4: 351–70.

Veltz, P. (1996) *Mondialisation, villes et territoires: l'économie d'archipel*, Paris: PUF.

Vuilleumier, M. (1988) *Horlogers de l'anarchisme. Emergence d'un mouvement: la Fédération Jurassienne*, Lausanne: Payot.

Wallerstain, I. (2004) *The Uncertainties of Knowledge*, Philadelphia: Temple University Press.

Wiener, N. (1956) *Cybernetics*, Cambridge, MA: MIT Press.

Williamson, O. (1985) *The Economic Institutions of Capitalism: Firms, Markets, Relational Contracting*, New York: Free Press.

Zolo, D. (1986) 'Function, meaning, complexity: the epistemological premises of Niklas Luhmann's sociological enlightenment', *Philosophy of Social Science*, 16: 115–27.

Zolo, D. (1990) 'Autopoiesis. Critique of a post modern paradigm', *Telos*, 86: 61–80.

4 Place is what we think with

Or spatial history, intellectual capital and competitive distinction

G. M. Peter Swann

Introduction

The title of this chapter is derived from a poem by one of Britain's outstanding poets, Roy Fisher (1994), which starts: 'Birmingham's what I think with'. That captures the theme of this chapter very succinctly, as I shall show in a moment. But, first, let us be clear what this chapter is *not* about. It's not about the idea that creative people need space. Nor is it about the idea that, 'new ideas need new space' because they conflict with existing orthodoxies, or because innovators locate apart from the cluster to avoid risk of information loss.[1] The chapter *is* about the idea that, even if space loses one part of its economic meaning through globalisation, it may acquire another economic meaning. With the growth of globalisation, place may no longer be the source of economic distinction that it was in the past. However, traders may find new sources of competitive distinction from their spatial history.

The chapter is organised as follows. The second section addresses what I call the *four ages of space*. The *first*, the *medieval* age, is one in which the cost of transport and communication over distance is sufficiently high that space is an enduring source of competitive distinction. Moreover, economies of agglomeration and scale, such as they are, are not sufficiently strong to lead to any 'clustering'. The *second*, the *industrial* age, is one in which transport and communication costs have fallen and economies of agglomeration and scale are sufficiently strong that clustering of production (plus transportation to local markets) is more cost-effective than local production at point of consumption. The *third* age, the age of *global clusters*, is one in which transport and communication costs decline towards zero, but economies of agglomeration and scale remain very important, so production is clustered into a small number of global clusters, which trade their outputs with the whole world. This is the world of today, and it is possible that this age will develop further and further without fundamental change. Another possibility is that there will be a *fourth* age. This could be called the *new global village*, where transport and communications costs decline to zero, and economies of agglomeration and scale fade away. Traditional economic forces lead to the dispersion of clusters, and product activity is once again dispersed with population.

At first sight, the third age and the fourth age may look similar, but they are very different in character. This chapter is concerned with the fourth age – if indeed it is ever to be seen. In this, space may not seem to have an important economic role – when compared with the first, second and third ages – but I shall argue that it does have such a role. In this apparently placeless world, spatial history shapes human capital, and hence economic distinction. Distance may have died, but location is not irrelevant.[2]

Then in the third section of this chapter, I examine why traders may need to turn to their spatial history as a possible source of competitive distinction when place itself no longer offers such distinction. This section uses some key results from the measurement of product competitiveness (Swann and Taghavi 1992). One of the most important of these is the assertion that, as the number of characteristics distinguishing a product from the competition falls, so also does the probability that a product will achieve sufficient competitive distinction to remain competitive. This is highly relevant in the context of globalisation. Geographical space is an obvious source of competitive distinction when transportation and communication over distance is costly. But space-shrinking technological change erodes this source of competitive distinction, and hence reduces the probability that a trader remains competitive.

The fourth section of the chapter then examines the issue of 'endogenous dimensionality' in economic models of product competition (Swann 1990). A key concept here is the assertion that traders seek to expand the dimensions of characteristics space when the existing space becomes congested, but if the existing space is not congested then there is less incentive to expand dimensions. Again, this is highly relevant to globalisation. If space-shrinking technologies remove the competitive distinction provided by location per se, then traders will need to seek other sources of competitive distinction to increase the dimensionality of characteristics space. However – and this is the key point – they do not do this until the existing space is congested.

The fifth section gives some examples of how spatial history may yield a source of competitive distinction when place in itself does not. The discussion in this section relates to the fourth age of place – a world in which the costs of transport and communication are zero and economies of agglomeration have vanished. If place no longer matters for producer–customer interaction, or as a source of agglomeration economies, then why should place matter at all? Here I consider two ways in which place can still matter in the fourth age. First, place may become a product/service characteristic in the eyes of the customer – when it was not previously a characteristic of any importance. Second, the history of place (or spatial history) shapes and enhances the intellectual capital of the trader: *place is what we think with*. The sixth section concludes.

The four ages of place

Building on Swann (1999, 2003), I find it helpful to identify four ages of place. These are distinguished by reference to two factors: first, the general costs of transportation and communication over distance; second, the extent of agglomeration economies.

Figure 4.1 provides a simple summary. As Swann (2003) shows, when transportation and communication costs are high and economies of agglomeration are low, then activity tends to be dispersed. As transportation and communication costs fall, then activity tends to become more clustered. Equally, as economies of agglomeration increase, then activity once again tends to become more clustered. When transport costs fall and economies of agglomeration rise together, then there is a strong tendency towards clustering. Figure 4.1 superimposes a path describing the four ages of place. These are labelled 1–4 in the figure, and are joined together in a curve to represent the possibility that some industries and economies at least will evolve along that hypothetical curve.

The first age: a medieval age

The first age is marked by a 1 in the top left-hand corner of Figure 4.1. In this age, costs of transport and communication are very high while agglomeration economies are very low. As a result, two producers, X and Y, located in distant towns are really no competition for each other. Geographical separation is a sufficient source of competitive distinction.[3] In this age, place clearly matters because a customer will generally buy from local producers, and hence distant producers are generally no competition. Place is a direct source of competitive distinction for that reason. However, there is also a sense in which place does not matter: agglomeration economies are not location specific, because there are indeed no agglomeration economies.

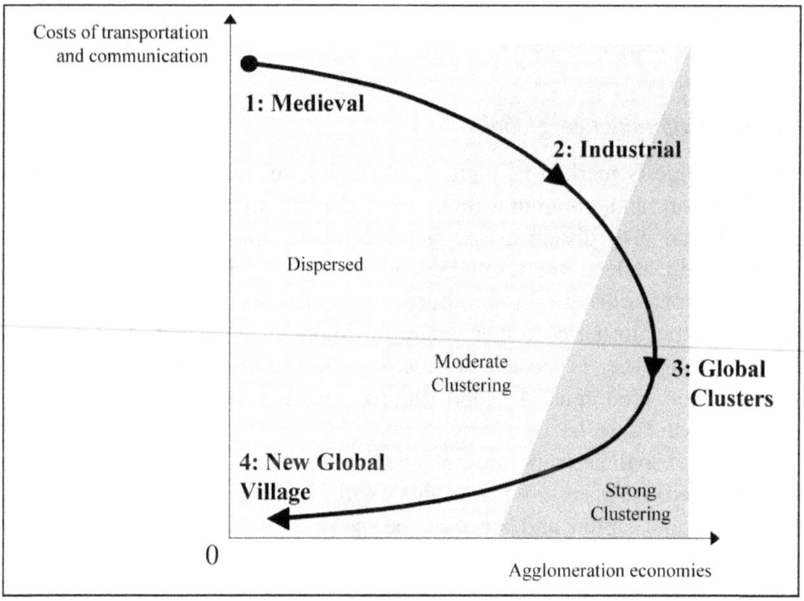

Figure 4.1 The four ages of place.

The second age: an industrial age

The second age is marked as point 2 in Figure 4.1. In this second age, transportation and communication costs have fallen somewhat and economies of agglomeration have grown somewhat. As a result there is some clustering, though not on the scale seen in the third age. Activities tend to crowd together in towns and cities that serve their region. But this is not yet the age of superclusters that achieve global dominance in their chosen industry. Inter-regional and international trade is higher than in the first age, but not as high as in the third age. Here place matters too, but for a different reason. In this second age, location is not such a strong source of competitive distinction as in the first age, and distant producers may be a threat to our local producer. However, place now matters as a source of agglomeration economies. The agglomeration economies are location specific.[4]

The third age: global clusters

The third age is marked as point 3 in Figure 4.1. Transport and communication costs have declined to a much lower level, but economies of agglomeration are even more important. For these reasons, clustering is now very strong. This is the age of global clusters and extensive international trade. In one sense place is irrelevant. In terms of access to customers, a local supplier enjoys no advantages over distant suppliers. In another sense, place is more important than ever. Agglomeration economies are highly location specific. Producers in a specific industry may find that there are only a few places worldwide where they can locate and remain competitive. This is where the economy is today, and it may be that this age will develop further and further without fundamental change. Alternatively, there may be a *fourth* age.

The fourth age: the new global village

The fourth age is marked as point 4, in the bottom left-hand corner of Figure 4.1. Transport and communication costs decline to zero and economies of agglomeration also disappear. As a result, there are no obvious reasons for clustering and, indeed, the normal economic force of the price mechanism will tend to dissipate clusters. In this fourth age, place does not appear to matter. It does not matter to the customer where the supplier is located. And it does not matter if a producer is located outside any cluster, because there is no loss of agglomeration economies. In short, the role of place in these four ages can be summarised in Table 4.1.

However, I shall argue below that, even in this fourth age, location may matter indirectly, because place is what we think with. Traders' locational history shapes their intellectual capital, and hence can be used to provide competitive distinction. Place matters because different locations shape their residents' intellectual capital in different ways. I return to this point later.

The outcome of the third age may seem surprising. Crude intuition suggests that as the costs of transportation and communication fall to zero then place

Table 4.1 The role of place

Age	*Producer–customer interaction*	*Agglomeration economies*
First	Important	Not important
Second	Moderately important	Moderately important
Third	Not important	Important
Fourth	Not important	Not important

becomes irrelevant. But this is a misunderstanding – partly right, of course, but also partly wrong. Customers may not care where their supplier is located. But place matters because producers located in the wrong place do not enjoy the same agglomeration economies as those located in the cluster, and hence will not be as efficient. This crude intuition fails to see the difference between the third age and the fourth age. The eradication of transport and communication costs leads only to the third age. To reach the fourth age, where place does not seem to matter, agglomeration economies must *also* be eradicated.[5]

It could be that the eradication of transport and communication costs would also eliminate agglomeration economies. And indeed, if this were true, then the third and fourth ages would be the same. But the eradication of transport and communication costs *need not necessarily* eliminate agglomeration economies. As will be clear in a moment, some economies of agglomeration are nothing to do with costs of transport and communication, and will remain even when the latter decline to zero.

Agglomeration economies here mean all the reasons why the collocation of production activities may entail lower production costs than if that production were dispersed. Some of these agglomeration economies may be sensitive to the costs of transport and communication. For example, one much discussed source of agglomeration economies is the ease with which employees from different organisations meet and exchange tacit knowledge. This requires face-to-face meetings, and hence will indeed be sensitive to the costs of transport. The advent of space-shrinking technologies can be expected to undermine these economies of agglomeration. But many plant-level economies of scale and scope are not influenced in this way by transport and communication costs. Rather, they derive from physically bound fixed costs. For example, economies of scale in a major semiconductor fabrication plant derive from the very large fixed costs incurred in installing the necessary capital in that plant. These scale economies are not destroyed by reducing transport and communications costs between two smaller (collaborative) plants.

A necessary condition for the eradication of all types of agglomeration economies would be that production processes are *infinitely reducible*, and without any economies of scale in the production of components. In general, it would take much more than the eradication of transport and communication costs to achieve that.

Take the example of PC manufacture. PC manufacture is highly reducible – it is split into many steps. But the process is not infinitely reducible, and there are strong economies of scale in the manufacture of each component. As a result, clusters are found which specialise in the production of particular components, and these are dispersed across many countries (Table 4.2). However, this is certainly *not* the sort of dispersion envisaged in the fourth age – the *new global village*.

Competitive survival

Competitive survival requires competitive *distinction*. It does not require absolute competitive advantage. It just requires that there is at least one competitive environment in which you have advantage. A zoological analogy illustrates this very clearly. In most environments within the UK, our native red squirrel cannot survive the competitive battle for survival against the (immigrant) grey squirrel. But in the right (mainly conifer) woodland, the red can survive because the grey does not find the food it likes. As a result, there are a few areas in England (and rather more in Scotland) where the red survives.

As Swann and Taghavi (1992) put it, competitive survival requires that traders lie on some part of the frontier of a competitive space. Another way of looking at this is to say that a product 0 is competitive if its price (P_0) is less than or equal to the maximum price at which it would find a buyer. The latter is defined as:

Table 4.2 Origin of components for a typical personal computer (2003)

Brand	USA
Final assembly and dispatch	Ireland
Main box	Ireland
Chips on motherboard	USA, Korea, Taiwan, Philippines
Battery on motherboard	Philippines
Power supply	China
CD ROM drive	China (assembled from Japanese parts)
CD-R (consumables)	Germany
Hard disk drive	Singapore
3.5" floppy disk drive	Philippines
Modem card	Netherlands (chips from USA, Korea, Taiwan)
Graphics card	China (chips from USA, Korea, Taiwan)
Specialist video card	USA
Monitor	UK (origin of components?)
Keyboard	Mexico
Mouse	Mexico
Child's mouse	Taiwan
Loudspeakers	Malaysia
Microphone	Mexico
Inkjet printer	Spain
Zip drive	Malaysia
Scanner	Taiwan
Web-cam	China
Power supplies (peripherals)	Taiwan, China, Malaysia, Mexico
Manuals	Scotland, Ireland, Wales, Germany
Environmental certification	Sweden

$$P_0^* = \max_{a \in A} \left\{ R_0 \mid V(Z_0; a) - R_0 \geq \max_{i \in I} \left[V(Z_i; a) - P_i \right] \right\} \tag{4.1}$$

where a describes the tastes of a consumer and A is the set of different consumer tastes to be found in a market; R_0 is a (dummy) price variable, to be maximised; $V(.)$ is a direct utility function, describing the value consumer a places on a product with characteristics defined by Z; and P_i defines the price of good i (from the set of all competing goods, I). Equation 4.1 defines the maximum price for product 0 such that the surplus on product 0 (as enjoyed by the *ideal consumer*, a) exceeds that surplus which consumer a could attain on any other product. Or this can be rewritten as:

$$P_0^* = \max_{a \in A} \left\{ V(Z_0; a) - \max_{i \in I} \left[V(Z_i; a) - P_i \right] \right\} \tag{4.2}$$

In this formulation, the solution values for a^* and i^* define (respectively) the tastes of the *ideal consumer* and the closest substitute to product 0 in the eyes of that *ideal consumer*. Swann and Taghavi (1992) show that $P^* - P$ increases (or at least, does not decline) as the number of characteristics (k) is increased. That is:

$$P^* - P = \phi(k) \tag{4.3}$$

where $\phi(.)$ is non-decreasing in k. It can be shown that the scope for traders to find sufficient competitive distinction for survival increases with k.

$$\text{Prob}\{P^* - P \geq 0\} = \pi(k) \tag{4.4}$$

where $\pi(.)$ is non-decreasing in k. Swann and Taghavi (1992) show that, when $\phi(.)$ is sharply increasing as a function of k, this means that the competitiveness of the product is highly dependent on its distinctive characteristics. But when $\phi(.)$ is barely increasing as a function of k, this means that the competitiveness of the product derives mainly from its low price, and is little affected by any distinctive characteristics.

These results are highly relevant to the present context. Space-shrinking technologies remove or reduce the effectiveness of geographical dimensions as a source of competitive distinction. As such, the chance of a trader achieving competitive distinction is likely to fall. In particular, those traders who previously survived because they offered a standard product/service at a standard price but in a new location will no longer survive. They have to introduce innovations in the product or service to achieve that. Figure 4.2 illustrates this quite clearly.

The first quadrant (upper left) shows an arbitrary distribution of products/services along a one-dimensional geographical space. The vertical axis measures value for money. The second quadrant (upper right) shows how all of these products/services can be competitive when consumers find it expensive to buy from traders

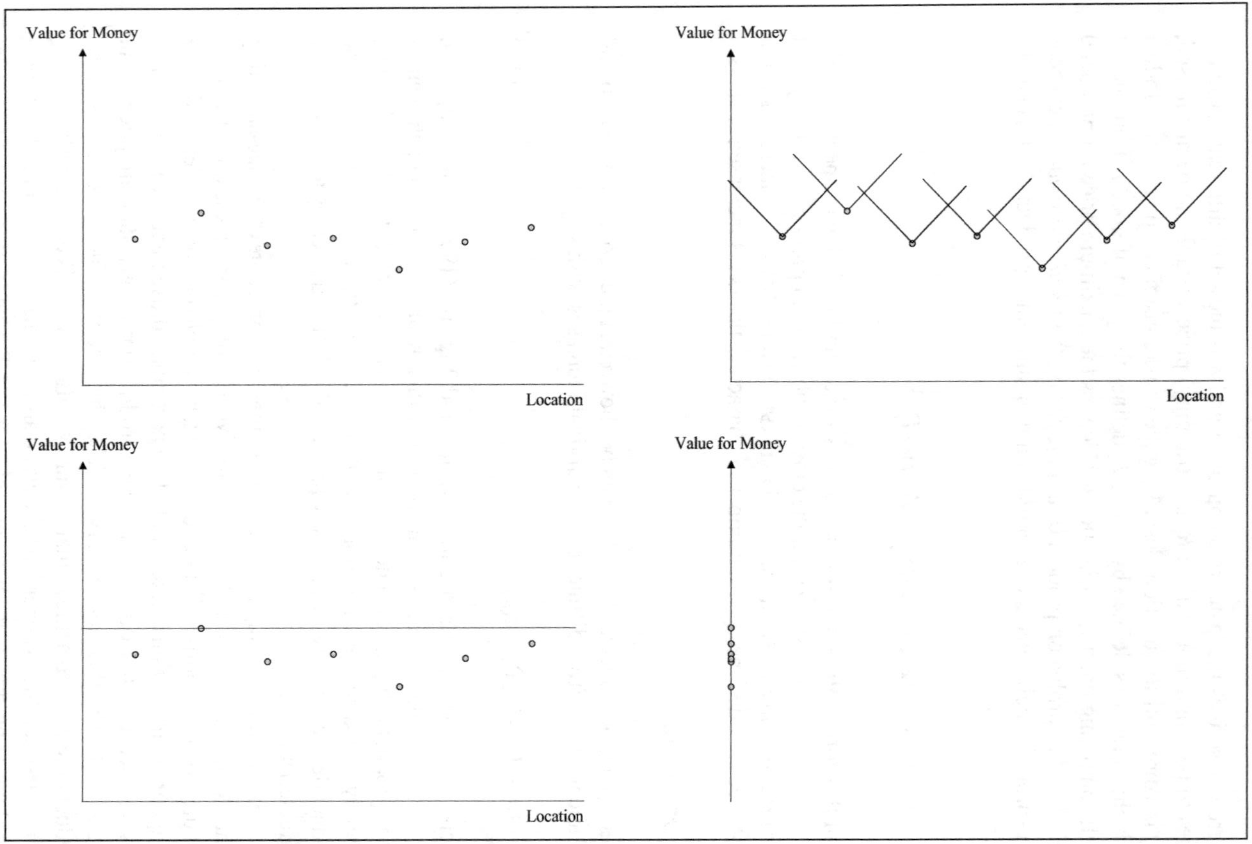

Figure 4.2 Space-shrinking technologies and competitive distinctions.

at distant locations. The V-shapes in this quadrant represent indifference curves for consumers located at particular points on the line. The apex of the V describes the value for money that is acceptable from a trader located at the consumer's home, so to speak. The consumer would be willing to travel to buy products from a distant trader, but these would have to offer better value for money. The V-shapes describe the trade-off between distance and value for money. Each of the different V-shapes represents the indifference curve for a consumer whose home is at the same location as a trader. As drawn, each of these consumers prefers to buy from their neighbourhood trader rather than travel to another trader – even if that trader offers better value for money. In each case the benefits of travelling to find better value for money are more than offset by the extra costs involved. Here, all traders are competitive.

The third quadrant (lower left) shows the relevant indifference curve when space-shrinking technologies reduce the cost of transacting over distance to nil. This indifference curve is flat. Here the only issue on the consumer's mind is value for money. The location of traders no longer matters. In this case every consumer will seek to buy from the trader offering the best value for money, and none of the other traders will make any sales. It is as if the dimension representing geographical space no longer exists so that competition between the different products is summarised as in the fourth quadrant (lower right). There is just one dimension, and in this one dimension *only one trader is competitive*. Compare this with the second quadrant (upper right), where all seven products could achieve sufficient competitive distinction to survive.

Dimensions of product space

What happens when one of the dimensions offering competitive distinction disappears? One common possibility is that traders will seek to add new dimensions by which they may – once again – distinguish themselves from the competition. In this context, much can be learnt from the analysis of 'endogenous dimensionality' – as summarised in Swann (1990). That source contains a number of generalisations from simulation studies, but these do not have the status of formal theorems. I shall just use one of these results here, which refers to *innovative entry* and *non-innovative entry*. The former describes market entry by a trader who increases the dimensions of product space (by adding one or more new characteristics). The latter describes entry by a trader who does not add new characteristics but finds a niche within the existing dimensions of product space.

Innovative entry becomes relatively profitable when any particular dimensional space becomes congested. But when the space is not congested, then the limited additional returns to innovative entry do not warrant the additional cost, and non-innovative entry is more profitable. Or, to put it another way, traders introduce new dimensions only when there is crowding in existing dimensions. Traders do not bother to differentiate themselves in *new* dimensions until they are unable to differentiate themselves in *existing* dimensions.

While this generalisation is couched in terms of *congestion*, it is also relevant to the case that one of the dimensions along which products are differentiated no longer serves as a source of distinction. This is relevant to the 'death of distance' that results from space-shrinking technologies. When space provides enough competitive distinction, traders will not necessarily find it worthwhile to seek distinction through product differentiation. But when space does not provide distinction – either because it is congested or because of the 'death of distance' – then traders will find it necessary to seek competitive distinction in other ways.

These new dimensions may be related to place. If they are, they can perhaps be of two sorts. First, the trader finds that he can turn place directly into new product characteristics, e.g. 'local' becomes a desirable characteristic for food. Second, the trader finds that his spatial history leaves a legacy in intellectual capital, and the trader can exploit this to generate competitive distinction. *Place is what you think with.*

Place in the fourth age

The discussion in this section relates to the fourth age of place – a world in which the costs of transport and communication are zero, and economies of agglomeration have vanished. I suggested above that such an age is not easily achieved, and is indeed a very different world from the third age. However, it is an important possible world within the context of this book, so I shall focus on it hereafter.

If place no longer matters for producer–customer interaction, or as a source of agglomeration economies, then why should place matter at all? But there are at least two ways in which place can still matter in the fourth age. First, place may become a product/service characteristic in the eyes of the customer – when it was not previously a characteristic of any importance. Second, the history of place (or spatial history) shapes and enhances the intellectual capital of the trader:[6] *place is what we think with.*

The examples that follow are only a few from the many possible. Moreover, in this short chapter, these are rather cursory and sometimes superficial. However, they are enough to demonstrate our main argument.

Place as a product/service characteristic

The experience of the holiday resort in the UK gives an excellent introduction to this phenomenon. Some holiday resorts have had to redefine themselves in the face of international competition. Or, to paraphrase a view that seems to be held by many in the tourism business: 'Bournemouth discovered it had a history when tour companies started to offer cheap packages to the Costa del Sol'. With the holiday resort, does place really matter? If a resort offers sunshine, clean beaches and warm water, does it really matter where it is? Judging from the way such resorts marketed themselves in the 1950s and 1960s, the answer would appear to be 'no'. The resort is a collection of product and service characteristics – and the three listed above are the key ones. If these are adequately supplied, then place does not matter. However, two factors have changed this emphatically in the subsequent forty to fifty years. First, the growth of international competition: cheap air travel led to competitive holiday packages in warmer climates, which could easily beat UK resorts on the three characteristics listed above. Second, the holiday has become for ever more of us an item of consumption in which distinction plays an important role. The customer does not want only the three characteristics described above: (s)he wants something more distinctive. Those on the producer side of tourism have tried to reinvent themselves so that place does matter. They do not just sell beaches; they sell place as history. Because international competitors can dominate UK resort X on each of the dimensions which X has to offer, X must reinvent itself as X plus something else.

Textbook economics tends to treat some foodstuffs (such as wheat) as the classic example of a commodity. After all, there exist commodity exchanges where standardised items are traded in million-dollar deals by traders who do not see the foodstuffs in which they are trading, certainly never taste their foodstuffs, and probably do not even know where their tonne of wheat is actually located, let alone where it was produced! Moreover, as Marx (1983 [1859]) observed: 'We cannot say from the taste of the wheat whether it was raised by Russian serf, French smallholder or English capitalist.' However, amongst some consumers at least, there is a revolt against the idea of foodstuffs as commodities. Partly this is a revolt against food miles (or food kilometres) and the attendant environmental damage. Partly it is a response to the sharply declining economic circumstances of farming as an industry. Suddenly the place in which food was produced becomes important.[7] That food is *locally produced* is a merit in its own right and/or it may be an indicator of quality (freshness, flavour, etc.). The supermarket chain Sainsbury label all its organic food with an instruction telling you how to find out about its origins. Increasing numbers buy their food from local farmers' markets. You can visit the farm, the vineyard or the distillery! The desirability of a particular foodstuff cannot be detached from the means of production.

Place is what we think with

Stewart (1997), amongst others,[8] has argued that intellectual capital is fast emerging as the principal source of competitive advantage – not natural resources, machinery or even financial capital. How can place shape that intellectual capital? I shall examine a number of examples below. In some of these cases, *variety* in spatial history and interaction is a virtue, while *purity* of spatial history and isolation is a hazard. But in other cases, *purity* of spatial history and isolation is a virtue, while *variety* in spatial history and interaction is a hazard.

The call centre looks like the ultimate virtual operation. The customer need not know where the centre is based, and (so it was thought) would not care. While there are presently some plant economies of scale in the call centre, it is possible to envisage a future call centre in which that is no longer true. The call centre is surely an organisation from the fourth age of place? And yet, perhaps not! Even for a call centre, location matters. It matters because of the small matter of local accents. In the UK, it was found that many callers responded best to regional accents from the periphery (north-east of England, parts of Scotland, south-west of England). More recent research found that callers were quite responsive to a wider range of regional accents,[9] but not, on the whole to accents from the south-east of England[10] or West Midlands. This is a simple but non-trivial example of the general phenomenon. Competitively speaking, accents are not neutral, and accents evolve from spatial history.[11] Hence spatial history shapes our intellectual capital – here our spoken voice and understanding of local culture – and thus competitive distinction.

Some studies of the success of Silicon Valley as a cluster (e.g. Saxenian 1994) have stressed the role of high job mobility in promoting the performance of the cluster. Mobility is important, so the argument goes, because mobile staff are the best mechanism for technology transfer. The fruitful exchange of tacit knowledge may be something of a myth in some so-called 'clusters', but if it is to happen, mobile labour is an essential component. The importance of mobile labour to the high-tech cluster can also be assessed by the salaries commanded by such labour. Some time ago, Forester (1980) commented on the extraordinary growth rates in earnings that could be achieved by the most mobile forms of labour in the Silicon Valley semiconductor industry. In the same fashion, many have commented on the extraordinary cultural richness and creativity to be found in New York City, and how that derives in large measure from the diverse cultural backgrounds and spatial histories of its inhabitants. Admittedly, Glazer and Moynihan (1970) and Steinfield (1973) have shown that the original conception of the 'melting pot' – a place where individuals from many different nations are 'melted' into a new race – is something of a myth. Strong ethnic divisions persist in New York. Nevertheless, the collocation of these diverse groups creates a diversity of cultures and spatial histories of substantial importance in cultural and economic life.

The division of academic labour becomes ever more specialised as competition increases. Most ordinary faculties can achieve a niche only in any one subdiscipline. Moreover, cross-disciplinary work generally brings low returns in short-term professional advancement. Nevertheless, the literature on creativity recognises that intellectual mobility can create some of the greatest advances. The recent creativity literature sees combination and reorganisation as fundamental to the process of creative thought. People create new knowledge or ideas by combining and reorganising *existing* concepts or categories (e.g. Mumford and Porter 1999). Koestler (1964) coined the term *bisociation* to describe what happens in creative thinking. Koestler's aim was to 'make a distinction between the routine skills of thinking on a single "plane" … and the creative act which … always operates on more than one plane'. Bisociation is about perceiving an idea or situation, 'in two self-consistent but habitually incompatible frames of reference' (Koestler 1964: 35).[12]

Bisociation is a combinatorial activity. It need not be a social activity. However, the scope for bisociation may be greatest when there can be creative social interaction in heterogeneous groups. Group interaction is important because it brings together individuals with different experience and backgrounds to exchange ideas. The more diverse the group, the greater the potential for creative bisociation because the group can in principle combine many different knowledge sets. This becomes increasingly important with the ongoing division of intellectual labour, and the attendant growing complexity of disciplines, because that makes it hard for any one individual to master more than one discipline, or at best a very small number of disciplines (Paulus 1999, Paulus *et al.* 1999).

A *hybrid* scholar is a researcher who transgresses the accepted boundaries of his/her home discipline and integrates concepts, theories, methods and results originating from other disciplines (Dogan and Pahre 1990, Dogan 1994, 1999). Disciplines vary in the reaction to hybrid scholars: some are highly suspicious and often very hostile towards scholars who have travelled to other 'lands' and seek to return. The hybridisation of disciplines means that elements from overlapping or adjacent disciplines are recombined into new specialised fields. Dogan (1994, 1999) goes further to argue that much of the invention in each discipline depends largely on exchanges with other fields. From this point of view, the *marginal scholars* play an especially important role in intellectual invention. These scholars are marginal in the sense that they live at the margins of their discipline. They may also be marginal in a social sense. Indeed, Dogan (1999) and Dogan and Pahre (1990) write of 'creative marginality', and go as far as to suggest that progress in academic disciplines is concentrated at the periphery, where there is cross-fertilisation with other disciplines. By contrast, the core of the discipline can become stagnant.

There has been much rhetoric to the effect that, with the growth of global telecommunications networks, internet companies above all could indeed start up anywhere. In fact, as Zook (2002) has shown, internet start-ups are quite highly clustered. Zook pays particular attention to the role of venture capital in this phenomenon, and finds that the uneven spatial pattern of internet companies reflects the uneven distribution of venture capital. In the same way, Virginia's Center for Innovative Technology (2000) found that internet companies in Virginia are highly clustered, often near major research universities. Golden (2000: B1) describes the experience of Lexeme, a company based near Harvard Square in Cambridge, MA, which provides natural language processing systems that can help to improve customer service. The unexpected key to their success was to recruit PhD graduates in linguistics. As Golden (2000: B1) puts it, 'traditionally, a linguistics degree has been among the least marketable of academic credentials'. Until very recently, very few software companies hired linguists at all. Lexeme, by contrast, has found these skills and recent developments in linguistics research indispensable to making some thoughtful advances in search engines. Lexeme succeeded because it was well placed to recruit graduates who had stayed around the Cambridge area because they originally hoped for an academic career. Place is what provides the skills necessary for creating imaginative software applications.

The novelist Virginia Woolf wrote of the famous Reading Room of the British Library (here quoted from Caygill 2000: 4): 'There is in the British Museum an enormous mind … hoarded beyond the power of any single mind to possess it'. This refers not just to the excellence of the book collection, but also to the fact that such a distinguished cast of great writers and statesmen had read and thought in that library. It is as if the reader can tap into this accumulation of historical thought, not just the written word. Even in the fourth age – when technology means that collocation is no longer required for access to the written word – a public reading space could still have this characteristic of an *enormous mind.*

This last example is rather different. It is about the advantage that arises from *purity and isolation* rather than variety and interaction. For the British academic today, a continuing source of criticism from our friends in business and government is that university people still live in an *ivory tower* – despite all the efforts made by successive governments to make us more business relevant. Many academics would dispute this, but my aim here is not to evaluate these claims, but rather to ask a different question. Is the *ivory tower* such a bad idea after all?

Some governments see an essentially instrumental role for the university: to support business in wealth creation. From that perspective, the research agenda should be designed by business, and hence demand led. This is a rather limiting perspective. From this point of view there would be little room for the linguistics research described in the previous example. Nor would there have been any room for Mendel's early research on what subsequently became genetics. Moreover, this perspective shows a splendid disregard for the long-established argument that the role of the university is not purely instrumental. This last view is best summarised by Ruskin (1996, vol. 22: 135):

> the object of University teaching is to form your conceptions ... It is to give you a notion of what is meant by smith's work, for instance, but not to make you blacksmiths. It is to give you a notion of what is meant by medicine, but not to make you physicians. The proper academy for blacksmiths is a blacksmith's forge; the proper academy for physicians is a hospital. Here you are to be taken away from the forge, out of the hospital, out of all special and limited labour and thought, into the 'Universitas' of labour and thought, that you may in peace, in leisure, in calm of disinterested contemplation, be enabled to conceive rightly the laws of nature, and the destinies of Man.

The ivory tower (or indeed the monastery) is actually quite a good way to achieve this objective. And, indeed, this cannot be dismissed purely as an outdated, nineteenth-century piece of elitism. For indeed, just as the creativity literature stressed the role of *bisociation* in creativity, so also it lays great emphasis on a degree of *autonomy*. Research on creativity has identified several characteristics of personality that are regularly correlated with creativity. These include (Amabile 1996, Abra and Abra 1999, Feist 1999): introversion; self-directedness and self-sufficiency; independence of mind and judgement; intrinsic (rather than extrinsic) motivation; no desire to conform for the sake of it; liking for solitude. I can perhaps summarise these in the term *autonomy*. Creative people are either autonomous by nature (or have it forced on them) or have to create such autonomy.

Sheldon (1999) argues that 'conformity and creativity don't mix'. Creativity of its very character involves breaking rules and disobeying norms. Sheldon argues that pressures to conform, broadly defined, have negative effects on creative effort. Sheldon makes a distinction between *informational* and *normative* social influences. *Informational* influence should be constructive if people use the information gained to sharpen their perception. In contrast, *normative* social influence can be destructive to the extent that it deters the creative person from his or her creative quest, back towards the conventional, flawed view. Those with a well-developed sense of autonomy are better able to take all external influence as informational – whether the intention was informational or normative. In short, the *autonomy* of the university is essential for the university to play the role for which it was designed. Reductions in that autonomy make the university less, rather than more, effective.

Conclusion

I can summarise the chapter very briefly. The chapter has talked of the *four ages* of place. In the *fourth age*, if it ever appears, place would in principle be of no relevance to economic activity. However, I have argued that place may take on a new economic function during that *fourth age*. *Place is what we think with.* Or, to spell it out, intellectual capital is what we think with, and intellectual capital is our source of competitive distinction. Our spatial history shapes our intellectual capital, and hence place is (still) a source of competitive distinction – even in the *fourth age*. This will continue until *all experiences are virtual* – unconnected with place – if such a future ever occurs.

One implication of the chapter is this. The question about the space-shrinking technologies discussed in this chapter is not 'do they make place irrelevant?'. The answer to that is, surely, 'no'. The right question to ask is, by contrast, '*how* do such technologies change the economic role of place?'. Place may become unimportant for some issues but may become more important (than before) for some other issues. In the fourth age, place (of the producer) is on the face of it no longer so important to the customer, nor indeed as a source of agglomeration economies to the producer. But place may become important for other reasons. As argued in the fourth and fifth sections, when space provides enough competitive distinction, traders will not find it necessary to seek further distinction. But when space does not provide distinction – either because it is congested, or because of the 'death of distance' – then traders will find it necessary to seek competitive distinction in other ways. Some will find this in place, or spatial history.

Notes

1 David Audretsch argued that 'new ideas need new space' at a conference in Cargèse, France (September 1995). See also Audretsch (1998). The later paper by Rodriguez-Palenzuela (1999) provides a fascinating exposition on this theme.
2 A reference to the book by F. Cairncross (1997).
3 This is not to suggest that there would be no trade at all, but this will tend to be concentrated where the exporter can produce products, or a level of quality, that the importer cannot obtain except by trade.
4 This scenario was especially relevant during the Industrial Revolution (see, for example, Deane 1965, Mathias 1983).
5 The advent of a 'weightless' economy would eradicate some, but not necessarily all, agglomeration economies. The weightless economy is discussed by Coyle (1997), Quah (2001), inter alia.

6 One leading example of how place shapes intellectual capital is the history of Manchester and its suburbs (see, for example, Chorley 1950).
7 As indeed, to some consumers, is the question of *how* it was produced, e.g. organic.
8 Stewart builds on Reich (1991).
9 Including some accents from the north-west of England (e.g. Liverpool), previously thought to be unsuitable for the purpose (see, for example, Ward 2000, Kahn 2003).
10 Including received pronunciation, or 'BBC English'.
11 Two important recent works on the economics of language are relevant here: Rubinstein (2000) and Lamberton (2002).
12 This idea is also found in areas of the literature more familiar to economists. Simon (1985) recognised that it is the process of problem solving and learning from diverse knowledge bases that is most likely to yield innovation. Cohen and Levinthal (1990) described the concept of absorptive capacity to capture how well organisations learn from their environment. Nelson and Winter (1982) showed us that an organisation's absorptive capacity was a function not so much of the individuals as of the *network of linkages* between individual capabilities.

References

Abra, J. and Abra, G. (1999) 'Collaboration and competition', in Runco, M.A. and Pritzker, S.R. (eds.) *Encyclopaedia of Creativity,* Vol. 1, San Diego: Academic Press.

Amabile, T.M. (1996) *Creativity in Context: Update to the Social Psychology of Creativity*, Boulder, CO: Westview Press.

Audretsch, D.B. (1998) 'Agglomeration and the location of innovative activity', *Oxford Review of Economic Policy*, 14: 18–29.

Cairncross, F. (1997) *The Death of Distance*, Boston: Harvard Business School Press.

Caygill, M. (2000) *The British Museum Reading Room*, London: British Museum.

Chorley, K.C. (1950) *Manchester Made Them*, London: Faber and Faber.

Cohen, W.M. and Levinthal, D.A. (1990) 'Absorptive capacity: a new perspective on learning and innovation', *Administrative Science Quarterly*, 35: 128–52.

Coyle, D. (1997) *The Weightless World*, Oxford: Capstone.

Deane, P. (1965) *The First Industrial Revolution*, Cambridge: Cambridge University Press.

Dogan, M. (1994) 'Fragmentation of the social sciences and re-combination of specialities', *International Social Science Journal*, 139: 27–42.

Dogan, M. (1999) 'Marginality', in Runco, M.A. and Pritzker, S.R. (eds.) *Encyclopaedia of Creativity,* Vol. 2, San Diego: Academic Press.

Dogan, M. and Pahre, R. (1990) *Creative Marginality: Innovation at the Intersection of Social Sciences*, Boulder, CO: Westview Press.

Feist, G.J. (1999) 'Autonomy and Independence', in Runco, M.A. and Pritzker, S.R. (eds.) *Encyclopaedia of Creativity,* Vol. 1, San Diego: Academic Press.

Fisher, R. (1994) *Birmingham River*, Oxford: Oxford University Press.

Forester, T. (1980) 'The jelly bean people of Silicon Valley', in Forester, T. (ed.) *The MicroElectronics Revolution*, Oxford: Basil Blackwell.

Glazer, N. and Moynihan, D.P. (1970) *Beyond the Melting Pot*, 2nd edn, Cambridge, MA: MIT Press.

Golden, D. (2000) 'No longer just Eggheads, linguists leap to the net', *The Wall Street Journal*, 30 May 2000.

Kahn, S. (2003) 'Number's up for the cut-glass accent: regional and foreign tones triumph as 118 rings the changes', *Observer*, 24 August.

Koestler, A. (1964) *The Act of Creation*, London: Hutchinson.

Lamberton, D. (ed.) (2002) *Economics of Language*, Cheltenham: Edward Elgar.

Marx, K. (1983 [1859]) *Critique of Political Economy*, London: Lawrence and Wishart.

Mathias, P. (1983) *The First Industrial Nation*, 2nd edn, London: Routledge.

Mumford, M.D. and Porter, P.P. (1999) 'Analogies', in Runco, M.A. and Pritzker, S.R. (eds.) *Encyclopaedia of Creativity,* Vol. 1, San Diego: Academic Press.

Nelson, R.R. and Winter, S.G. (1982) *An Evolutionary Theory of Economic Change*, Cambridge, MA: Harvard University Press.

Paulus, P.B. (1999) 'Group creativity', in Runco, M.A. and Pritzker, S.R. (eds.) *Encyclopaedia of Creativity,* Vol. 1, San Diego: Academic Press.

Paulus, P.B., Brows, V. and Ortega, A. (1999) 'Group creativity', in Purser, R.E. and Montuori, A. (eds.) *Social Creativity*, Creskill, NJ: Hampton Press.

Quah, D. (2001) 'The weightless economy in economic development', in Pohjola, M. (ed.) *Information Technology, Productivity, and Economic Growth: International Evidence*, Oxford: Oxford University Press.

Reich, R.B. (1991) *The Work of Nations: Preparing Ourselves for 21st Century Capitalism*, New York: Alfred A. Knopf.

Rodriguez-Palenzuela, D. (1999) 'New ideas need new space', Department of Economics and Business Working Paper 390, Barcelona: Universitat Pompeu Fabra.

Rubinstein, A. (2000) *Economics and Language*, Cambridge: Cambridge University Press.

Ruskin, J. (1996) *The Works of John Ruskin*, CD-ROM version. Cook, E.T. and Wedderburn, A. (eds.), Cambridge: Cambridge University Press.

Saxenian, A. (1994) *Regional Advantage: Culture and Competition in Silicon Valley and Route 128*, Cambridge, MA: Harvard University Press.

Sheldon, K.M. (1999) 'Conformity', in Runco, M.A. and Pritzker, S.R. (eds.) *Encyclopaedia of Creativity,* Vol. 1, San Diego: Academic Press.

Simon, H. (1985) 'What do we know about the creative process?', in Kuhn, R.L. (ed.) *Frontiers in Creative and Innovative Management*, Cambridge, MA: Ballinger.

Steinfield, M. (1973) *Cracks in the Melting Pot*, 2nd edn, New York: Glencoe Press.

Stewart, T.A. (1997) *Intellectual Capital: The New Wealth of Organisations*, London: Nicholas Brealey.

Swann, G.M.P. (1990) 'Product competition and the dimensions of product space', *International Journal of Industrial Organisation*, 8: 281–95.

Swann, G.M.P. (1999) 'The internet and the distribution of economic activity', in Macdonald, S., Nightingale, J. and Allen, D. (eds.) *Information and Organisation: A Tribute to the Work of Don Lamberton*, Amsterdam: Elsevier.

Swann, G.M.P. (2003) 'High technology clusters: specialisation, interaction and transportation', paper presented at the Accademia dei Lincei Conference on Districts, Pillars, Networks: Italy and Europe, Rome, April 2003.

Swann, G.M.P. and Taghavi, M. (1992) *Measuring Price and Quality Competitiveness: A Study of 18 British Product Markets*, Aldershot: Avebury.

Virginia's Center for Innovative Technology (2000) *A Snapshot of Virginia's Internet Companies*, Herndon, VA (available online at www.cit.org/publications/Snapshot_VA_Companies.pdf).

Ward, D. (2000) 'Scousers put the accent on success', *Guardian*, 22 September.

Zook, M.A. (2002) 'Grounded capital: venture financing and the geography of the internet industry, 1994–2000', *Journal of Economic Geography*, 2: 151–77.

Part II

Empirical evidence

5 The boom and the bombshell

The New Economy bubble and the San Francisco Bay Area

Richard A. Walker

> In the known world, this 49-square mile patch of land is Ground Zero of the Internet. The whole world is watching what we're doing.
>
> Derek Gordon, DigitalThink, San Francisco (Seligman 2000: A14)

The attacks of September 11, 2001, that brought the destruction of the twin towers of the World Trade Center forever changed the urban landscape of New York. That event was sudden, violent, monstrous. Yet the economic forces at work in all great cities are just as inexorable in reworking the lay of the land from generation to generation. Anyone who lives in the modern world comes to a realization that the landscapes we inhabit are built on sand. Known and familiar buildings, streets, storefronts, homes, and factories have a way of disappearing without a trace, and often memory fails to recreate the image of what used to be. This relentless redevelopment of cities moves to the rhythms of capital accumulation. The manic logic of capitalism is capable of spectacular bouts of building that surpass anything in the past, and equally capable of laying low skyscrapers, blocks, city centers, and factory districts in short order (Harvey 1982).

Such was the case in the San Francisco Bay Area in the 1990s. An economic boom of unparalleled ferocity hit the place like a bombshell. The city was picked up, shaken until it rattled, and then dropped into a new configuration. Although other observers have chronicled what took place (Solnit and Schwartzenberg 2000, Beitel 2003, Carlsson 2004, Olsen 2004), I nonetheless have four reasons for plowing the same ground. First of all, most of the attention has been confined to San Francisco, when in fact the boom and the bubble was centered in Silicon Valley not San Francisco and affected the whole Bay Area. Second, the boom by the Bay has been too much interpreted in local political terms and insufficiently linked to larger movements of finance capital, which in this instance were volcanic. The eruption in the Bay Area was, ironically, linked directly to the financial wizards of Wall Street, many of whom were housed in New York's Twin Towers, and who oversaw the greatest financial bubble in history. Third, the connection of the New Economy to Silicon Valley has not been adequately appreciated. As the world center of high-tech in the emerging internet age, the Bay Area became the paragon of the New Economy and the iconic space of the neoliberal 1990s. Finally, all this renders the Bay Area of the 1990s a perfect case study for scholars of the geography of the capitalist economy and the dialectics of place (Cox 1997).

Ground Zero of the New Economy

John Doerr, the venture capital kingpin of Silicon Valley, is credited with being the first to utter the phrase "the New Economy" to describe what was going on in the Bay Area during the roaring nineties (Miles 2001). The Bay Area's economic strength and innovative energy was the solid base on which the hyperbole of the New Economy, American revival, and dot-com dottiness were constructed. It was Ground Zero of the New Economy.

The domain of high-tech

Silicon Valley was already the principal global center of electronics when the internet age struck. It led the world in electronics and information technology, which had become the leading industrial sector at the end of twentieth century. Many a book has been written lauding the Valley's exceptional mix of technical talent, business acumen, and openness to new ideas (Hanson 1982, Freiberger and Swaine 1984, Rogers and Larsen 1984, Caddes 1986). By the 1990s, the high-tech economy had come to dominate the whole Bay region (Bay Area Economic Forum 1996, 1999).

Technologically, the new thing of the 1990s was the internet. By the end of the decade, everyone was agog about the possibilities unleashed by this astonishing system linking up computers everywhere at the blink of an eye. The Bay Area was the heartland of the World Wide Web as it became commercially operational, with the densest wiring, most domains, and most intensive population of users (Zook 2000, 2001, 2002). New York, London, Washington, Seattle, and Los Angeles followed. The geography of the network society – so called by Castells (1996), the sociological siren of the brave new world of IT – began and ended in Silicon Valley. Moreover, Bay Area high-tech companies were seen as exemplars of business organization for the new era. They were celebrated for their open, diversified, and strategic systems of doing business (Peters and Waterman 1985, Peters 1992, Packard 1995). In the early 1990s, "the virtual corporation" became the buzzword to capture the ongoing shift from manufacturing to product and system design, marketing, and branding that was taking place in the high-tech industries (Davidow and Malone 1992). By the end of the decade, no other sector better illustrated new methods of integrating global networks of subcontracting and contract manufacturing (Dedrick and Kraemer 1998, McKendrick *et al.* 2000, Sturgeon 2005).

At the same time, the idea of industrial districts was flourishing, with its compelling vision of interactive firms, flexible specialization, and external economies. Silicon Valley became the prime example of the post-Fordist industrial region, replete with dense linkages among high-tech manufacturers, designers, suppliers, and business services (Saxenian 1994, Kenney 2000, Patton and Kenney 2005).

Added to this were venture capital and a free-wheeling culture of start-ups, which nurtured technical innovation and entrepreneurial liberation (Kenney and Florida 2000, Zook 2002, 2004). Ironically, the Bay Area had, in the meantime, grown more Fortune 500 blockbuster corporations than anywhere else except New York City.

The New Economy also rested on new forms of work and employment. Silicon Valley has long been noted for its utilization of a highly educated technical labor force enjoying an exceptional degree of freedom to work and create within the capitalist enterprise (Rogers and Larsen 1984). It has sucked in some of the world's best talent (Saxenian 2002) and made the most of their collective labor in a consummate "learning region" (Storper 1997). With the rise of the web world of the internet, San Francisco came to epitomize the liberty and libertine lives of this "creative class" of workers (Florida 2002). Of course, not all workers are so favored in high-tech. There are many ordinary workers of modest skill, whose wages barely budged in the 1990s despite the boom (Benner *et al.* 1999, Greenwich and Niedt 2001). The new age of labor relations has given companies maximum flexibility in hiring, firing, deploying, and overworking all workers. It is, furthermore, a place where temporary agencies are used for every type of labor and independent contractors offer their skills on the open market – where, in short, long-term employment relations are rare. In the 1990s, the use of "contingent labor" approached the unprecedented level of one-quarter of the local workforce (Benner *et al.* 1999).

As the USA rebounded smartly in the 1990s, its bounce came, above all, from high-tech. Computing and information technology led the USA to a long-awaited revival from the profit and productivity doldrums of the 1970s and 1980s (Gordon 2000, Brenner 2002[1]). High-tech, representing 8 percent of gross domestic product (GDP), accounted for no less than one-third of US economic growth in the second half of the decade (Brenner 2004). If you wanted to bet on the future of capitalism, the Bay Area was double zero on the roulette wheel.

Firewater in the Valley

Silicon Valley fever is not a new syndrome (Freiberger and Swaine 1984, S. Levy 1984, Rogers and Larsen 1984). In the 1990s, however, the "fire in the valley" hype surpassed anything previously imagined. The ballyhoo over the New Economy allowed enthusiasts far and wide to join in a kind of "imagined community of nerds" enthralled by the internet revolution (Bronson 1999, Miles 2001, Frank and Mulcahey 2003). The Bay Area was the Never-Never Land of the New Thing (Lewis 2000). San Francisco became the cultural capital of the virtual world. Semidelusional ideas were the ordinary provenance of the young gnomes hooked to The Well, Salon.com, and Craigslist in the early 1990s, and spread far and wide over the rest of the decade via the city's new media mavens at *Wired, Red Herring* and *The Industry Standard.* Soon techno-babble had become the everyday cant of the rich and powerful around the country (Perkins and Perkins 1999, Miles 2001, Henwood 2003).

People spoke of the New Gold Rush, and they were not far from the mark. John Doerr claimed that Silicon Valley was "the largest legal creation of wealth in the history of the planet" (Miles 2001: 9). The roaring nineties threw up a whole new generation of millionaires at Netscape, Yahoo, and other high-flyers of the internet era, thanks to Silicon Valley's insider trick of granting stock options to all its key technical employees.[2] The Bay Area zoomed past New York and Los Angeles to lead the country in the number of super-rich on the Forbes 400 list (forty-three compared with thirty-eight for New York in 2001).[3] The super-rich were the princes of the New Economy (Micklethwait 1997, Wilson 1997).

The local hype intersected decisively with the nationalist cant of American economic revivalism. American business and the state were engaged in a fearsome competition with Europe and Japan over economic supremacy in the new global capitalist order. Things had gone badly for the USA in the 1970s and early 1980s, and it was eagerly trying to prove that "America is back," as Ronald Reagan put it. Another recession in the early 1990s cost George Bush his job and put Bill Clinton in office on the premise that "it's the economy, stupid" (Pollin 2003). Fortunately for American boosters, Europe and Japan remained sluggish throughout most of the decade, while the USA seemed to be breaking into a run (though its performance would later be shown to have been artificially enhanced) (Brenner 2002, Henwood 2003).

As the USA peddled its neoliberal wares, proclaiming the wonders of capitalism and free markets, governments around the globe wanted to know how to get some of that vaunted American technology, entrepreneurship, flexibility, and thrill of capitalism. What better model than Silicon Valley? Wherever the myth of US supremacy and capitalist renewal went, the legend of Silicon Valley was not far behind (Massey *et al.* 1992, Saxenian and Hsu 2001, Bresnahan and Gambardella 2004). The New Economy of the Bay Area was the Great White Hope for the restoration of American global primacy and for revival of the entrepreneurial myth in America.

Dot-com delusions

If Silicon Valley was the supernova of the New Economy, San Francisco was its neutron star twin. Although the city has slipped in economic power vis-à-vis the upstart Valley, San Francisco nonetheless retained a thriving intellectual, artistic, cultural, and political milieu, of which Silicon Valley – indeed, most American cities – could only dream (Solnit and Schwartzenberg 2000, Carlsson 2004). The old central city still attracted a dynamic array of young people seeking outlets for their energy and imagination. What happened, beginning in the 1980s, was a synergy between such people's talents and the growing electronics wizardry of the Valley, with a big dollop of Hollywood thrown in. By the mid-1990s, people came to speak of a new phenomenon, "multimedia," taking place South of Market (SoMa), including movie special effects, video games, and electronic publishing. By 1995 there was a robust cluster of over 15,000 employees in the new sector. Then the era of the "dot-coms" – new internet-related companies – hit, and by

1999 employment in the sector had ballooned to 40,000, in over 1,000 companies, with a payroll of US$2 billion; in 2000 that payroll reach an eye-popping US$5.7 billion (Saracevic 2000). The workforce was overwhelmingly young, informal, and enthusiastic.

The whole culture of San Francisco was inflected by a rapid influx of young "dot-commers" hoping to change the world, or make a million bucks – whichever came first (Ledbetter 2003, Lowenstein 2004). The dot-com frenzy raging around the Bay Area represented a significant shift in the classic character of high-tech. In a few quick years the internet graduated from the fantasy of a few techno-droids to a fantasy of mass sales over the World Wide Web. The American technological sublime (Nye 1994) embraced America's money culture, had joyous intercourse, and gave birth to the hellspawn of the dot-coms. This commercial castle was built on profitless clouds, however, and would ultimately fall to earth (Perkins and Perkins 1999, Frank and Mulcahey 2003, Henwood 2003).

In the meantime, the Bay Area was primed to be the darling of the wheelers and dealers of hot-house capital in the 1990s. It would be the primary object of affection for the financiers of the American empire as their cups ran over with money. Financialization and futurism would collide on the eve of the new millennium, and the resulting stock market tsunami would clobber the heartland of the New Economy.

The financial tidal wave hits the bay shore

If the New Economy was being bottled and sold like firewater, the hype would still have meant little without a powerful surge of finance capital that made everything seem possible. Financial markets run amuck would propel the boom by the bay into a bubble of monumental proportions.

Surfing waves of risk capital

The rosy dawn of the New Economy and of the internet bubble was signaled by the 1995 launch of Netscape, the most successful launch in stock market history. Netscape was the first commercial search engine for the World Wide Web, and its financial father-figure was venture capitalist John Doerr. As Netscape went ballistic, it minted the first of thousands of New Economy millionaires created during the boom (Lewis 2000).

The Bay Area gave birth to the financial means of its own expansion. The current form of venture capital developed in the 1960s in Silicon Valley, born of a former New York banker and special funds earmarked for start-ups by the founders of Intel. Once east coast financiers got wind of what was happening, they began pumping money into specialized venture firms located on Sand Hill Road behind Stanford. By the 1980s, there was nothing like it in the world – a multi-billion-dollar pool of risk-taking capital searching out new ideas (Florida and Kenney 1988). In the 1990s, Silicon Valley venture capital became legendary, and highly sophisticated in its creation of whole management teams for start-ups (Kenney and Florida 2000, Zook 2002, 2004). By the end of the decade, the number of venture firms had grown to over 800 and venture capitalists numbered over 8,000 (Shinal 2003).

The start-up culture of Silicon Valley also gave birth to the modern fad for IPOs (initial public offerings of stock). Although Wall Street dominates American investment banking, a trio of specialized investment houses arose in San Francisco's financial district in the 1980s to become major players in moving high-tech start-ups into the stock markets: Montgomery Securities, Robertson Stephens, and Hambrick and Quist. They specialized in electronics, biotechnology, and high-end retailing, developing an expertise that none of the distant Wall Street giants could match. By the late 1990s, the local bankers were doing so well that the financial giants of New York and Europe crashed the party, buying out the boutiques. This opened up new conduits from Wall Street and global financial markets straight into the heart of the Bay Area, down which eager investors could pour the accumulated wealth of the world.

As a consequence, the Bay Area could tap into an unparalleled amount of capital eager to make a killing off the New Economy (Kenney and Florida 2000, Patton and Kenney 2005). As total venture capital investment in the USA rocketed from US$30 billion in 1998 to US$60 billion in 1999 and to over US$100 billion in 2000, the Bay Area went along for the ride, with venture capital peaking at US$33 billion in 2000 (Abate 2004). Of all the venture investments in the USA in the 1990s, the Bay Area was creaming off one-quarter to one-third, by far the most of any place (Zook 2002).[4] IPOs were less concentrated on the Bay Area than was venture capital; nevertheless, at the peak of the bubble in 1999, one-quarter of all IPOs in the USA occurred here, accounting for one-sixth of the total IPO stock value. The average gain that year was 350 percent or more, twice the levitation of IPOs issued elsewhere in the country, for a total value of over US$300 billion (Hua 2000, Sinton 2000).

Riding the NASDAQ

The stock markets began their long rise in the 1980s, propelled by the neoliberal revolution of the Reagan administration. After a nasty shock in October 1987 and the recession of 1989–92, stocks began to soar again in the 1990s. By 1996, Federal Reserve Chairman Alan Greenspan was already taking public note of the "irrational exuberance" of the markets. But the Asian financial crisis of 1997 put a scare into the world's financiers, and led Greenspan to lower interest rates. For the next two years, the Federal Reserve continued to fill the stock markets' sails to keep the ship of state moving ahead. The managers of American capitalism had been converted to "stock market Keynesianism" to keep the economy buoyant (Schiller 2000, Brenner 2002, Henwood 2003, Pollin 2003, Lowenstein 2004).

The NASDAQ was the principal vehicle of stock speculation in the 1990s (Figure 5.1). Its rise was more precipitous than that of any other market in the world during that decade (Ingebretsen 2002). The NASDAQ index rose from around 500 in 1990 to 1,000 in 1995, at the time of the Netscape launch; it sur-

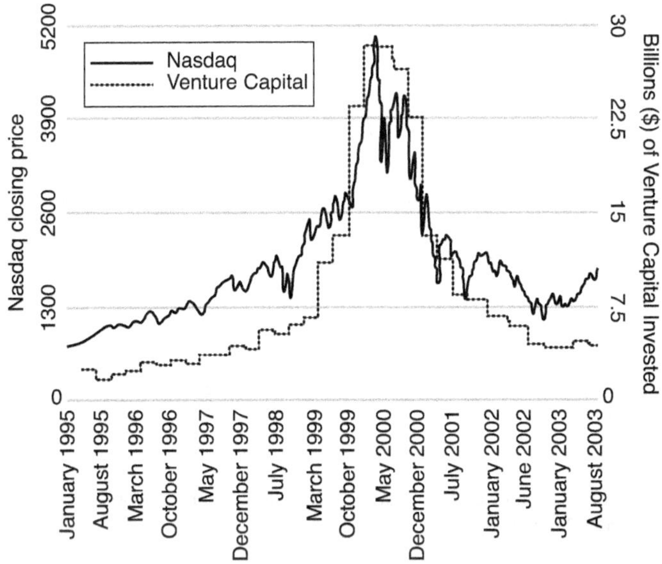

Figure 5.1 NASDAQ index vs. US venture capital, 1995–2003. Sources: NASDAQ Exchange, PriceWaterhouseCoopers, Moneytree survey and Matthew Zook.

passed 2,000 in 1998, then skyrocketed above 5,000 in early 2000.[5] The venture capital and IPO booms closely tracked the rise of the NASDAQ (Zook 2002).

Although the stock market bubble has been much commented on, the radically skewed geography of its money flows has hardly been noticed. Economists are too wedded to thinking in national units and geographers are unused to thinking about stock markets.[6] In fact, the Bay Area was the eye of the storm in the stock market bubble of the 1990s. The Bay Area was more closely tied to the NASDAQ and the world of electronic stock trading than any other region. Most electronics companies, such as Microsoft, Oracle, and Cisco, prefer to list on the NASDAQ rather than the New York Stock Exchange (NYSE). In their early days, these companies also liked the NASDAQ because it kept IPOs afloat better than conventional markets. Their rise to prominence among US corporations in the 1980s propelled the NASDAQ from an exchange for also-ran companies to a rival to Wall Street (Ingebretsen 2002).

Alongside the increasing popularity of the NASDAQ came the low-margin stock trading revolution begun by Charles Schwab in San Francisco in 1974 (Kador 2002). Schwab rode to prominence in national stock trading in part because of the widely dispersed wealth of California investors. The first fully internet trader was the 1994 start-up, E*trade, in Palo Alto, with eSchwab following in 1996. E-trading exploded on the back of the internet (Kador 2002, Henwood 2003, Lowenstein 2004).

There are no certain figures on the influx of bubble money into the Bay Area, but there are several indicators. The most spectacular might be the way in which stocks of individual star companies rocketed into the stratosphere. In

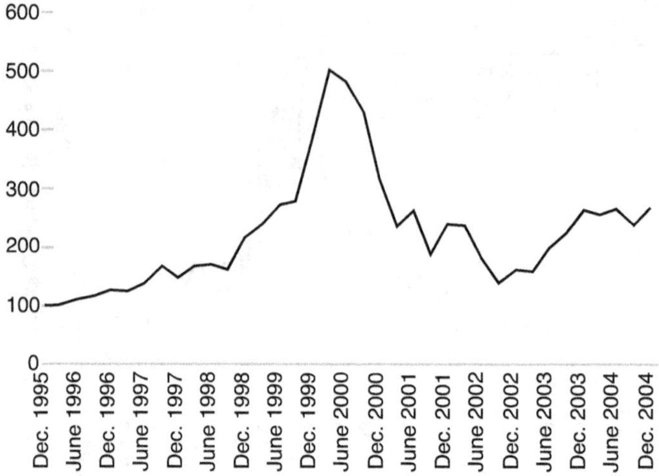

Figure 5.2 Bloomberg San Francisco index, 1995–2004. Source: Bloomberg LP index of 232 Bay Area stocks.

1998, San Jose's Cisco Systems, maker of internet hardware, became the fastest company to reach US$100 billion in total stock value, a record surpassed in 1999 by Sunnyvale's Yahoo. More astounding, Cisco Systems overtook Microsoft briefly to become the most hyper-valued company in the world – at over US$555 billion in mid-1999. Overall, Bay Area stock performance was nothing short of miraculous. The Franklin 250 California growth index shot up from 250 in 1990 to 1,300 in mid-1999 to a peak of almost 2,900 in March 2000. The Franklin's gain of 1,200 percent exceeded the NASDAQ's 1,000 percent and the S&P's 300 percent. The Bloomberg San Francisco index gained over 500 percent between 1995 and 2000 (Figure 5.2). The *San Francisco Chronicle* report on the top firms in the Bay Area for calendar year 1999 defies belief: the total value of the region's 500 largest public corporations nearly *tripled* in one year, from US$1.3 trillion to US$3.5 trillion. By contrast, the NASDAQ doubled in the same period, while the Dow Jones index rose by only 6 percent (Sinton 2000).

Wipe-out!

At the same time as the world was discovering the New Economy in the Bay Area, surfers discovered that the world's largest waves were not in Hawaii or Australia but just south of the Golden Gate, at a place they called "Mavericks." Winter storm winds blowing across the northern Pacific can push walls of water upwards of ninety feet high (similar to the Indian Ocean tsunamis of December 2004). The waves are wickedly dangerous and have claimed the life of more than one world-class surfer. So, too, did surfing the financial mavericks of the 1990s turn out to be a risky enterprise for many an entrepreneurial genius.

The speculative wave broke in April 2000. The NASDAQ fell 1,500 points in a nonce, then slid below 3,000 by June; after a brief recovery in mid-summer it went into a long, steady slide that dragged the index below 2,000 by April 2001 and on down to a low of 1,119 on October 9, 2002 – putting it back where it was in 1997. That comes out as a loss of more than 77 percent of stock values. By late 2000 the Dow index, too, was falling and would continue downward for another two years, losing over 30 percent of its value; the S&P 500 index fell 40 percent in the same period. The three-year decline would prove the worst since 1929–32 in the USA. By the end of 2002, the combined markets had vaporized US$7 trillion out of the US$17.8 trillion gained during the long run-up. The Bay Area was Ground Zero of the financial implosion of 2000. The Franklin 250 California stock index collapsed, cascading down over 1,000 points in the month of April 2000 – a plunge of over one-third. The year 2000 witnessed the pricking of the dot-com bubble in an astonishingly short time (Kirby 2000, Saracevic 2000). Nine-tenths of the dot-coms in San Francisco would be gone by the middle of 2001. Wags began referring to the "dot-gones." But beyond lay a deeper sickness that would lay low the elephants of the high-tech game parks. By the end of the year 2000, the Chronicle 500 had evaporated an astronomical US$2.2 trillion, to US$1.28 trillion. After a calm in 2001, the storm hit again in 2002, and the Chronicle 500 shrank back to 200, some US$409 billion poorer than before – another annual loss of one-third of total stock values, The overall losses added up to a breath-taking 75 percent since early 2000 (Fost 2003).

The Bay Area suffered by far the largest hit of anywhere in the country in the meltdown. A report in 2001 showed the top 100 corporations in the Bay Area having evacuated nearly US$2 trillion in value from their 2000 peaks, compared with a national loss for the Wilshire 5000 of US$4.45 trillion (Liedtke 2001). That would mean that Bay Area firms accounted for at least 45 percent of all the stock losses for the USA in the first round of the markets' collapse. The Bay Area's total loss of US$2.63 trillion on the Chronicle 500/200 amounted to well over one-third of the national total. That is a spatial distribution that should impress even the most geographically obtuse economist. Amazingly, it took investors a while to wake up to the crisis. Even after April 2000, venture capital continued to flow in record quantities to risky San Francisco start-ups (Abate 2004) and IPOs continued to raise hundreds of millions for Silicon Valley companies (Minton 2001). By the end of the year, New York and Boston capitalists had finally seen the light. Venture investment fell off the cliff in the first quarter of 2001, dropping by 40 percent from the previous quarter (Emert 2001); it ended up 60 percent lower for the year, at under US$40 billion, and then fell to a pitiful US$7.8 billion in 2002 (Shinal 2003). The investment banking houses in San Francisco had closed their doors by 2002.

Why the great fall in stock values? Certainly not the acts of September 11, 2001, since the crash had come six months earlier. The reasons lay in the normal abnormality of business cycles and financial enthusiasms. In retrospect, the markets had overshot any reasonable assessment of corporate profits as early as 1996, and bore no relation to classic evaluations of price–earnings ratios thereafter (Schiller 2000, Brenner 2002, Lowenstein 2004). Electronics and telecommunications were the worst offenders in this regard. When the dust had settled by 2003, total losses incurred in those sectors were equal to all the profits rung up in the boom years (Brenner 2004). Hence, stock values fell back to where they had been in 1996–97, before the absurd run-up of the bubble. But in Silicon Valley the debacle was worse: in one year the top 150 companies lost a combined US$90 billion, wiping out all the profits they had made in the previous eight years (Sylvester 2002).[7]

Rocketing real estate

So far we have established the Bay Area's importance in the age of the New Economy and its place in the record-breaking financial speculations of the late twentieth century. Industrial capital and finance capital are thus accounted for. But for the urbanist there is always a vital third piece of the capitalist puzzle: property development and real estate markets (Harvey 1985, 2003). The Bay region has, overall, the priciest real estate of any metropolitan area in the country, including greater New York and Los Angeles (Walker *et al.* 1990). But the run-up of prices that occurred in the time of the bubble exceeded anything previously imaginable.

Prices take off

Real estate values in the Bay Area started to motor upward in the early 1970s and hit their stride in the 1980s, as Silicon Valley roared into prominence and downtown San Francisco business and finance thrived. Downturns in electronics and banking in 1985 threw the regional real estate market into a doldrums from which it did not recover for almost a decade. Then things turned back up and local businesses started filling space and bidding up rents on commercial properties. As the boom accelerated, vacancy rates fell to microscopic levels and prices spiraled ever upward.

An outrageous spike occurred in commercial rents in San Francisco and Silicon Valley in 1999 and 2000 (Figure 5.3). A classic bottleneck had developed as vacancies fell below 1 percent in central San Francisco and buildings were being leased before they were off the drawing boards (Seligman 2000). In a CB Richard Ellis global survey of class A office rents in late 2000, Silicon Valley's US$87.48 per square foot ranked fourth in the world, behind London, Tokyo, and Hong Kong. San Francisco's US$73.75 per square foot came in seventh, just behind Paris and Mumbai – and ahead of midtown Manhattan (Morrissey 2001). Bay Area realtors and landlords crowed, and enjoyed a moment of unparalleled power over tenants. At the height of the dot.com mania in San Francisco, landlords were being given stock options in tenant companies as a move-in bonus!

As commercial real estate skyrocketed, housing could not be far behind. Apartment rents hit unprecedented levels, with San Francisco leading the charge. Rents rose by more than 225 percent from 1996 to 2000, as the city became the nation's most expensive rental market. The rent on a two-bedroom apartment by 2000 was typically over U$2,000 per month, or three times what it had been in

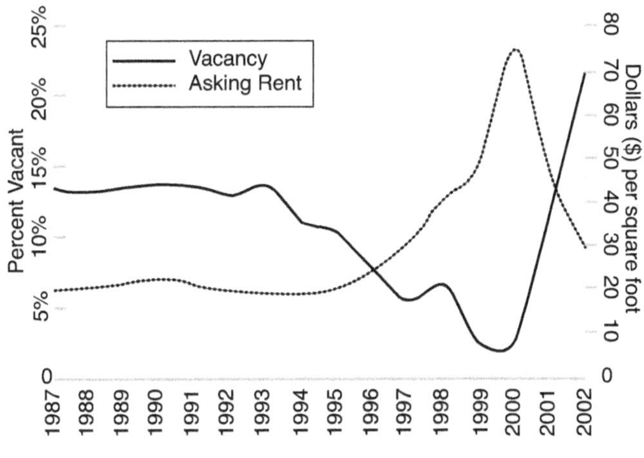

Figure 5.3 San Francisco office vacancies vs. rents, 1987–2002. Source: San Francisco Planning Department (after Olsen 2004).

1993 (Beitel 2003). House price rises also accelerated. The median price of a home in the Bay Area rose from US$215,000 in 1995 to US$364,000 in 2000, jumping 20 percent at the peak of the bubble in 2000. By 2002, Bay Area housing was almost three times the national average, that is, the median house sold for over US$400,000, compared with a California median of US$260,000 and a national standard of US$144,000 (Zito 2002). In 1999 the West Bay (Silicon Valley to Marin) had eight towns with median house prices higher than in Beverly Hills and Malibu.[8] Why such absurd prices? On the commercial side, the Bay Area was generating new companies by the score in the boom and filling their coffers with easy money. Office rents tracked the NASDAQ very closely throughout. As for residential real estate, the explanation is not that the Bay Area is short of land. Most important, the region is filthy rich, boasting the highest per capita income and wealth in the country over most of the last generation (Walker *et al.* 1990). Second, the Bay Area is saturated with finance capital, so mortgage loans are easy to obtain – and became easier in the bubble times (Zito 2002). Third, very fast growth creates a bottleneck effect in housing markets that squeezes prices upward.[9]

It is not easy to trace financial flows into the Bay Area for the purposes of mortgage lending and property development. Developers were raising fast money by turning themselves into real estate investment trusts (REITs), as the Bay Area became one of the largest centers of REITs in the country (Shilton *et al.* 1996). Other important sources of finance were insurance companies and pension funds, which also favored the region (Kaufman 1998, Rosen and Anderson 1999). The scale of property companies grew so fast that they came to be valued in the billions, and numbered among the largest real estate operators in the nation. Here again, the pipelines of capital investment and speculation had been opened wide.

Building blasters kick in

In every building cycle, rising prices and falling vacancies trigger new construction. Normally, there is a time lag of a year or two between price rises and new building projects as the time from conception to completion of any major commercial project is considerable, time needed to secure options on land, round up financing, draw up architectural plans, win city approval, and arrange for prospective tenants.

Because the Bay Area had become badly overbuilt in the last real estate cycle, peaking in the mid-1980s, there was lots of underused space to absorb before the full force of the price wave could be felt. In Silicon Valley, for example, some 30 million square feet of industrial and R&D space remained vacant in 1990, 18 percent of its total of 169 million square feet.[10] Moreover, new arenas of office space were opening up in the former industrial zones in SoMa, in Downtown San Jose, and over in Oakland because of intervening changes in the outlook of business, which had previously avoided such places like the plague.

But as the economic boom built up momentum, construction took off, creating millions of new square feet of commercial space around the region. San Francisco would add 10 million square feet of offices, an increase of about 16 percent. Silicon Valley would expand its supply of office space from 39 to 47 million square feet between 1990 and 2000, a jump of 20 percent, and its industrial/R&D space to 197 million square feet, an increase of 22 percent in a decade.[11]

Into the wide open spaces

The real estate bubble was punctured by the same shot that brought down the New Economy. Like venture capital and investment banking, it took the commercial real estate market a while to see the writing on the wall, so it levitated over the NASDAQ crash of spring 2000. Then reality hit realty in 2001. As companies withered on the vine, vacancy rates in commercial space vaulted upward and prices plunged. 'For Rent' signs sprouted like mushrooms on rotting logs. This was by far the worse disaster to befall San Francisco real estate since the Great Depression. Downtown office vacancies went from 4 to 16 percent in one year, and prices fell from US$78 to US$38 per square foot. Vacant class A office space remained at over 20 percent from 2002 to 2004, with a peak at around 24 percent.[12] Rents slumped badly, bottoming out at less than US$30 per square foot – more than a 60 percent drop from the 2000 peak – about where they stood in 1995 (in real terms). South of Market the carnage was worse: vacancies shot up from 10 to 46 percent and rents fell from US$67 to US$22 per square foot (D. Levy 2001); vacancies remained at nearly 40 per cent for the next three years (D. Levy 2002, 2003a,b, 2004).

Silicon Valley's plight was more severe than the city's. Commercial vacancies soared to almost 30 percent across Santa Clara and San Mateo counties (D. Levy 2003a). Prime office space in the Valley fell from US$70 per square foot to US$28,[13] while industrial/R&D space fell below U$5, and remained at these rates as late as 2005.[14] The wide open spaces are still easy to spot in the see-through buildings formerly occupied by thriving companies such as Excite@Home in Redwood City.

A paragon of New Economy excess was the international terminal at the San Francisco Airport (SFO) (Figure 5.4). During the boom, traffic at all three Bay Area airports grew rapidly, but none more so than SFO; passenger traffic was the fifth highest of any airport in the country. Flights became so numerous that delays threatened to overwhelm operations at peak hours. Airport planners, ever ahead of the curve, set their sights high and designed one of the grandest of international air terminals in existence. Finished in 2002, it boasted a vast canopied space 500 feet long, 100 feet high, and backed up by sweeping new freeway interchanges, two huge garages, an inter-terminal people mover, and a BART (Bay Area Rapid Transit) station. But air travel had collapsed – well before 9/11. For its first three years, the international terminal felt like a mausoleum – a suitable monument to the passing of the New Economy.[15]

Residential markets behaved more strangely. Apartment rents fell as expected in a business downturn. In March 2001, average rents peaked at US$1,628 for the central Bay Area and at US$1,956 in Silicon Valley, then both began to sag downward with the departure of hordes of dot-commers and their fast bucks. By 2002, San Francisco rents had fallen 12 percent and those in Silicon Valley by 18 percent; by 2003, they were down 18 and 34 percent respectively; and both stayed flat through 2004 (Rosen and Bishop 2002, Zito 2003a,b, Liedtke 2005). House prices, on the other hand, never stopped booming, creating a secondary boom and bubble in the midst of recession.[16]

Reconfiguring the urban landscape

The face of the city bears the scars of every epoch of capitalist development. Urban space is created according to the technologies, tastes, and profit calculus of every generation, then reworked into new configurations as the social order

Figure 5.4 International terminal at the San Francisco airport in 2004.

changes. One era is layered onto the next, like an artist building up the oil paint on a canvas into new forms, colors, and textures. Only the process is less clearly thought out or harmonious than that. Instead, greed, conflict, and political maneuvering intrude to shape the city into a collective product that no one person can ever quite get a grip on (Harvey 1985, 2003). The bubble by the bay put its mark all over the urban landscape, with the greatest impact on the inner cities of San Francisco and San Jose. Although every business cycle does its work on the city, this one was more dramatic than most. As Solnit and Schwartzenberg (2000: 34) put it, "... the earthquake that has come at the millennium has been a temblor of capital and its unstable distribution, altering San Francisco more than could almost any natural disaster."

Lofty spaces of San Francisco

San Francisco's landscape was thoroughly reworked by the bubble. The dot.com boom was centered in the SoMa area, achieving at a stroke what had been fought over for fifty years: expanding downtown deep into territory along the southern waterfront and around Mission Bay once held by industry and the working class (Hartman 1984, Walker 1998). The bubble economy unleashed a kind of urban bulldozer by means of financial speculation rather than the state, leaving the SoMa district radically transformed and the Mission district on the verge of wholesale displacement. There were several dimensions to how this urban renewal by market means played out. The first element in the transformation of SoMa was the conversion of warehouses and industrial space into dot-com offices. This began at the foot of the Bay Bridge on Rincon Hill around South Park, the techies' favorite meeting spot, and continued all the way out through the Inner Mission, the city's principal Latino district. The last vestiges of manufacturing were swept aside, along with artist spaces, non-profits, and relict bars. By the time the bubble burst, the tide of conversions had washed up all the way to the heart of the Mission Street commercial district (Cohen 1998, Solnit and Schwartzenberg 2000, Beitel 2003).

The second facet of SoMa's makeover was the quick build-out of residential lofts, or live/work units (Figure 5.5). Lofts began as an alternative space for artists and bohemians in former industrial districts, for which city planners had been willing to allow variances from housing standards. But then the hip ran smack into the hop in the real estate market and a crowd of young dot-commers with lots of cash to spend on nifty digs close to work. Add to the mix the political pop of the developers, who saw live–work lofts as a fantastic way to build quickly and profitably, and hundreds of new buildings went up (Solnit and Schwartzenberg 2000, Beitel 2003, Olsen 2004). A third aspect of the reworking of SoMa was the high-rise explosion on its eastern flank, east of Third Street. This part of the city has been converted into a little Sao Paolo with a radically transformed skyline of office and apartment towers. Here, the old city's landscape has not just been made over, but virtually erased. This has been continued to the present because of unrelenting demand for housing, which is being met by high-rise apartments and condominiums (King 2004).

Figure 5.5 SoMa loft.

Meanwhile, the residential neighborhoods of the Mission district, packed into mid-rise Victorian houses and flats, felt the heat of gentrification in the late 1990s. Dot-com adventurers were seeking out homes near their warehouse workplaces and the trendy clubs and restaurants sprouting along Valencia Street. Tenant expulsions for wholesale building conversions were rampant. Simultaneously, many locals were losing their jobs as warehouse conversions eliminated blue-collar manufacturing jobs and social service agencies (Godfrey 1997, Solnit and Schwartzenberg 2000, Beitel 2003). The last piece of the conversion puzzle was to clear the way for the gigantic Mission Bay project on the southern flank of SoMa, on eighty acres of former Southern Pacific rail yards. This is by far the biggest new land development in the city in fifty years. Once too far from downtown to feel connected, Mission Bay is now accessible by a new light rail system and just a shout away from the lofts of SoMa. The key to winning approval was to anchor the project with a University of California San Francisco Medical School research campus. The hope is that this will attract biotechnology firms (Beitel 2003, King 2004, Olsen 2004). Thus is the ground prepared for the next New Thing.

Not that all this is bad. Downtown San Francisco is quite small by the standards of world cities and the new SoMa developments have added a surprisingly vigorous new layer of density and high style to the urban core. The lofts and warehouse makeovers of the late 1990s often feature techno-modern designs, combined with a good deal of eclectic retro elements (Lloyd 1997, Sardar 2000, Johns 2004). These can be quite good because of the money available to pay for first-class architects. Similarly, some of the high-rise offices are better than the post-modern edifices of the 1980s because they are fitted out in modernist revival glass and metal exoskeletons (King 2004). San Francisco's dowdy reputation in design has undergone a retrofit, as Silicon Valley futurism overtook classically conservative San Francisco tastes in architecture.

On the other hand, the triumphant march of gentrification through SoMa and into the Mission District did a lot of permanent damage to San Francisco's subcultures in the arts, politics, and immigrant life, replacing it with a shallower cult of techno-capitalism. Beitel (2003: 172) captures the defects of the new city of what the locals derisively called "the silicon implants":

> [The] recasting of entrepreneurialism as a type of transgressive practice … reach[ed] its extremes in the fantasies of a self-styled avant garde of anarcho-capitalists … [in which] the central city is (re)presented and imagined as a site within which these new impulses are circulated through a dense network linked by microchips, high speed digital connections, and rapidly formed partnerships perpetually dissolved in a fluid flux of change and transition. The semiotics of "industrial chic" pervades the living and work environments of SF's digital economy through which the industrial wasteland is reappropriated as a playground for entrepreneurial capital and the techno-salariat … [where] the techno-gentry dines and cuts business deals surrounded by the stylistic chic of the digital cutting edge – polished galvanized pipes suspended from the high wooden beam ceiling, [and other refurbished bits of machinofacture] compose the space within which the "New Economy" is reproduced.

Fortunately, the cultural and ethnic cleansing of the area was not as thorough as many people feared at the height of the bubble. It was cut short by the puncturing of the New Economy bubble. Civic life, like a ravaged forest, proved to be more resilient than expected and with a surprising capacity for recuperation.

A capital city for high-tech

In a remarkable reversal of the historic pattern of metropolitan dominance, San Francisco lost its place atop the urban hierarchy to San Jose and Silicon Valley during the bubble years. During the recessions of the early 1980s and 1990s, the old-line corporate powerhouses of San Francisco fell like redwoods before the ax, leaving only a couple of megaliths such as Chevron and Bechtel still standing (Walker *et al.* 1990). Meanwhile, electronics companies from the South Bay littered the Fortune 500 list. San Francisco lost virtually its entire manufacturing base, while Santa Clara County held the most intensive concentration of manufacturing in the country (Bay Area Economic Forum 1996, 1999). In the 2000 census, San Jose counted 900,000 souls and San Francisco only 775,000. The US Census Bureau recently designated the region as, officially, the *San Jose*–San Francisco–Oakland Consolidated Metropolitan Statistical Area.

The New Economy building boom had a dramatic effect on Silicon Valley, although the vast spaces of the South Bay disperse the impact compared with compact San Francisco. The most pervasive effect of high land values in a growing city is densification, and Silicon Valley is no exception. The Santa Clara Valley is no longer the suburban sprawl of our imaginations. It is home to a true city, and a dense one by American standards. By the 2000 census San Jose Metro had become the third densest urban area in the USA, after – surprise, surprise! – Los Angeles and San Francisco–Oakland.[17] What this means is that the New

York metropolitan region is more sprawling today than either LA or the Bay Area – quite the reverse of expectations.

To accommodate the Valley's tremendous growth it has been necessary to build upward. This shows up in hundreds of mid-rise housing complexes, especially along the major transportation corridors. The number of apartment, condominium, and townhouse units in San Jose passed 50 percent by 2000, compared with less than 30 percent in 1970.[18] Some of the new developments offer spectacular new urbanist concoctions that mix residential, office, and retail space, as in the Santana Village complex in San Jose (Calthorpe and Fulton 2001). Almost every town center in the Valley, long neglected as farm towns were transformed into suburbs, has been rebuilt to attract residents and shoppers, and infuse a bit of urban life into the sterile suburban landscapes.

The boom put a new face on the electronics industry, as high-tech companies started using their immense wealth to project an image of corporate stature. High-rise headquarters began to appear in the 1980s and became the norm in the 1990s, replacing the low-rise, slap-up look of the previous generation for which the Valley was notorious (Banham 1980). As a result, architecture took a turn for the better. This can be seen in the comely designs of corporate headquarters and office complexes. Some of the newer buildings have even been designed by name architects (although Silicon Valley remains largely a no-man's land of design fame). Even in speculative buildings, architecture improved. While these are still suburban high-rises rather than city skyscrapers, they measure up favorably as exercises in post-modern and techno-modern styling, thick with colored glass, metallic sheathing, and curved surfaces.

The most astonishing transformation of the landscape of Silicon Valley in the 1990s was the vast makeover of downtown San Jose. Long the country cousin to San Francisco – and eclipsed even by Palo Alto and Stanford as the key center of the Valley – San Jose began parading itself as "the capital of Silicon Valley" in the 1980s. It has never quite achieved this lofty goal, but it did make a stunning bid for the honors by recreating itself as few American downtowns have. A redevelopment program was put in place to tear down and rebuild the city's derelict downtown. It got off the ground in the boom of the 1980s, and came to fruition a decade later. Downtown San Jose now sports a bevy of gleaming new skyscrapers and civic buildings. All this has been paid for (or leveraged by) the richest redevelopment agency in California, using tax revenues drawn from the vast electronics belt cutting across north San Jose. More than US$1.5 billion has been siphoned from the industrial lands to the downtown over twenty years (Rhee 2006). Downtown San Jose now has 9 million square feet of office space.

In short, the Bay Area's urban landscape was in violent upheaval through the 1990s as a result of the New Economy boom and financial bubble. Real estate values shot up, and so did new buildings, at a markedly higher density than before. This came at a real cost in displacement of people and disarray in cultural life. The great urban beast arose and shook off many a poor soul like so many fleas. By the time it settled down again, the region would never be the same.

The rubble of the bubble

The aftermath of the boom and the bubble has done more than left the Bay Area geographically reconfigured. It has meant serious unemployment, dislocation, and despair among workers. It threw the state of California into fiscal chaos at all levels of government. It stilled the sirens of the New Economy. And it served as midwife to a political upheaval that has captured worldwide attention.

Economic hangover

The Bay Area economy has taken a tremendous beating since 2000. Markets dried up as corporate America (and Asia) cut back on purchases of electronic equipment. Companies have bled red ink until they have shrunk to shadows of their former bloated selves. Hints of recovery in 2002 proved ephemeral, and the downward spiral took off again with a vengeance in early 2003. Massive layoffs came in the wake of the passing financial tidal wave as high-tech corporations sought to stave off the grim reaper. In the Valley (San Jose metropolitan area) 176,000 jobs vaporized from the peak of 1,035,000 at the end of 2000 to the bottom of the slump in fall 2003, or over one-sixth of the total; in San Francisco metropolitan area (San Francisco plus San Mateo and Marin Counties) the loss was 129,000 out of 1,085,000, or 12 percent. The East Bay (Oakland metropolitan area) was less hard-hit because it is the least dependent on electronics. The total job loss amounted to 322,000 around the Bay Area on a base of 3,540,000, or 9.1 percent of all jobs. The jobless rate in Silicon Valley hovered in the 7–8 percent range for three years; in San Francisco it was around 5 percent, despite the departure of tens of thousands of dot-commers (no precise figure exists on the outflow).[19]

In terms of geographic impact, the Bay Area truly reaped the whirlwind. Its job loss represents an astonishingly high proportion of all layoffs in the USA during the 2000–03 recession, the area accounting for 322,000 out of a total of 2.45 million jobs lost nationally (Figure 5.6). That means the Bay Area, with less than 3 percent of the national population, suffered 13 percent, or one-seventh, of the nation's job loss. This ought to go down in the annals of economic geography, along with the shriveling of Detroit in the early 1980s and the burning of recession-torn Los Angeles in 1992, as a recent urban disaster born of a major recession.[20] Figure 5.6 shows that unemployment in Silicon Valley reached a much higher level than in either California or the USA.

The secondary effects of the drying up of electronics have been quite stark. Retailing has been socked, from Stanford Shopping Center to Union Square in San Francisco. The Gap, retailing's second biggest success story in the 1990s after Wal-Mart, took a three-year dive. One of San Francisco's biggest law firms, Brobeck, Phleger and Harrison, with 500 attorneys focused on electronics and high-tech investment, declared bankruptcy. Talk of the New Economy has been stifled as such vocal advocates as *Red Herring* and *The Industry Standard* have disappeared from the internet. On the other hand, homelessness surged, leaving upwards of 20,000 people on the streets in San Francisco, Oakland, Berkeley, and San Jose combined. They are still being swept off the streets, this human rubble of the bubble.

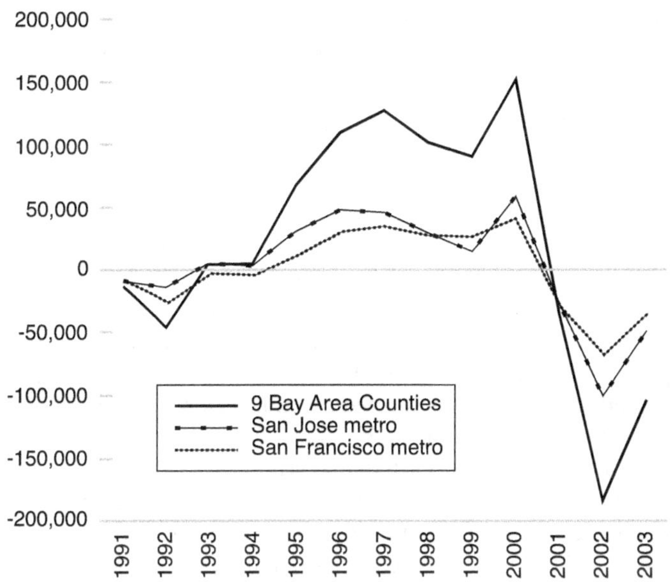

Figure 5.6 Annual employment change in the Bay Area, 1991–2003. Source: State of California Employment Development Department.

Faustian politics

The boom and bust of the turn of the millennium shook Bay Area politics to its roots. The high times gave rein to the lustiest of pro-development politicians and their cronies, while the subsequent economic earthquake left more than a few cracks in the edifice of the state. Through those weakened walls have passed those with the ruthless political ambition to steal in and grab the keys to the vault. Locally, the boom was seized upon by Mayor Willie Brown of San Francisco, and other like-minded politicians, as a means of aggrandizing their careers. There's nothing truer to American local politics than vigorous promotion of business and land development (Logan and Molotch 1986) and so they made lusty concourse with the New Economy and its financiers and real estate schemes. They eagerly greased the wheels of planning boards and other government agencies, allowing a great deal of slippery dealing to enrich business, developers, and their campaign funds, and left a tainted legacy for both.

Willie Brown is the former Speaker of the Assembly, and the most powerful politician in Sacramento during the 1980s. Some say that terms limits were passed expressly to end his tenure (Clucas 1995, Richardson 1996). So, in 1995, Brown ran for Mayor, serving two terms. Brown had a liberal reputation in the state, but by San Francisco standards he is a business Democrat (Walker *et al.* 1990). He cobbled together an alliance of downtown and Pacific Heights capital with African-Americans at the forgotten south edge of the city, plus the ambitious new money of Chinese San Francisco. He kept the labor movement quiet by granting living wages to city employees and wooing the building trades into his pro-development alliance. And he put his muscle behind real estate developers in the beefy alliance with the Residential Builders' Association. Brown installed a pro-development Planning Commission that rubber-stamped all the warehouse conversions and loft projects developers could muster in the boom times. He was able to sell the new baseball park to the voters and to follow that with voter approval of the Mission Bay scheme, after two failed efforts in the 1980s (Blackwell 2000, Beitel 2003, Brahinsky 2004).

The political machinations of the bubble period triggered a popular response of impressive proportions in San Francisco. Many on the left had worried that steadily rising rents had driven all but the leftovers of the counterculture and the political activists out of the city. But the artists, Mission Latinos, and others put up a surprisingly fierce fight against the dot-coms, lofts, and developers. As the warehouse and loft conversions washed up on the shores of the Mission District, it created solid opposition from a still vibrant working-class and immigrant area (Blackwell 2000, Beitel 2003, Carlsson 2004).

Willie Brown's regime took the brunt of the anger. This figures, since Brown showed not the least compassion for displaced tenants in the Mission and nearby neighborhoods where he had twice been outgunned for votes by his mayoral opponent, gay Supervisor Tom Ammiano. In a remarkable election at the end of 2000, neighborhood activists and leftists won seven out of eight Supervisoral seats in San Francisco and dealt Brown a political defeat the likes of which he had never experienced in his brilliant, charmed career. The city lurched dramatically to the left (Beitel 2003, Carlsson 2004). The powers-that-be bounced back, however. They began grooming young, photogenic Supervisor Gavin Newsom as Brown's successor. Newsom is well connected to Pacific Heights wealth and is an up and coming entrepreneur in his own right. Newsom found his headline-grabbing issue with a campaign to eliminate city handouts to the homeless, in a ballot measure deftly entitled "Care Not Cash," because the human rubbish accumulating in the streets was scaring off tourists and shoppers. Newsom was elected in fall 2003, though not without a scare from a polyglot assemblage of the left, headed by equally young, smart, and charismatic Supervisor Matt Gonzales. Not surprisingly, Newsom outspent Gonzales 10 to 1 to earn his narrow victory (Carlsson 2004).

In comes the smiling terminator

The biggest political news from California in recent years was the recall of Governor Gray Davis and election of Arnold Schwarzenegger in October 2003. The presence of Arnold, star of *The Terminator* series and other violent revenge and humiliation flicks, captured the attention of the world. His victory was a *coup d'état* of surpassing brilliance and bloodless efficiency.

The state Republican Party had been in the doldrums since Davis's election in 1998. It had lost a big portion of the immigrant vote because of Governor Pete Wilson's attempt to blame immigrants for California's fiscal crisis of the early 1990s (Walker 1995). The legislature was still firmly in Democratic Party hands.

George Bush lost the state decisively in 2000. But the bursting bubble-by-the-Bay made Davis and the Democrats suddenly vulnerable. The state of California was broke, with a staggering 2003–04 budget deficit of US$25–35 billion (out of US$100 billion). California's deficit was larger than that of all the other states put together. To cover the shortfall, Davis was proposing to cut US$8 billion from expenditures, raise US$5 billion by taxes on car registrations, and borrow US$16 billion short term on the bond markets. In the face of this disaster, the Republicans argued that irresponsible spending was responsible for the deficit and, moreover, Democrats were going to close the gap on the backs of the citizenry by raising taxes.

The real reason for the deficit was not overspending but the precipitous collapse of revenues (Rosen *et al.* 2003). A huge part of the increase in state income in the late 1990s was derived from capital gains taxes, which had ballooned on all the paper stock wealth generated during the bubble. Those taxes had become vital to paying the state's bills for education, health, and infrastructure because Californians have been living in a neoliberal fantasy world for twenty-five years of declining tax effort (California Tax Reform Association 2005). To make matters worse, the legislature – backed solidly by mainstream business opinion – took the view that the New Economy was permanent, and its revenues could be put to use without worry.

The Republicans hit upon the recall to unseat Davis, an obscure law that had been on the books since 1911 but never before employed. California's is an exceedingly facile recall system that allows for no major malfeasance in office and a petition by a small proportion of the voters. The petition drive for the recall was paid for out of the personal fortune of Darryl Issa, a man made rich selling car alarms. Republicans filled up their campaign coffers with millions of dollars and started drawing up lists of candidates. Schwarzenegger was not the obvious choice for governor. But it soon became apparent that his star-power and personal

Figure 5.7 The New Economy Cleaners, Berkeley, CA, in 2004.

charm made him an ideal candidate. He had the further asset of being a Hollywood libertine, in a state where reactionary Christian values do not carry much weight. Arnold was helped immeasurably by the dull response of Davis. The governor was a classic New Democratic: a big fund-raiser weighing political payoffs to the fraction. He was utterly mute about issues of importance to an electorate suffering great strain in the face of the state's economic and fiscal meltdown. So in walked the smiling terminator, who swiftly put in place a pro-business agenda – making the budget deficit worse by rescinding the car registration tax. The Bay Area, to its credit, opposed the rest of the state on the recall and voted against Schwarzenegger.

Truly, California has been taken to the cleaners, in this case the New Economy Cleaners – which is just down the road from my home in Berkeley (Figure 5.7). Here is a business that is willing to partake of the ideological fervor without forgetting first principles. It has outlived both the Davis administration and the dot-coms because it has a sound basis in the old economy and provides people with a real service.

Notes

1 Gordon (2000) calculates that virtually all the productivity gains of the late 1990s were concentrated in the computer sector.
2 As Lowenstein (2004: 17) says "Silicon Valley made stock options especially fashionable." When the Securities and Exchange Commission tried to crack down on options in 1993, John Doerr led the Valley's successful lobbying effort to hold them at bay (ibid: 44).
3 Despite the economic crash, the Bay Area had added one billionaire to register forty-four of the Forbes 400 in 2004, putting it ahead of New York and Los Angeles. San Francisco still runs neck and neck with the Valley in the number of super-rich.
4 The percentage had been even higher in the 1980s, nearly 50 percent.
5 At its peak, the NASDAQ's stock traded at an average of ninety times earnings, compared with a peak of eighty times on the Nikkei just before it crashed in 1989 (Ingebretsen 2002: 219). By 2002, the NASDAQ had become biggest US stock exchange in trading volume.
6 Most observers have noted the significance of international capital flows in the great NYSE stock run-up of the 1990s, when around 25 percent of the funds supporting the bubble came from abroad (Brenner 2002, Pollin 2003). Data are readily available at the national level, but not the regional.
7 The catastrophic losses of 2001 are somewhat misleading in that they include some enormous write-offs of bogus gains of the late 1990s, when profits were already falling but the fact was being covered up. In fact, US manufacturing profits had been falling sharply since 1997 (Brenner 2004) and Silicon Valley had been generating more and more profitless start-ups (Sylvester 2002). By the end of 2001, US manufacturing profits were down to one-third from 1997 and computer equipment profits down by 80 percent (Brenner 2004).
8 Based on data from California Association of Realtors.
9 Because housing turnover is relatively low, prices are leveraged higher than they would be in a perfect market, rather like oil in a time of panic buying.
10 Based on data from Colliers International real estate reports.
11 Data from Urban Land Institute and courtesy of Colliers International's San Jose office.

12 This compares with a national average office vacancy rate of 17 percent (Bardhan and Kroll 2003). By no means was the real estate bubble and crash confined to the Bay Area. But it was worse here than anywhere else, as had been the case in Los Angeles in the late 1980s and in Houston before that.
13 Data courtesy of Grubb & Ellis solicitors.
14 Data courtesy of Colliers International's San Jose office.
15 Airport managers also wanted more runways and proposed a doubling of the tarmacs, by filling the bay. This plan has been on hold since the bubble burst, but will be back. It is fiercely opposed by environmentalists.
16 House prices have continued to rise, in large part because of the most drastic reduction in interest rates since the Great Depression. Home buyers can afford much more as their monthly payments fall markedly. This is quite a general phenomenon nationally (Brenner 2004). In the Bay Area, the rise in house values has actually been slower than in many cities since 2000, but still esceeded all other metro areas, surpassing US$600,000 in 2005. But two things have added to the increase in prices. The upper classes were pulling their considerable savings out of stocks and putting them into bigger homes. At the same time, many middle market purchasers panicked as they saw this as their last chance to sneak into a starter home under the half-million mark (soon to be a distant memory).
17 Based on census data for "urbanized areas" (metropolitan areas minus open space). Tables can be found at www.demographia.com.
18 City and county data. In fact, multiples have outrun single-family houses in most years since the late 1960s.
19 Employment figures were repeatedly readjusted downward during the long fall, which was the worst since the Great Depression and proportionately a good deal worse than the horrendous job shrinkage in Los Angeles in the early 1990s.
20 Employment remained stagnant through 2004 (Armstrong 2004) and was worsened by the eagerness of electronic capitalists to offshore work to cut labor costs (Bardhan and Kroll 2003).

References

Abate, T. (2004) 'Recovery moves in fits, starts', *San Francisco Chronicle*, November 14.

Armstrong, D. (2004) 'Few new jobs in weak recovery', *San Francisco Chronicle*, 10 July.

Banham, R. (1980) 'The architecture of Silicon Valley', *New West*, September 22.

Bardhan, A. and Kroll, C. (2003) 'A New Wave of Outsourcing', Research Report no. 1103, Berkeley, CA: Fisher Center for Real Estate and Urban Research, Haas Business School, University of California.

Bay Area Economic Forum (1996) *The Bay Area: Leading the Transition to a Knowledge Based Economy*, San Francisco: Bay Area Economic Forum.

Bay Area Economic Forum (1999) *The Bay Area: Winning in the Global Economy*, San Francisco: Bay Area Economic Forum.

Beitel, K. (2003) 'Community and capital in the era of globalization: the case of San Francisco, 1956–2001', unpublished thesis, University of California.

Benner, C., Brownstein, B. and Dean, A. (1999) *Walking the Lifelong Tightrope: Negotiating Work in the New Economy*, San Jose: Working Partnerships and Economic Policy Institute.

Blackwell, S. (2000) 'The battle for San Francisco', *San Francisco Bay Guardian*, October 18.

Brahinsky, R. (2004) 'The great housing hoax', *San Francisco Bay Guardian*, February 11.

Brenner, R. (2002) *The Boom and The Bubble: The US in the World Economy*, London: Verso.

Brenner, R. (2004) 'New boom or new bubble? The trajectory of the US economy', *New Left Review*, 25: 57–100.

Bresnahan, T. and Gambardella, A. (eds.) (2004) *Building High-Tech Clusters: Silicon Valley and Beyond*, Cambridge: Cambridge University Press.

Bronson, P. (1999) *The Nudist on the Late Shift, and Other Tales of Silicon Valley*, New York: Random House.

Caddes, C. (1986) *Portraits of Success: Impressions of Silicon Valley Pioneers*, Palo Alto, CA: Tioga Publishing Company.

California Tax Reform Association (2005) *Tax Policy for the 21st Century: Resolving California's Long Term Structural Deficit*, Sacramento: CTRA.

Calthorpe, P. and Fulton, W. (2001) *The Regional City: Planning for the End of Sprawl*, Washington, DC: Island Press.

Carlsson, C. (ed.) (2004) *San Francisco: The Political Edge*, San Francisco: City Lights.

Castells, M. (1996) *The Rise of the Network Society*, Malden, MA: Blackwell Publishers.

Clucas, R. (1995) *The Speaker's Electoral Connection: Willie Brown and the California Assembly*, Berkeley, CA: Institute of Governmental Studies, University of California.

Cohen, P. (1998) 'Transformation in an industrial landscape: San Francisco's Northeast Mission', unpublished thesis, San Francisco State University.

Cox, K. (ed.) (1997) *Spaces of Globalization: Reasserting the Power of the Local*, New York: Guilford Press.

Davidow, W. and Malone, M. (1992) *The Virtual Corporation: Structuring and Revitalizing the Corporation for the 21st Century*, New York: HarperCollins.

Dedrick, J. and Kraemer, K. (1998) *Asia's Computer Challenge: Threat or Opportunity for the United States and the World?*, New York: Oxford University Press.

Emert, C. (2001) 'Venture-capital bubble bursts in 2001', *San Francisco Chronicle*, May 3.

Florida, R. (2002) *The Rise of the Creative Class*, New York: Basic Books.

Florida, R. and Kenney, M. (1988) 'Venture capital, high technology and regional development', *Regional Studies*, 22: 33–48.

Fost, D. (2003) 'Top firms lose $409 billion in market capitalization', *San Francisco Chronicle*, May 5.

Frank, T. and Mulcahey, D. (eds.) (2003) *Boob Jubilee: The Cultural Politics of the New Economy*, Chicago: W.W. Norton.

Freiberger, P. and Swaine, M. (1984) *Fire in the Valley: The Making of the Personal Computer*, Berkeley, CA: Osborne; and New York: McGraw-Hill.

Godfrey, B. (1997) 'Urban development and redevelopment in San Francisco', *Geographical Review*, 87: 309–33.

Gordon, R. (2000) 'Does the New Economy measure up to the great inventions of the past?', *Journal of Economic Perspectives*, 14: 49–74.

Greenwich, H. and Niedt, C. (2001) *Decade of Divide: Working, Wages and Inequality in the East Bay*, Oakland, CA: East Bay Alliance for a Sustainable Economy.

Hanson, D. (1982) *The New Alchemists: Silicon Valley and the Microelectronics Revolution*, Boston: Little Brown.

Hartman, C. (1984) *The Transformation of San Francisco*, Totowa, NJ: Rowman and Allenheld.

Harvey, D. (1982) *The Limits to Capital*, Oxford: Blackwell Publishers.

Harvey, D. (1985) *The Urbanization of Capital*, Baltimore: Johns Hopkins University Press.

Harvey, D. (2003) *Paris, The Capital of Modernity*, London: Routledge.

Henwood, D. (2003) *After the New Economy*, New York: The New Press.

Hua, V. (2000) 'Bay Area led pack in IPOs in 1999', *San Francisco Examiner*, May 1.

Ingebretsen, M. (2002) *NASDAQ: A History of the Market that Changed the World*, Roseville, CA: Forum.

Johns, M. (2004) 'Urban retro', *New York Times*, January 4.

Kador, J. (2002) *Charles Schwab: How One Company Beat Wall Street and Reinvented the Brokerage Industry*, Hoboken: John Wiley & Sons.

Kaufman, S. (1998) 'Prime real estate trust', *San Jose Mercury*, April 12.

Kenney, M. (ed.) (2000) *Understanding Silicon Valley: The Anatomy of an Entrepreneurial Region*, Stanford, CA: Stanford University Press.

Kenney, M. and Florida, R. (2000) 'Venture capital in Silicon Valley: fueling new firm formation', in Kenney, M. (ed.) *Understanding Silicon Valley*, Stanford, CA: Stanford University Press.

King, J. (2004) '15 seconds that changed San Francisco: the sweeping makeover that transformed the city began 15 years ago today with the Loma Prieta earthquake', *San Francisco Chronicle*, October 17–22.

Kirby, C. (2000) 'Dot-Com downfall takes new victims', *San Francisco Chronicle*, October 3.

Ledbetter, J. (2003) *Starving to Death on $200 Million a Year: The Short, Absurd Life of the Industry Standard*, New York: Public Affairs.

Levy, D. (2001) 'Office boom goes bust: Bay Area commercial rents suffer record slide and vacancies soar to new heights', *San Francisco Chronicle*, December 28.

Levy, D. (2002) 'The big slide', *San Francisco Chronicle*, January 18.

Levy, D. (2003a) 'SF commercial rents fall: vacancy rates rise to record high with no relief in sight', *San Francisco Chronicle*, April 2.

Levy, D. (2003b) 'Empty hallways: SF commercial real estate at low ebb', *San Francisco Chronicle*, July 3.

Levy, D. (2004) 'Prime offices sit empty', *San Francisco Chronicle*, May 7.

Levy, S. (1984) *Hackers: Heroes of the Computer Revolution*, New York: Anchor/Doubleday.

Lewis, M. (2000) *The New New Thing: A Silicon Valley Story*, Chicago: Norton.

Liedtke, M. (2001) 'Tech firms' $2 trillion paper loss', *San Francisco Chronicle*, August 13.

Liedtke, M. (2005) 'Apartment rents hold steady in the Bay Area', *San Francisco Chronicle*, January 20.

Lloyd, P. (1997) *San Francisco: A Guide to Recent Architecture*, London: Ellipsis.

Logan, J. and Molotch, H. (1986) *Urban Fortunes: The Political Economy of Place*, Berkeley, CA: University of California Press.

Lowenstein, R. (2004) *The Origins of the Crash: The Great Bubble and Its Undoing*, London: Penguin.

McKendrick, D., Doner, R. and Haggard, S. (2000) *From Silicon Valley to Singapore: Location and Competitive Advantage in the Hard Disk Drive Industry*, Stanford, CA: Stanford University Press.

Massey, D., Quintas, P. and Wield, D. (1992) *High-Tech Fantasies: Science Parks in Society, Science and Space*, London: Routledge.

Micklethwait, J. (1997) 'The valley of the money's delight', *The Economist*, March 29.

Miles, S. (2001) *How to Hack a Party Line: The Democrats and Silicon Valley* (revised edition), Berkeley: University of California Press.

Minton, T. (2001) 'IPOs raised a fortune but most plummeted', *San Francisco Chronicle*, May 6.

Morrissey, J. (2001) 'SF, Silicon Valley in office cost top 10', *San Francisco Chronicle*, February 14.

Nye, D. (1994) *American Technological Sublime*, Cambridge: MIT Press.

Olsen, A. (2004) *Boom, Bust and Land-Use Planning in San Francisco*, Copenhagen: Geografisk Institute, University of Copenhagen.

Packard, D. (1995) *The HP Way*, New York: Harper Business Books.

Patton, D. and Kenney, M. (2005) 'The spatial configuration of the entrepreneurial support network for the semiconductor industry', *R&D Management* (in press).

Perkins, A. and Perkins, M. (1999) *The Internet Bubble*, New York: Harper Business Books.

Peters, T. (1992) *Liberation Management: Necessary Disorganization for the Nanosecond Nineties*, New York: Knopf.

Peters, T. and Waterman, R. (1985) *In Search of Excellence: Lessons from America's Best-Run Companies*, New York: Harper and Row.

Pollin, R. (2003) *Contours of Descent: U.S. Economic Fractures and the Landscape of Global Austerity*, London: Verso Books.

Rhee, N. (2006) 'Searching for working class politics: labor, community and urban power in Silicon Valley', forthcoming unpublished thesis, University of California, Berkeley.

Richardson, J. (1996) *Willie Brown: A Biography*, Berkeley, CA: University of California Press.

Rogers, E. and Larsen, J. (1984) *Silicon Valley Fever*, New York: Basic Books.

Rosen, K. and Anderson, M. (1999) 'Equity REIT strategies', *Wharton Real Estate Review*, 3: 1–13.

Rosen, K. and Bishop, A. (2002) 'The San Francisco area apartment market: a renters market', Working Paper no. 281, Fisher Center for Real Estate and Urban Economics, University of California, Berkeley.

Rosen, K., Van Dyke, D. and Beller, E. (2003) 'Anatomy of the California fiscal crisis: facts and figures do matter?', Working Paper no. 287, Fisher Center for Real Estate and Urban Economics, University of California, Berkeley.

Saracevic, A. (2000) 'Fallout.Com: economy comes down with the dot com flu', *San Francisco Chronicle*, December 10.

Sardar, Z. (2000) *San Francisco Modern*, San Francisco: Chronicle Books.

Saxenian, A. (1994) *Regional Advantage: Culture and Competition in Silicon Valley and Route 128*, Cambridge, MA: Harvard University Press.

Saxenian, A. (2002) *Local and Global Networks of Immigrant Professionals in Silicon Valley*, San Francisco: Public Policy Institute of California.

Saxenian, A. and Hsu, J.-Y. (2001) 'Transnational communities and industrial upgrading: The Silicon Valley–Hsinchu connection', *Industrial and Corporate Change*, 10: 893–920.

Schiller, R.J. (2000) *Irrational Exuberance*, Princeton, NJ: Princeton University Press.

Seligman, K. (2000) 'Dot-coms dominate space in SoMa', *San Francisco Examiner*, March 26.

Shilton, L., Stanley, C., Tandy, J. (1996) 'The top thirty counties of institutionally owned real estate', *Real Estate Review*, 25: 54–60.

Shinal, J. (2003) 'VC firms endure changing times', *San Francisco Chronicle*, September 7.

Sinton, P. (2000) 'Torrential flow of venture money', *San Francisco Chronicle*, May 10.

Solnit, R. and Schwartzenberg, S. (2000) *Hollow City: Gentrification and the Eviction of Urban Culture*, London: Verso Press.

Storper, M. (1997) *The Regional World*, New York: Guilford Press.

Sturgeon, T. (2006) 'What really goes on in Silicon Valley? Spatial clustering and dispersal in modular production networks', *Journal of Economic Geography* (in press).

Sylvester, D. (2002) 'Survey reveals staggering tech plunge: year's losses exceeded eight years of profits', *San Jose Mercury News*, April 14.

Walker, R. (1995) 'California rages against the dying of the light', *New Left Review*, 209: 42–74.

Walker, R. (1998) 'An appetite for the city', in Brook, J., Carlsson, C. and Peters, N. (eds.) *Reclaiming San Francisco: History, Politics and Culture*, San Francisco: City Lights Books.

Walker, R. and the Bay Area Study Group (1990) 'The playground of US capitalism? The political economy of the San Francisco Bay Area in the 1980s', in Davis, M., Hiatt, S., Kennedy, M., Ruddick, S. and Sprinker, M. (eds.) *Fire in the Hearth: The Radical Politics of Place in America*, London: Verso/Haymarket.

Wilson, M. (1997) *The Difference Between God and Larry Ellison*, New York: William Morrow.

Zito, K. (2002) 'Expanding or ready to burst? Experts wonder if Bay Area home prices will continue to rise', *San Francisco Chronicle*, May 26.

Zito, K. (2003a) 'Bay Area apartment rents fall farther', *San Francisco Chronicle*, January 21.

Zito, K. (2003b) 'Bay Area renters relishing clout', *San Francisco Chronicle*, April 21.

Zook, M. (2000) 'The web of production: the economic geography of commercial internet content production in the United States', *Environment and Planning A*, 32: 411–26.

Zook, M. (2001) 'Old hierarchies or new networks of centrality? The global geography of the internet content market', *American Behavioral Scientist*, 44: 1679–96.

Zook, M. (2002) 'Grounded capital: venture financing and the geography of the internet industry, 1994–2000', *Journal of Economic Geography*, 2: 151–77.

Zook, M. (2004) 'The knowledge brokers: venture capitalists, tacit knowledge and regional development', *International Journal of Urban and Regional Research*, 28: 621–41.

6 The role of regional innovation systems in a globalising economy

Comparing knowledge bases and institutional frameworks of Nordic clusters

Bjørn T. Asheim and Lars Coenen

Introduction

Over the past two decades social scientists and policy-makers have been paying more and more attention to regions as designated sites of innovation and competitiveness in the globalising economy. The popularity of this argument can be traced back to various empirical studies of regional success stories, such as the rapid economic growth of networked small and medium-sized enterprises (SMEs) in industrial districts in the 'Third Italy' (Asheim 2000), the exemplar industrial system of Silicon Valley (Saxenian 1994) as well as other examples of successful regional clustering in most developed as well as developing economies (Porter 1990). These studies all draw on the common rationale that territorial agglomeration provides the best context for an innovation-based learning economy promoting localised learning and endogenous regional economic development (Asheim 2002).

In this discourse, two concepts belonging to the territorial innovation theory family (Moulaert and Sekia 2003) demonstrate particular resonance: clusters and regional innovation systems. Even though the two concepts are closely related, they should not be conflated. Therefore, we argue for an analytical distinction not the least against the background of a rising popularity of both concepts in policy and consultancy circles. It can, in fact, be observed that many regions have been treated with off-the-shelf, 'best-practice' cluster or regional innovation system solutions drawn 'from the experience of successful regions or some expert manual' (Amin 1999: 371) without due regard for its specific context and circumstances. This chapter seeks to take the issue of contextualisation along two tracks. First, from a bottom-up perspective, it discusses the linkage between regional innovation systems and clusters on the basis of the cluster's knowledge base and, second, from a top-down perspective, it positions regional innovation systems in their wider national frame.

The second section introduces the notion of the learning economy as well as the two main contextualisation tracks: industrial knowledge base and institutional frameworks. The third section elaborates on the two main concepts, clusters and regional innovation systems. The fourth section provides the empirical illustrations from a Nordic comparative project on SMEs and regional innovation systems. Conclusions and implications for further research are given in the final section.

Providing context: the learning economy, industrial knowledge bases and institutional settings

Both the knowledge-based as well as the learning economy rationale argue that, in the globalising economy, knowledge is the most strategic resource and learning the most fundamental activity for competitiveness (Lundvall 1992, OECD 1996). However, in academic as well as policy-oriented discourses, these two concepts have from time to time taken on different meanings with potential importance for the theoretical understanding of the contemporary economy as well as for policy implications. Lundvall has always preferred to talk about the contemporary global economy as a 'learning economy', whereas the Organization for Economic Cooperation and Development (OECD) (at least the economic sections), being strongly influenced by the USA, has instead more often used 'the knowledge-based' economy. The difference between the two can basically be traced back to the threefold taxonomy of high-, medium- and low-tech industries as suggested by the OECD (1986). This taxonomy reflects the R&D intensity between industries, with those spending more than 5 per cent of turnover being classified as high-tech. Though the initial discussion was carefully launched, offering many necessary qualifications, it still seems that the high-tech fascination has taken on a life of its own, equating R&D intensity with innovation at large (Hirsch-Kreinsen *et al.* 2003). Because of its more inclusive notion of innovation, we prefer to argue in terms of the learning economy rather than the more exclusive and high-tech-focused knowledge-based economy. Thus, we follow Cooke *et al.* (2003) in their broad definition of innovation as the transformation of knowledge into novel wealth-creating technologies, products and services through processes of learning and searching.

In a learning economy, innovation is basically understood as an interactive learning process, which is socially and territorially embedded and culturally and institutionally contextualised (Lundvall 1992). This conceptualisation of innovation means an extension of the range of branches, firm sizes and regions that can be viewed as innovative, also to include traditional, non R&D-intensive branches (e.g. the importance of design in making furniture manufactures competitive and moving them up the value-added chain). An important implication of this broad perspective on innovation is to re-establish the focus on the 'enormous untapped growth potential that could be mobilized to solve social and economic problems' if the necessary 'institutional reforms and organizational change that promote learning processes' were implemented (Lundvall 2004: 1). This implies that the introduction of advanced technologies has to be accompanied by organisational change and competence-building among employees in order for firms to become successful. Furthermore, the outsourcing to subcontractors and suppliers within a production system as a result of the development from vertical integration to disintegration of production is accompanied by a transition from an internal knowledge base in specific industries to a distributed knowledge base of firms (Smith 2000). Knowledge flows, within a distributed knowledge base, can take place between industries with very different degrees of R&D intensity, further weakening the analytical and substantial distinction between high-tech and low-tech industries (e.g. when food and beverage firms produce functional food based on inputs from biotechnology firms).

Despite the generic trend towards increased diversity and interdependence in the knowledge process, we argue that the innovation process in firms and industries is dependent on their specific knowledge base (Asheim and Gertler 2005). Here we will distinguish between two (ideal) types of knowledge base: 'analytical' and 'synthetic' (Laestadius 1998). These types indicate different mixes of tacit and codified knowledge, codification possibilities and limits, qualifications and skills, required organisations and institutions involved, as well as specific innovation challenges and pressures from the globalising economy. Table 6.1 provides a summary of some important differences.

An analytical knowledge base refers to industrial settings, where scientific knowledge is highly important, and where knowledge creation is often based on cognitive and rational processes, or to formal models. Examples are genetics, biotechnology and information technology. Both basic and applied research, as well as systematic development of products and processes, are relevant activities. Companies typically have their own R&D departments but they rely also on the research results of universities and other research organisations in their innovation process. University–industry links and resultant networks are thus important and more frequent than in the other type of knowledge base.

Knowledge inputs and outputs in this type of knowledge base are more often codified than in the other type. This does not imply that tacit knowledge is irrelevant, since both kinds of knowledge are always involved and needed in the process of knowledge creation and innovation (Nonaka *et al.* 2000; Johnson and Lundvall 2001). Codification is more frequent for several reasons: knowledge inputs are often based on reviews of existing studies, knowledge generation is based on the application of scientific principles and methods, knowledge processes are more formally organised (e.g. in R&D departments) and outcomes tend to be documented in reports, electronic files or patent descriptions. Knowledge application takes the form of new products or processes, and there are more radical innovations than in the other knowledge type. An important route of knowledge application is new firms and spin-off companies, which are occasionally formed on the basis of radically new inventions or products.

A synthetic knowledge base refers to industrial settings, where the innovation takes place mainly through the application of existing knowledge or through new combinations of knowledge. Often this occurs in response to the need to solve specific problems coming up in the interaction with clients and suppliers. Industry examples include plant engineering, specialised advanced industrial machinery and ship-building. Products are often 'one-off' or produced in small series. R&D is in general less important than in the first type and often takes the form of applied

Table 6.1 Industrial knowledge bases

Synthetic	*Analytic*
Innovation by application or novel combination of existing knowledge	Innovation by creation of new knowledge
Importance of applied, problem-related knowledge (engineering) often through inductive processes	Importance of scientific knowledge often based on deductive processes and formal models
Interactive learning with clients and suppliers	Research collaboration between firms (R&D department) and research organisations
Dominance of tacit knowledge due to more concrete know-how, craft and practical skill	Dominance of codified knowledge due to documentation in patents and publications
Mainly incremental innovation	More radical innovation

research, but more often product or process development. University–industry links are relevant, but they are clearly more important in the field of applied research and development than in basic research. Knowledge is created less in a deductive process or through abstraction, and more often in an inductive process of testing, experimentation, computer-based simulation or through practical work. Knowledge embodied in the technical solution or engineering work is at least partially codified. However, tacit knowledge seems to be more important than in the first type, in particular because knowledge often results from experience gained at the workplace, and through learning by doing, using and interacting. Compared with the first knowledge type, more concrete know-how, craft and practical skill are required in the knowledge production and circulation process. These are often provided by professional and polytechnic colleges, or by on-the-job training.

The innovation process is often oriented towards the efficiency and reliability of new solutions, or the practical utility and user-friendliness of products from the perspective of the customers. Overall, this leads to a rather incremental way of innovation, dominated by the modification of existing products and processes. Since these types of innovation are less disruptive to existing routines and organisations, most of them take place in existing firms, whereas spin-offs are relatively less frequent.

Lam (2000) emphasises that learning and innovation cannot be separated from broader societal contexts when analysing the links between knowledge types, organisational forms and societal institutions in order to meet the needs of specific industries, in particular with respect to learning and the creation of knowledge in support of innovations. Soskice (1999) argues that different national institutional frameworks support different forms of economic activity, i.e. that coordinated market economies (e.g. the Nordic and (continental) West European welfare states) have their competitive advantage in 'diversified quality production' (Streeck 1992), based on problem-solving and engineering-based knowledge developed through interactive learning and accumulated collectively in the workforce (e.g. the machine tool industry), while liberal market economies (e.g. the USA and UK) are most competitive in production relying on scientific based knowledge, i.e. industries characterised by a high rate of change through radical innovations (e.g. IT, defence technology and advanced producer services). Following Soskice, the main determinants of coordinated market economies are the degree of non-market coordination and cooperation that exists inside the business sphere and between private and public actors, the degree to which labour remains 'incorporated' as well as the ability of the financial system to supply long-term finance (Soskice 1999). This represents a situation in direct conflict with a preference for unilateral control over work processes, generated by certain finance and governance systems found in liberal market economies, where competitive strength is based on institutional freedom as well as financial incentives to continuously restructure production systems in light of new market opportunities (Gilpin 1996). While coordinated market economies at the macro level support cooperative, long-term and consensus-based relations between private as well as public actors, liberal market economies inhibit the development of these relations but instead offer the opportunity to quickly adjust the formal structure to new requirements using temporary organisations frequently.

Such differences – due to the impact of the specific modes of organisation of important societal institutions such as the market, the education system, the labour market, the financial system and the role of the state – both contribute to the formation of divergent 'business systems' (Whitley 1999) and constitute the institutional context within which different organisational forms with different mechanisms for learning, knowledge creation and knowledge appropriation have evolved. Through its emphasis on institutional complementarities, the varieties of capitalism approach focuses on dynamic ensembles of mutually reinforcing sets of institutions rather than isolating individual forms and their impact. As such it pieces together consistent configurations of institutions and the implications for innovative performance (Nooteboom 2000). However, despite the emphasis on institutional complementarities, it takes predominantly institutions at the national level into consideration, leaving 'the multi-scaled set of institutional forms' (Martin 2000: 89) unaddressed.

In a learning economy, which indeed is also a knowledge-based economy, competitive advantage is based on the exploitation of unique competencies and resources. A firm or a region competes on the basis of what it has that is unique in relation to its competitors. A strategic perspective in the contemporary global economy is, thus, how to develop such unique competencies and resources in order to foster competitiveness based on competitive advantage (Porter 1990). Hall and Soskice (2001) partly criticise this position by arguing that the theory of competitive advantage identifies factors that improve the performance of any economy, while not taking its comparative advantage sufficiently into account. This refers to the aforementioned idea that the distinct institutional structure of a political economy favours specific types of firm activities. Moreover, they contend that such institutional structures are difficult to change. The institutional landscape invoked here can in turn be criticised for being overly inert and inherited (Peck 2003). It is generally recognised that the theory of competitive advantage is more dynamic than the theory of comparative advantage and, thus, can be more easily influenced by innovation policies and supporting regulatory and institutional frameworks. In this way innovation plays a central role in attaining and sustaining competitive advantage.

To understand the difference between competitive and comparative advantage it is important to acknowledge the multiple and interrelated layers by which institutions tend to work (Rogers Hollingsworth 2000). At the high end of the hierarchy of the institutional setting of a society we find deeply embedded norms and values which are more permanent and durable. Changes at this level are highly likely to influence the lower levels of the institutional spheres, which are more open and susceptible to change. While the theory of comparative advantage stresses the persistence of institutional structures, the theory of competitive advantage allows to a greater extent for institutional change. In order to understand both the competitive and comparative advantages of a region it is important to recognise the duality of institutional frameworks by interpreting them as 'enabling constraints' (Nooteboom 2000: 94).

Regional innovation systems and clusters: differences and connections

An important tool for analysing regional performance in the learning economy is the concept of regional innovation systems (RIS) that emerged in the early 1990s (Cooke 1992, 1998, 2001), a few years after Chris Freeman first used the national innovation system concept – originally developed by Bengt-Åke Lundvall – in his analysis of Japan's blooming economy (Freeman 1987). Characteristic of a systems approach to innovation is the acknowledgement that innovations are carried out through a network of various actors underpinned by an institutional framework. This dynamic and complex interaction constitutes what is commonly labelled systems of innovation (Edquist 1997), i.e. systems understood as interaction networks (Kaufmann and Tödtling 2000). A set of variations on this approach have been developed over time, taking as their point of departure either territories (national and regional) or specific sectors or technologies (Fagerberg *et al.* 2005).

The national innovation systems (NIS) approach highlights the importance of interactive learning and the role of nation-based institutions in explaining the difference in innovation performance and, hence, economic growth across various countries. Regions are, nonetheless, seen as important bases of economic coordination and governance at the mesolevel between the national and the local (cluster or firms): 'the region is increasingly the level at which innovation is produced through regional networks of innovators, local clusters and the cross-fertilising effects of research institutions' (Lundvall and Borras 1997: 39).

To a large extent the 'system' dimension in RIS was inspired by this literature. In the case that the following two subsystems of actors are systematically engaged in interactive learning (Cooke *et al.* 1998), it can be argued that a regional innovation system is in place:

- the regional production structure or knowledge exploitation subsystem, which consists mainly of firms, especially where these display clustering tendencies;
- the regional supportive infrastructure or knowledge generation subsystem, which consists of public and private research laboratories, universities and colleges, technology transfer agencies, vocational training organisations, etc.

As it refers to 'regional', it is geographically defined by the boundaries of the region, i.e. an administrative division of a country yet above the local or municipal level (Cooke and Leydesdorff forthcoming). Nonetheless, the level of regional administration can differ quite a lot across countries. Furthermore, regional governance is expressed in both private representative organisations, such as branches of industry associations and chambers of commerce, and public organisations such as universities, polytechnics and regional ministries with devolved powers concerning enterprise and innovation support, particularly for SMEs. The RIS approach does not only exist as a framework for studying economic and innovative performance, but is also in use as a concrete tool for policy-makers to systemically enhance localised learning processes to secure regional innovativeness in practice (which in turn influences the functioning of the RIS as such) (Asheim *et al.* 2003a).

Clusters and RIS are indeed closely related. In order to delineate the concepts, we argue that it is essential to acknowledge sector specificity and a high density of functionally related firms as necessary cluster conditions. Therefore, we prefer Isaksen and Hauge's (2002: 14) definition – 'a concentration of interdependent firms within the same or adjacent industrial sectors in a small geographic area' – rather than the traditional Porterian definition, which conflates both concepts.[1] Through processes of localised learning, clustered firms enjoy advantages in terms of innovation performance. An RIS can in principle stretch across several sectors in the regional economy and is more lenient in terms of necessary conditions. An RIS is in place as soon as there are firms and knowledge organisations that interact systematically on the regional level. This means that clusters and RIS may coexist in the same territory. The RIS may in fact contain several clusters.

Furthermore, research has revealed that the regional level is neither always nor even normally sufficient for firms in a cluster to stay innovative and competitive (Isaksen 1999). Under pressure of processes of globalisation the learning process becomes increasingly inserted into various forms of networks and innovation systems (at regional, national and international levels). The continuous importance of the regional level is, however, confirmed by results from a European comparative cluster survey (Isaksen 2005), which shows that regional resources and collaboration are of major importance in stimulating economic activity in the clusters. Nonetheless, the survey found an increased presence of multinational corporations (MNCs) in many clusters, and also that firms in the clusters increasingly source major components and perform assembly manufacturing outside the clusters (Isaksen 2005). In addition, Tödtling *et al.* (2005) found support for clustering, because of the importance of social interaction, trust and local institutions. Yet, they also note that both local and distant networks are often needed for successful cooperative projects, in particular for projects of innovation and product development, when it is usually necessary to combine both local and non-local skills and competencies in order to go beyond the limits of the region (see also Cooke *et al.* 2000, Asheim and Herstad 2003, Bathelt *et al.* 2004).

A central point that this chapter seeks to put forward is that clusters drawing on a predominantly synthetic knowledge base are more loosely coupled with the RIS than are clusters that draw on a predominantly analytic knowledge base. The latter case can thus be typified as an *integrated* cluster–RIS configuration. In the former case, the RIS is contingently supportive to innovation in the cluster but the two parts do not form an integrated whole and can thus be typified as an *auxiliary* cluster–RIS configuration. It needs to be noted that this proposition does not exclude the importance of non-regional knowledge linkages. It primarily entails the argument that in auxiliary cluster–RIS configurations, based on industries with a synthetic knowledge base, the logic behind building a regional innovation system is to support and strengthen the localised learning of an existing industrial specialisation, i.e. to promote historical technological trajectories based on 'sticky' knowledge. In contexts of an integrated cluster–RIS configuration, it is a question of promoting new economic activity based on industries with an analytical knowledge base, requiring close and systemic industry–university cooperation and interaction in the context of, for example, science parks, located in proximity of knowledge-creating organisations (e.g. (technical) universities). The difference between auxiliary and integrated cluster–RIS configurations is illustrated below on the basis of a comparative analysis of five clusters in three Nordic countries: Denmark, Sweden and Norway.

First, however, it is important, in a general institutional framework, to realise that Sweden, Norway and Denmark are coordinated market economies (Hall and Soskice 2001), in contrast to the UK and USA, which are the liberal market economies. The overall effect of this is that firms tend to rely more on strategic interaction among firms and other actors. In an innovation system context, the prime mode of firm conduct is 'voice', in contrast to the 'exit' mode that is typical of liberal market economies (Nooteboom 2000). Systemic relationships between the production structure and the knowledge structure embedded in networking governance structures are therefore characteristic of innovation systems in the Nordic countries. In comparison, exit-based innovation systems lack these strong systemic elements and are to a greater extent based on individual entrepreneurialism, flexibility and venture capital. Hall and Soskice's (2001) argument that both Sweden and Denmark show modest results in term of radical innovation while being better in incremental innovation confirms Edquist and Lundvall's findings (1993) about the Danish and Swedish systems of innovation.

> [In Denmark] the survival of small-scale and artisan-like production has fostered a kind of corporatism, very different from the Swedish. Small, independent entrepreneurs in Denmark will often be quite negative to cen-

> tral union power, but at the same time, often willing to cooperate locally with their workers and their representatives. [...] This small-scale corporatist model often involving a flexible use of reasonably advanced production equipment and a continuous development of incremental product innovations has its strength in flexible adaptation.
>
> (Edquist and Lundvall 1993: 275)

In contrast, the authors describe the Swedish innovation system as comparatively more advanced in process innovation against the backdrop of a dominating position of large firms and heavy investments in R&D on a national level. In general, Denmark tends to fit best with the institutional features of a 'coordinated industrial district' whereas Sweden would belong to the 'collaborative' national business system (Whitley 1999). The Norwegian general framework seems to be quite similar to the coordinated industrial district system of Denmark due to the large number of SMEs. However, a key difference that stands out is the national specialisation in process industries that follows from the importance of petroleum to the Norwegian economy.

These rather static macro-level tendencies represent the comparative advantages of nations and, as regions are, by definition, part of the national system, they also influence innovation processes at the regional level. However, this top-down perspective does not take full account of the competitive advantage of firms at the regional level which emphasises to a greater extent the exploitation of unique competencies and resources through processes of localised learning as discussed below.

Comparison of Nordic clusters

Empirically the analysis builds on a set of studies that have been conducted on various regional clusters/RIS in three Nordic countries:[2]

- in Denmark the furniture cluster of Salling and the wireless communication cluster of North Jutland;
- in Sweden the functional food 'cluster' of Scania;
- in Norway the Rogaland food cluster and the Horten electronic cluster.

On the issue of method, Cooke (1998: 12) argues that one of the distinct advantages of the RIS approach is that it allows for a systematic comparison of innovation activities across various regions: 'Conducting such comparable studies can lead to identification of some functional equivalents for specific as well as generic problems within the innovation process.' However, various other researchers remain critical and argue that the rise of the 'Silicon Valley fever' (Benneworth and Hardy 2003) has confined much work to textbook cases in high-tech sectors (Doloreux 2002). It is argued that more attention should be paid to applying the approach to regions other than the stereotypical 'happy few' and, more importantly, theory must be informed by the lessons drawn from such ordinary regions. Reflecting on the applicability of the concept, Kaufmann and Tödtling (2000) question whether regional innovation systems can be found only in exemplar regions or also in less ideal situations. Their comparative study of old traditional industrial regions shows that the concept does not necessarily embrace extraordinary regions only but allows for utilisation in ordinary regions as well. The scope of this chapter does not allow for detailed analyses of the individual cases.[3] Instead, we focus on the most important characteristics which are required to illustrate our previous argument that whether coupling between clusters and RIS is loose or tight depends on the type of industrial knowledge base.

Over the past decades, the furniture-producing sector in *Salling*[4] has demonstrated considerable economic growth despite high factor costs. Between 1972 and 1992 employment in the cluster tripled (while overall employment in Denmark decreased) and the number of firms grew by approximately 80 per cent. In 1996, fifty-four firms, the majority of which could be classified as SMEs, employed 2,388 employees (Lorenzen 2003). This remarkable performance is ascribed to the strong ability of the cluster to collectively penetrate new markets, brand products and develop new designs. This high level of low-tech innovativeness is in turn underpinned by a combination of stable and at the same time flexible inter-firm relationships held together by a high level of trust and shared norms and conventions. The high-tech wireless communication cluster in *North Jutland*[5] consists of roughly thirty-five firms employing around 3,220 people. In terms of firm size, the cluster is composed of both SMEs as well as branches of major multinationals. In 1997, the private sector, Aalborg University and the science park NOVI established the formal cluster association NorCOM, reflecting successful cooperation between the various actors (Dalum *et al.* 2002).

The case for Sweden is represented by functional foods in *Scania,*[6] a region that is by tradition an important national centre for agricultural production, hosting some of the country's largest food-processing industries. Previous empirical research identifies the food sector as well as the life science sector as constituting the two internationally competitive clusters in Scania (Nilsson *et al.* 2002). Functional foods[7] are regarded as an area of high future growth and innovation in a sector that is traditionally considered as having low growth and low levels of innovation. Against this background, several small, R&D-intensive companies dedicated to functional food have emerged around the University of Lund. Furthermore, these companies work together with the traditional large food companies for the production and marketing of functional foods as well as with regional research groups and organisations in the area of scientific research. It would be going too far to consider this a full-fledged cluster, but it can be argued that a highly innovative and knowledge intensive embryonic cluster is taking shape.

The cases for Norway are constituted by the *Rogaland*[8] food cluster and the *Horten*[9] electronics cluster. Rogaland is a leading production area for food in Norway. Onsager and Aasen (2003) distinguish three partially differentiated, partially integrated subsystems: agrofood production, seafood production and livestock production. Although these subsystems are internally differentiated, each exploiting separate raw materials, production technologies and end markets, functional connections and interrelations are in place across the subsystem with regard to subcontracting, common customers and support organisations (R&D, training and professional fora). Given this differentiation, it is debatable whether one can consider this a true cluster. Despite this, Rogaland makes an interesting case because of the geographical concentration of companies and a support organisation, which together constitute an 'agglomerated sector environment' (Onsager 1999) that displays a high degree of local collaboration in terms of innovation. Finally, the case of Horten can rightfully be defined as a real yet small cluster, hosting approximately twenty-five firms and 1,900 employees in the electronics sector (Asheim and Isaksen 2002, Isaksen 2003). The cluster contains a few large enterprises but is dominated by SMEs. The power factors in the local electronics industry are the large system houses and suppliers of original equipment manufacturers (OEMs). These mainly collaborate with national and international research organisations, universities and customers when innovating. Even so, localised learning can be said to occur through the movement and personal networks of individuals between different Horten firms. However, a third group of firms in the cluster, the local subcontractors, displays clear regional linkages by delivering for the system houses and OEM suppliers in Horten. As specialised producers of components and software they play a significant role in co-innovation processes with their customers by transferring prototypes into effective industrial production as well as through joint problem-solving.

In this section we analyse the industrial knowledge base of each of the clusters in relation to loose or tight coupling between the cluster and the RIS. Table 6.2 summarises the result of this analysis.

From an analysis of the case study conducted by Lorenzen (2003), the characteristic knowledge base of the furniture cluster in Salling can be classified as synthetic. In terms of technological product innovations, Salling firms mainly design variations on the existing product line that differ in, for example, style, materials and colours. Totally new product types and designs are typically introduced once a year. Process innovations necessarily follow such new product designs. The shift from hardwood to other materials, notably plywood, is considered to be the most dramatic shift that the cluster has witnessed. The synthetic nature of the knowledge base is further illustrated by the way in which the companies innovate internally: through experimentation on the shop floor and product revision based upon employees' ideas. The most important innovation mechanism is, however, local inter-firm relations. These appear to be highly conducive to both user–producer innovation as well as horizontal networks. In terms of direct knowledge flows and learning processes, the Salling cluster appears to be almost exclusively firm based, with few connections outside the cluster or other knowledge organisations. However, two local organisations are indirectly important for the innovative performance of the cluster. First, the skills needed by the workforce are largely provided through education at the local technical school, which is considered to be highly specialised in furniture production. Second, another organisation important to the cluster is the local cabinetmakers' guild. The guild provides a

Table 6.2 RIS cluster configuration vs. industrial knowledge base

	Analytical knowledge base	*Synthetic knowledge base*
Integrated RIS cluster	Functional food, Scania Wireless communication, North Jutland	
Auxiliary RIS cluster	Electronics, Horten	Furniture, Salling Food, Rogaland

crucial forum for firms to exchange information and form inter-firm relationships. However, interactive learning occurs nearly exclusively between firms directly involved in furniture production.

The Rogaland regional food cluster provides a somewhat more complex picture even though the general argument holds: the linkage between the cluster and the RIS can be characterised as auxiliary in the light of the predominantly synthetic knowledge base of the regional food industry. As Onsager and Aasen (2003) show, Rogaland hosts important R&D bodies involved in innovation activities with the cluster companies. An example is Nordconserv (the Norwegian Institute for Fish Processing and Preservation Technology), which serves as an important centre of expertise for regional companies involved in changing and developing production processes. The institute is renowned for its emphasis on hands-on research of relevance to industry. However, these R&D bodies are often divisions of national organisations. This is characteristic of the situation in Norway, where there is a long tradition of public R&D programmes being implemented at the national level, although there has recently been a move towards greater regionalisation in this area. Thus, in Norway clusters are not exclusively embedded in the RIS. Learning and knowledge transmission 'depend extensively on an ability to make use of knowledge resources from many different players, centres and levels' (Onsager and Aasen 2003: 28).

The above examples of low-tech innovation can be contrasted with the high-tech cluster of Northern Jutland and the embryonic functional food cluster in Scania. These cases are prime examples of analytic knowledge base clusters in which the regional knowledge infrastructure plays a crucial role. The historical overview of the development of the wireless communication cluster in North Jutland provided by Dalum *et al.* (1999, 2002) clearly shows how the presence of Aalborg University and the NOVI science park have been requisites for the cluster's growth. This interdependence has even been formalised through the NorCOM cluster association, founded in 1997. Since the university was established in 1974, a central feature of its role in the cluster has been the provision to the region of skilled engineers. Moreover, Dalum *et al.* (2002: 16) argue that the university's research orientation ('basic research with a sufficiently application-oriented touch') in close interaction with local industry constitutes a core asset of the region, attracting the attention of major MNCs. In addition, the NOVI science park can be considered as an indication of successful integration between private and public organisations around wireless communication in North Jutland.

The story for functional foods in Scania is similar, albeit the scale, in terms of companies, is much more modest. Holmberg (2003) identifies three dedicated functional food firms that constitute the core of this embryonic cluster. In line with findings for the Swedish biotechnology–pharmaceutical sector in general (McKelvey *et al.* 2003), inter-firm knowledge linkages are weak despite the firms' proximity. Instead, the firms cooperate with firms and research organisations at the regional, national and international level. Notwithstanding this, the firms' location close to Lund University remains of fundamental importance because of the presence in the university of world-class research and education facilities in the field of functional foods. This has been further reinforced by the recent establishment of the cross-faculty Functional Foods Science Centre. It can, therefore, be argued that Lund University serves as the backbone of the commercial exploitation of functional foods in Scania as well as of the further development of a true functional foods cluster.

As Table 6.2 indicates, the Horten case serves as an exception to the suggested proposition. Right from the beginning, in the 1960s, knowledge linkages among the pioneering firms in this cluster were largely embedded in the national system of innovation. These firms were in fact spin-offs from important national knowledge organisations and were established based on product ideas that originated in these organisations. Later (radical) product development relied mainly on cooperation with technological R&D institutes and large public and private clients in Norway, in projects often partly financed by the National Research Council (Isaksen 2003). Again, this should be viewed in the context of the Norwegian tradition for national R&D programmes. In contrast, the regional knowledge infrastructure was of little value to the electronics cluster. For the technologically advanced system houses and OEM suppliers this is still the case. According to Isaksen (2003), these companies have even outgrown the national innovation system from which they arose and are increasingly collaborating at an international level with firms and R&D institutes. What, then, ties these firms to Horten? The answer lies in the build-up of unique competencies among key personnel attached to the locality (Asheim and Isaksen 2002). Furthermore, the role of local subcontractors appears to be highly important. These have arisen since the beginning of the 1980s when system firms closed down their in-house production facilities. While the knowledge base of the system houses and OEM suppliers tends to be more inclined to an analytical knowledge base, the innovation activities of these local subcontractors typically build on a synthetic knowledge base.

Conclusions

In this chapter we have argued that, in a learning economy, clusters and RIS are two different yet closely interrelated concepts. The fundamental distinction is that the cluster concept is substantially narrower than the RIS concept because the former has a strong sectorial connotation whereas an RIS can transcend multiple sectors. From a policy perspective it is important to remember this distinction and bear in mind that some policies may be sector specific whereas others are generic. In addition, we analysed the relationship between clusters and RIS from an industrial knowledge base perspective on the basis of a comparison of Nordic clusters. This indicated that clusters drawing on an analytical knowledge base tend to be more integrated in the RIS than are clusters drawing on a synthetic knowledge base, which tend to be more loosely connected to the RIS (i.e. an auxiliary configuration). Furthermore, Cooke's (2003) finding that biotechnology clusters (which is a prime example of an analytical industry) are intrinsically tied to regional knowledge 'fountainheads' corroborates this proposition. Despite this, the case of the electronics cluster in Horten showed weak linkages with the regional knowledge infrastructure. This needs to be viewed against the background of Norway's traditionally national science and technology orientation.

However, as a result of empirical studies that have emphasised the significance of the regional level in economic development (in addition to – and sometimes taking precedence over – the national level), a strong case has been made for an approach geared to region-specific innovation activities. The core of the argument is that close proximity between actors and organisations strongly facilitates the creation, acquisition, accumulation and utilisation of knowledge rooted in inter-firm networking, interpersonal relationships, local learning processes and 'sticky' knowledge grounded in social interaction (Asheim and Isaksen 2002).

In a globalising learning economy characterised by vertical disintegration and distributed knowledge bases, the important perspective ought to be the inter-dependences between regions and nations, with the deciding criteria being the location of core activities (rather than the whole value chain) and the relative importance of their connections to regional knowledge infrastructures. The argument that 'production configurations are often dependent on structures and developments which are shaped and take place outside' the actual regional territory (Bathelt 2003: 796) applies as readily to most small and medium-sized countries as to regions, especially if they are members of supranational organisations such as the EU. Also, from an institutional perspective, it is essential to recognise the intertwined nature of a region in a wider geographical context (Howells 1999). It acknowledges the importance of institutions negotiated and designed at the supraregional level but, at the same time, it also allows for differentiation in terms of the impact of overarching institutions on the regional level as well as for differing degrees of regional institutional autonomy. More research across geographical scales is needed to avoid the kind of spatial fetishism that deals with territorial innovation systems in a confined way.

Notes

1 'A geographic concentration of interconnected companies, specialized suppliers and service providers, firms in related industries and associated institutions (e.g. universities, standard agencies and trade associations) in particular fields that compete but also cooperate' (Porter 2000: 253).

2 These studies were carried out through the common research project 'Nordic SMEs and Regional Innovation Systems' financed by the Nordic Industrial Fund (currently Nordic Innovation Centre).

3 For this, see Asheim *et al.* (2003b).
4 The case of Salling in Denmark draws predominantly on the work of Mark Lorenzen at Copenhagen Business School.
5 This case draws on studies carried out by Michael Dahl, Christian Pedersen and Bent Dalum at Aalborg University.
6 This case draws for the most part on work by Gustav Holmberg at Lund University.
7 Artificially developed food with added ingredients that demonstrate scientific evidence of positive health-related effects.
8 This case draws mainly on a study carried out by Knut Onsager and Berit Aasen at the Norwegian Institute for Urban and Regional Development (NIBR).
9 This case draws mainly on a study carried out by Arne Isaksen at Agder University College.

References

Amin, A. (1999) 'An institutionalist perspective on regional economic development', *International Journal of Urban and Regional Research,* 23: 365–78.

Asheim, B.T. (2000) 'Industrial districts: the contributions of Marshall and beyond', in Clark, G.L., Feldman, M.P. and Gertler, M.S. (eds.) *The Oxford Handbook of Economic Geography,* Oxford: Oxford University Press.

Asheim, B.T. (2002) 'Temporary organizations and spatial embeddedness of learning and knowledge creation', *Geografiska Annaler: Series B Human Geography*, 84: 111–24.

Asheim, B.T. and Gertler, M.S. (2005) 'Regional innovation systems and the geographical foundations of innovation', in Fagerberg, J., Mowery, D. and Nelson, R. (eds.) *The Oxford Handbook of Innovation*, Oxford: Oxford University Press, pp. 291–317.

Asheim, B.T. and Herstad, S.J. (2003) 'Regional innovation systems, varieties of capitalism and non-local relations: challenges from the globalizing economy', in Asheim, B.T. and Mariussen, Å. (eds.) *Innovations, Regions and Projects*, Stockholm: Nordregio.

Asheim, B.T. and Isaksen, A. (2002) 'Regional innovation systems: the integration of local "sticky" and global "ubiquitous" knowledge', *Journal of Technology Transfer*, 27: 77–86.

Asheim, B.T., Isaksen, I., Nauwelaers, C. and Tödtling, F. (eds.) (2003a) *Regional Innovation Policy for Small-Medium Enterprises*, Cheltenham: Edward Elgar.

Asheim, B.T., Coenen, L. and Svensson-Henning, M. (2003b) *Nordic SMEs and Regional Innovation Systems – Final Report.* Available online at www.keg.lu.se/forska/projekt/nordic.htm (accessed 23 June 2004).

Bathelt, H. (2003) 'Geographies of production: growth regimes in spatial perspectives 1 – innovation, institutions and social systems', *Progress in Human Geography*, 27: 789–804.

Bathelt, H., Malmberg, A. and Maskell, P. (2004) 'Clusters and knowledge: local buzz, global pipelines and the process of knowledge creation', *Progress in Human Geography*, 28: 31–56.

Benneworth, P. and Hardy, S. (2003) 'In celebration of the "ordinary" region', paper presented at the RGS-IBG International Annual Conference, London, September 2003.

Cooke, P. (1992) 'Regional innovation systems: competitive regulation in the new Europe', *Geoforum* 23: 365–82.

Cooke, P. (1998) 'Introduction: origins of the concept', in Braczyk, H., Cooke, P. and Heidenreich, M. (eds.) *Regional Innovation Systems*, London: UCL Press.

Cooke, P. (2001) 'Regional innovation systems, clusters, and the knowledge economy', *Industrial and Corporate Change*, 10: 945–74.

Cooke, P. (2003) 'The evolution of biotechnology in three continents: Schumpeterian or Penrosian?', *European Planning Studies*, 11: 757–64.

Cooke, P. and Leydesdorff, L. (forthcoming) 'Regional development in the knowledge-based economy: the construction of advantage', *Journal of Technology Transfer*.

Cooke, P., Uranga, M.G. and Etxebarria, G. (1998) 'Regional systems of innovation: an evolutionary perspective', *Environment and Planning A*, 30: 1563–84.

Cooke, P., Boekholt, P. and Tödtling, F. (2000) *The Governance of Innovation in Europe. Regional Perspectives on Global Competitiveness*, London: Pinter.

Cooke, P., Roper, S. and Wylie, P. (2003) ' "The golden thread of innovation" and Northern Ireland's evolving regional innovation system', *Regional Studies*, 37: 365–79.

Dalum, B., Holmén, M., Jacobsson, S., Præst, M., Rickne, A. and Villumsen, G. (1999) 'The formation of knowledge-based clusters in North Jutland and Western Sweden', paper presented at the DRUID Conference on National Innovation Systems, Industrial Dynamics and Innovation Policy, Rebild, June 1999.

Dalum, B., Pedersen C. and Villumsen, G. (2002) 'Technological life cycles: regional clusters facing disruption', DRUID Working Paper 02-10, Aalborg: Aalborg University.

Doloreux, D. (2002) 'What we should know about regional systems of innovation', *Technology in Society*, 24: 243–63.

Edquist, C. (1997) 'Introduction', in Edquist, C. (ed.) *Systems of Innovation: Technologies, Institutions and Organisations*, London: Pinter.

Edquist, C. and Lundvall, B.-Å. (1993) 'Comparing the Danish and Swedish systems of innovation', in Nelson, R. (ed.) *National Innovation Systems: A Comparative Analysis*, Oxford: Oxford University Press.

Fagerberg, J., Mowery, D. and Nelson, R. (eds.) (2005) *The Oxford Handbook of Innovation*, Oxford: Oxford University Press.

Freeman, C. (ed.) (1987) *Technology Policy and Economic Performance: Lessons from Japan*, London: Pinter.

Gilpin, R. (1996) 'Economic evolution of national systems', *International Studies Quarterly*, 40: 411–43.

Hall, P. and Soskice, D. (2001) *Varieties of Capitalism: The Institutional Foundations of Comparative Advantage*, Oxford: Oxford University Press.

Hirsch-Kreinsen, H., Jacobson, D., Laestadius, S. and Smith, K. (2003) 'Low-tech industries and the knowledge economy: state of the art and research challenges', Oslo: STEP Report 16-2003.

Holmberg, G. (2003) 'Functional foods in Scania, Sweden'. Available online at www.keg.lu.se/forska/projekt/nordic.htm (accessed 23 June 2004).

Howells, J. (1999) 'Regional systems of innovation?', in Archibugi, D., Howells, J. and Michie, J. (eds.) *Innovation Policy in a Global Economy*, Cambridge: Cambridge University Press.

Isaksen, A. (ed.) (1999) 'Regionale innovasjonssystemer: innovasjon og læring i 10 regionale næringsmiljøer', Oslo: STEP Report 02-1999.

Isaksen, A. (2003) 'Learning, globalization, and the electronics cluster in Horten: discussing the local buzz – global pipeline argument'. Available online on at www.keg.lu.se/forska/projekt/nordic.htm (accessed 23 June 2004).

Isaksen, A. (2005) 'Regional clusters between local and non-local relations: a comparative European study', in Lagendijk, A. and Oinas, P. (eds.) *Proximity, Distance and Diversity: Issues on Economic Interaction and Local Development*, Aldershot: Ashgate, pp. 129–52.

Isaksen, A. and Hauge, E. (2002) 'Regional clusters in Europe', Observatory of European SMEs report 2002 No. 3, Luxembourg: European Communities.

Johnson, B. and Lundvall, B.-Å. (2001) 'Why all this fuss about codified and tacit knowledge?', paper presented at the Druid Academy winter conference, Korsør, January 2001.

Kaufmann, A. and Tödtling, F. (2000) 'Systems of innovation in traditional industrial regions: the case of Styria in a comparative perspective', *Regional Studies*, 34: 29–40.

Laestadius, S. (1998) 'Technology level, knowledge formation and industrial competence in paper manufacturing', in Eliasson, G. and Green, C. (eds.) *Micro Foundations of Economic Growth*, Ann Arbor, MI: University of Michigan Press.

Lam, A. (2000) 'Tacit knowledge, organizational learning and societal institutions: an integrated framework', *Organization Studies,* 21: 487–513.

Lorenzen, M. (2003) 'Low-tech localized learning: the regional innovation system of Salling, Denmark'. Available online at www.keg.lu.se/forska/projekt/nordic.htm (accessed 23 June 2004).

Lundvall, B.-Å. (ed.) (1992) *National Systems of Innovation: Towards a Theory of Innovation and Interactive Learning*, London: Pinter.

Lundvall, B.-Å. (2004) 'Why the New Economy is a learning economy', DRUID Working Paper 04-01, Aalborg: Aalborg University.

Lundvall, B.-Å. and Borras, S. (1997) *The Globalising Learning Economy: Implications for Innovation Policy*, Luxembourg: European Communities.

McKelvey, M., Alm, H. and Riccaboni, A. (2003) 'Does co-location matter for formal knowledge collaboration in the Swedish biotechnology–pharmaceutical sector?', *Research Policy*, 32: 483–501.

Martin, R. (2000) 'Institutional approaches in economic geography', in Sheppard, E. and Barnes, T. (eds.) *A Companion to Economic Geography*, Oxford: Basil Blackwell.

Moulaert, F. and Sekia, F. (2003) 'Territorial innovation models: a critical survey', *Regional Studies* 37: 289–302.

Nilsson, M., Svensson-Henning, M. and Wilkenson, O. (2002) *Skånska Kluster och Profilområden – En Kritisk Granskning*, Malmö: Region Skåne.

Nonaka, I., Toyama, R. and Konno, N. (2000) 'SECI, Ba and leadership: a unified model of dynamic knowledge creation', *Long Range Planning*, 33: 5–34.

Nooteboom, B. (2000) *Learning and Innovation in Organisations and Economies*, Oxford: Oxford University Press.

OECD (1986) *OECD Science and Technology Indicators (R&D, Innovation and Competitiveness)*, Paris: OECD.

OECD (1996) *The Knowledge-based Economy*, Paris: OECD.

Onsager, K. (1999) 'Matindustrien i innovative nettverk i Rogaland', in Isaksen, A. (ed.) *Regionale innovasjonssystemer: innovasjon og læring i 10 regionale næringsmiljøer*, Oslo: Step Rapport 2-1999.

Onsager, K. and Aasen, B. (2003) 'The case of Rogaland regional food cluster'. Available online at www.keg.lu.se/forska/projekt/nordic.htm (accessed 23 June 2004).

Peck, J. (2003) 'Economic sociologies in space', paper prepared at the School of Geography, Nottingham, April 2003.

Porter, M.E. (1990) *The Competitive Advantage of Nations*, Worchester: Billing and Sons.

Porter M.E. (2000) 'Locations, clusters and company strategy', in Clark, G.L., Feldman, M.P. and Gertler, M.S. (eds.) *The Oxford Handbook of Economic Geography*, Oxford: Oxford University Press.

Rogers Hollingsworth, J. (2000) 'Doing institutional analysis: implications for the study of innovations', Vienna: ICE Working Paper No. 9.

Saxenian, A. (1994) *Regional Advantage: Culture and Competition in Silicon Valley and Route 128*, Cambridge, MA: Harvard University Press.

Smith, K. (2000) 'What is "the knowledge economy"? Knowledge-intensive industries and distributed knowledge bases', paper presented at the DRUID summer conference The Learning Economy – Firms, Regions and Nation Specific Institutions, Aalborg, June 2000.

Soskice, D. (1999) 'Divergent production regimes: coordinated and uncoordinated market economies in the 1980s and 1990s', in Kitschelt, H., Lange, P., Marks, G. and Stephens, J.D. (eds.) *Continuity and Change in Contemporary Capitalism*, Cambridge: Cambridge University Press.

Streeck, W. (1992) *Social Institutions and Economic Performance – Studies of Industrial Relations in Advanced Capitalist Economies*, New York: Sage Publications.

Tödtling, F., Trippl, M. and Brathl, H. (2005) 'Networking and project organization in the automotive industry: the case of Styria', in Lagendijk, A. and Oinas, P. (eds.) *Proximity, Distance and Diversity: Issues on Economic Interaction and Local Development*, Aldershot: Ashgate, pp. 89–110.

Whitley, R. (1999) *Divergent Capitalisms – the Social Structuring and Change of Business Systems*, Oxford: Oxford University Press.

7 Spatial externalities and local employment dynamics

Raffaele Paci and Stefano Usai

Introduction

Over the last decade a vast body of literature has addressed the issue of the influence of externalities on local growth (starting with Glaeser *et al.* 1992, until Henderson 2003, to mention just a few). Such literature has, however, paid relatively little attention to the wider scenario in which such phenomena are rooted, that of an ongoing process of structural change that is transforming our economies from manufacturing to service ones.[1] Such a process has important implications for the analysis of the geography of economic activities. In fact, the spatial distribution and functioning of industrial economies have been shaped by the characteristics of prevailing levels of production and distribution technology, modes of work organisation, labour and capital mobility. All these features are currently changing dramatically as a result of the relocation and deverticalisation of mass production industries followed by the development of new service activities, the transformation of cultural and leisure activities from pastimes into economic businesses and the emerging role of information and communications technologies. These trends are modifying both the economic geography of local production systems and the manner in which these are linked to a broader economy. Economic landscapes are increasingly being shaped by a complex mixture of forces operating simultaneously at a global, national and local level, with the common denominator being the structural shift from manufacturing to services in the most developed economies.

The main aim of this chapter is to analyse local short-term economic performance, as expressed by employment dynamics, in both the service and the manufacturing sectors. Working with a large set of variables and data, we attempt to explain some of the differences in the economic performance of sectors[2] by assessing the role of several potential determinants of local employment dynamics.

In particular, we aim to introduce a useful classification of determinants in order to present a general setting for testing different potential explanatory scenarios. Such a classification includes the usual distinction between specialisation–Marshall externalities, resulting from the scale of local, own-industry activity, and urbanisation–Jacobs economies attributable to cross-fertilisation enhanced by the scale or diversity of activity outside the own industry. Moreover, other important phenomena are included both at the local industry level (scale and competition effects) and at the local level (population size effects, human and social capital, among others). The use of spatial econometric techniques, moreover, allows us to avoid placing artificial bounds on agglomeration economies. We, therefore, do not consider our geographical units as isolated closed economies[3] by taking into account the possibility of some externalities crossing borders.

The chapter is organised as follows. In the next section we briefly survey the literature background. In the third section the databank is presented along with a descriptive picture of the phenomenon under examination. In the fourth section the theoretical underpinnings are presented. In the fifth section we discuss the main econometric results. In the last section, we put forth some concluding remarks.

Some theoretical and empirical issues

In the last decade, the influence of regional externalities on local economic growth has been under recurrent investigation. Glaeser *et al.* (1992) were the first to focus on employment growth as a proxy for local economic performance and to study its dynamics at both the city and the sectoral level. The empirical analysis was based on the discrimination between static externalities, associated with cost efficiencies or pecuniary externalities, and dynamic externalities, related to knowledge spillovers. Static externalities are those that affect industry localisation[4] but not growth. Since then, the debate about dynamic externalities has mainly focused on two competing theories:[5] those of Marshall (1990 [1890]), Arrow (1962) and Romer (1986) (MAR) and those of Jacobs (1969).

The main difference between these theories concerns the effects of specialisation (the degree to which a location specialises in one industry) and diversity (the range of different industries in a location). The MAR framework maintains that most spillovers occur among firms in the same industry. Specialised locations with high levels of industry concentration should experience more innovation and faster growth. In contrast, Jacobs posits that the most important knowledge transfers take place across different industries. Jacobs's theory predicts that industries will innovate more and grow faster in locations with greater diversity. Empirical tests addressing this debate have produced conflicting results.

Glaeser *et al.* (1992) found that both competition and diversity fostered industry growth and innovation, whereas specialisation discouraged them. The evidence collected for other countries, mainly in the EU, seems to support these findings although it should be noted that common features of such studies are that the analysis typically covers a short time span and that, owing to a lack of data, they focus on employment dynamics as a proxy of productivity growth. In the case of Italy, Usai and Paci (2003) found that growth had a positive effect on diversity and specialisation a negative effect, at the local labour system level. In the Netherlands, at the city level and for the top industries only, van Soest *et al.* (2002) obtained similar results, as did Combes (2000a),[6] for France, and Almeida (2001), for Portugal, these being the only authors to have examined both the manufacturing and service sectors. The consistency of the finding that diversity tends to have a positive effect and specialisation a negative is interesting, given that externalities are different across sectors and countries.

However, these results conflict with those of Henderson *et al.* (1995), who reported that both diversity and specialisation externalities had positive effects on high-tech industries whereas only MAR spillovers were found among mature industries. Similar results were also obtained by Forni and Paba (2002), who found that specialisation and diversity are important for growth in most manufacturing sectors although each industry needs its own diversity in terms of input–output relations. These interesting outcomes are, however, subject to Combes' critique (2000b), according to which the simultaneous inclusion of a specialisation index and of total employment among the regressors introduces a positive bias to the specialisation coefficient.[7] The positive effect of specialisation is, therefore, questionable.

More compelling is the contribution of more recent studies (Dekle 2002, Cingano and Schivardi 2003, Henderson 2003) that manage to avoid some of the typical flaws affecting the aforementioned studies. The flaws result from the idea that employment growth can be used as a proxy of productivity changes whereas this may prove to be unrealistic when: (i) local capital stock is not constant with time (Dekle 2002); (ii) productivity shocks have a negative impact on employment growth because demand elasticity is low and production does not expand enough at the same time (Combes and Overman 2004); (iii) the sources of externalities and agglomeration influence the labour supply (Dekle 2002, Cingano and Schivardi 2003); and (iv) capital and labour have a high degree of substitutability and technological change is labour saving.

In fact, recent empirical studies (Dekle 2002, Cingano and Schivardi 2003) have cast serious doubts on the idea that changes in productivity reflect proportional variations in employment. In particular, such studies, by using total factor productivity (TFP) measures of productivity growth, show that specialisation may prove to be positively linked to economic performance whereas diversity is not.[8] Similar results were obtained by De Lucio *et al.* (2002), who concluded that diversity had no effect on labour productivity growth and obtained an interesting U-shaped curve for specialisation effects. Finally, Henderson (2003), by estimating plant-level production functions in a panel context, found that localisation/MAR scale externalities have strong productivity effects in high-tech but not in machinery industries. Again, he found no evidence of urbanisation economies resulting from the diversity of local economic activity outside the industry concerned and limited evidence of urbanisation economies from the overall scale of local economic activity. Henderson also studied the spatial extent of externalities and found that they are relatively localised within any particular county, so that there are no external benefits from plants in other counties. Similarly, Cingano and Schivardi (2003) found that neighbourhood specialisation at a higher level of territorial aggregation has no effect on TFP.

The use of TFP measures in these studies is a notable improvement, although data availability remains a problem. Both Dekel (2002) and De Lucio *et al.* (2002), in order to obtain sufficient data, had to extend their analysis from the city or the local labour system level typical of such studies to a more aggregated level, that is administrative regions, where the labour market and good markets do not necessarily coincide. In contrast, Henderson (2003) and Cingano and Schivardi (2003) were able to maintain a very disaggregated level of analysis, that of metropolitan areas and counties in the former and that of local labour systems in the latter, with the acknowledged problem that both studies relied on samples of plant data with the associated serious problems of selection bias.

Another interesting issue raised in the literature is whether the role of externalities varies with respect to some concurrent economic phenomena. Glaeser *et al.* (1992), for instance, suggested that there might be an industry life cycle in which externalities are important only in the early development stages. Similarly, Krugman (1991) proposed that, as an industry develops, it might become less dependent on pooled labour, specialised inputs and knowledge spillovers. Moreover, externalities that foster the initial development of a location might not be the same as those that cultivate its subsequent growth (Duranton and Puga 2001). In other words, the nature of externalities is not independent of the product cycle. Experimental activity is initially found in large, diverse, urban areas (Jacobs externalities), whereas traditional production, which is more standardised, can be more decentralised in smaller, more specialised, urban areas with lower costs (Marshall externalities). This line of interpretation has been used by both Combes (2000a) and Usai and Paci (2003) to make sense of some differences in results among sectors in the former case and among regions in the latter case.

Most importantly for the purposes of this chapter, the role of externalities may be very different across industries and most of all between the two macro-sectors: manufacturing and service. The reason, as argued by Krugman and Venables (1995),[9] is that goods that are essentially non-tradable (i.e. services) have to be produced close to customers, leading to activities remaining spread out. In contrast, the production of tradable goods, i.e. manufacturing, can enjoy agglomeration economies by locating where it is more convenient and therefore can be more concentrated in space. This view, according to Desmet and Fafchamps (2003), may have interesting dynamic implications. As transport costs fall, goods become tradable, allowing production to take advantage of agglomeration economies by concentrating. However, if transport costs continue to drop, those agglomeration economies may exceed a threshold at which activities start to spread back out to less congested areas. If this holds true, then service sectors, with their non-tradable nature, will initially be more spread out, but, as transport costs fall, there should be an increase in concentration. In contrast, manufacturing goods are eminently tradable and have been for a long time. Falling transport costs should, therefore, result in manufacturing industries becoming less concentrated. Finally, the dynamics of the service sector are linked to the evolution of the economy and, in particular, of the manufacturing compound. One can distinguish two possible effects of the interaction of the dynamics of the two macro-sectors. On the one hand, service firms may replace manufacturing firms as the latter rely more and more on the market because of, for instance, decreasing transaction costs. There is, therefore, in this scenario, an inverse relationship between the two sectors. On the other hand, as long as the two macro-sectors remain complementary, which may be the case because the manufacturing sector is a customer of the service sector, the two dynamics may be positively related. However, one should bear in mind that service sectors are extremely heterogeneous: for example, business services may follow an altogether different dynamics and localisation process from personal services.

Business services are typically concentrated in close proximity to the firms to which they sell their products. This is usually explained by the importance of intangible aspects of localised knowledge, with a reliance on day-to-day and face-to-face contact to facilitate exchanges of essential information. In contrast, personal services are usually more spread out. And there may be other important differences in dynamics, depending on other characteristics. For example, some services may prove to have the characteristics of inferior goods such that their consumption decreases with increasing income, for example transport services may be replaced by durable goods, i.e. private cars. Conversely, other services, such as culture and tourism, are closer to the nature of luxury goods and their general consumption increases as income increases. The complexity of the nature of the two macro-sectors and of their relationship is bound to be reflected in our results.

The data and the descriptive analysis

Our empirical analysis makes use of a comprehensive database on socioeconomic indicators for the Italian local labour systems (LLS). LLS are 784 groupings of municipalities identified by the Italian Institute of Statistics (ISTAT) by means of commuting data from the population census: the geography of where people live overlaps the geography of where people work, that is the local labour market and local goods market coincide (Sforzi 1997). This high level of geographical breakdown appears to be particularly useful for the analysis of local growth as production activities have, by construction, a high degree of self-containment that makes it easier to identify explanatory factors at a local level. The information on local labour systems is also disaggregated with respect to thirty-four sectors at the two-digit ATECO 91-ISIC 3 level. In particular, we distinguish between twenty-one manufacturing sectors (including building) and thirteen service sectors (excluding the public sector, for which data are available only for 1991).

The data, which consist mainly of units of labour and number of firms and plants, refer to the five-year period from 1991 to 1996. The reason for our decision to confine our analysis to such a short period, which is obviously bound to limit our result, is that we preferred to use territorial units that do not vary over time. To extend backwards (to 1981) the definition of LLS based on 1991 information would have required us to ignore the fact that in 1981 LLS in Italy were determined differently and numbered 944.

Employment figures at the aggregate level in Italy during the 1990s show a loss of 287,000 units of labour with an average annual fall of 0.43 per cent. This aggregate trend hides a highly differentiated pattern at the sectoral level. In particular, the manufacturing sector reported an average employment fall of 1.47 per cent per year, whereas employment in the service sector increased by 0.17 per cent per year. Employment growth in the service sector was strictly related to a process of structural change and outsourcing, common to all advanced economies. Between the 1980s and the present day, a large number of manufacturing firms, in order to improve their productivity in the core business, transferred some auxiliary internal activities, such as cleaning, accounting, engineering, marketing and security, to external service firms.

However, the most striking feature of this general employment decline was its considerable geographical variation. Employment dynamics follow the usual north–south pattern, although some important qualifications emerge from the data, especially among northern regions. In fact, if one distinguishes six macro-areas and two macro-sectors (manufacturing and services) some interesting findings emerge (Figures 7.1, 7.2 and 7.3 and Table 7.1).

Comparing the macro-sectors and Italy as a whole, we can see from Table 7.1 that the only area with rising employment was the north-east; the centre-north, in comparison with the other areas, reported a smaller decrease in employment; and the south and islands were the poorest performers. It is, in addition, worth noting the dichotomy in the north: whereas the north-east showed a good performance, with employment growth of 0.33 per cent per year, in the north-west employment fell by 0.48 per cent per year, which is worse than the national average. Employment growth in the north-east came mostly from the localisation in that area of growing services sectors such as real estate, computer activities and tourism activities (hotels and restaurants). The recent story of the north-east is one of industrial and service development based on local networks of small and medium-sized dynamic firms and plants scattered throughout the area. This is the widely studied development model of the 'industrial districts' (see, among many others, Brusco 1982, Piore and Sabel 1984). Performance in the regions of the centre-north was similar, suggesting that the Italian model of agglomeration systems composed of small and medium enterprises, which are typical of these two areas, has been relatively successful during what was a troublesome period. In contrast, the story of the north-west very much reflects its development history as the Italian industrial centre, with the main metropolitan centres, Turin, Milan and Genoa, constituting the so-called 'industrial triangle', which is dependent on large heavy industries. Services growth in this area has not been able to compensate for the deep industrial crisis. At the other extreme, the south and the islands show the worst performance, with employment falling by, respectively, 0.8 per cent and 1.7 per cent per year during the period 1991–96. The crisis in the industrial sector in these areas can be attributed to government policy that favoured the location of large firms in capital-intensive industries (chemicals, oil, steel) in these areas. This had the effect of crowding out a weak domestic network of firms. When these heavy industries experienced structural crisis, recovery and growth of a renewed structure of endogenous firms did not occur sufficiently quickly and this, together with a lack of infrastructure, had a negative effect on employment.

Let us now examine changes in employment in the two macro-sectors. Table

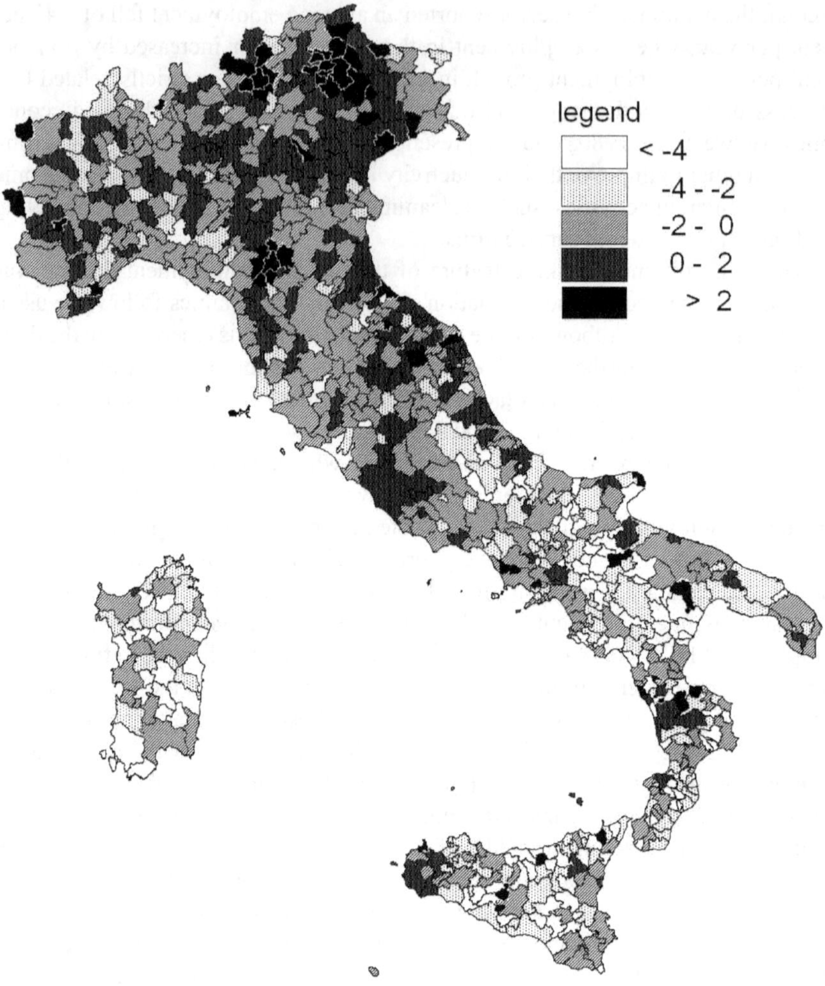

Figure 7.1 Total employment dynamics in the local labour systems in Italy, 1991–96 (% annual average growth rate).

7.1 shows that the fall in manufacturing employment in the north-east was more similar to that in the centre-north, in both cases being lower than the national average (as a result of the presence of small dynamic firms in the industrial districts), than to that in the north-west (which remains characterised by the presence of large heavy industries). Once again, as for overall employment, the worst performance was found in the islands and the south. In the country as a whole, employment in the service sector increased, but again the pattern varied across the macro-regions. The best positive result occurred in the north-west, followed by the north-east and centre-north. In the three remaining macroregions employment in the services sector fell, with the islands again showing the worst performance.

Consider now the performance of individual LLS (Table 7.2). Very often, the

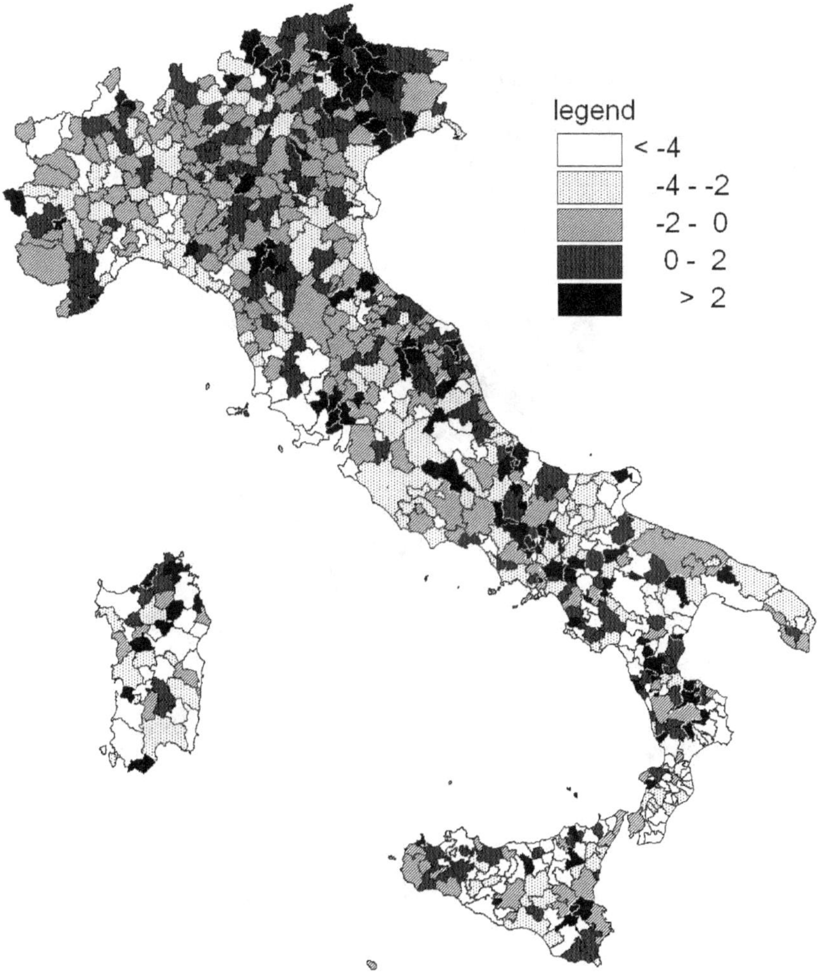

Figure 7.2 Employment dynamics in manufacturing in the LLS in Italy, 1991–96 (% annual average growth rate).

difference between success and disaster depends on idiosyncratic shocks that affect certain sectors which are (or become) prevalent in certain regions. Most of the best-performing LLS are in the north (especially in Trentino). An exception is provided by Melfi, where the multinational car manufacturer, Fiat, acted as a so-called 'large developer' by building a car production plant with the help of financial and fiscal incentives available to the Objective 1 regions of the EU. Most of the worst-performing LLS are in the south (especially in Calabria and Basilicata).

In Table 7.3, we turn our attention to employment figures across the thirty-four sectors under consideration. It can bee seen that variability between sectors is as great as between areas. The best-performing service sector by far was real estate

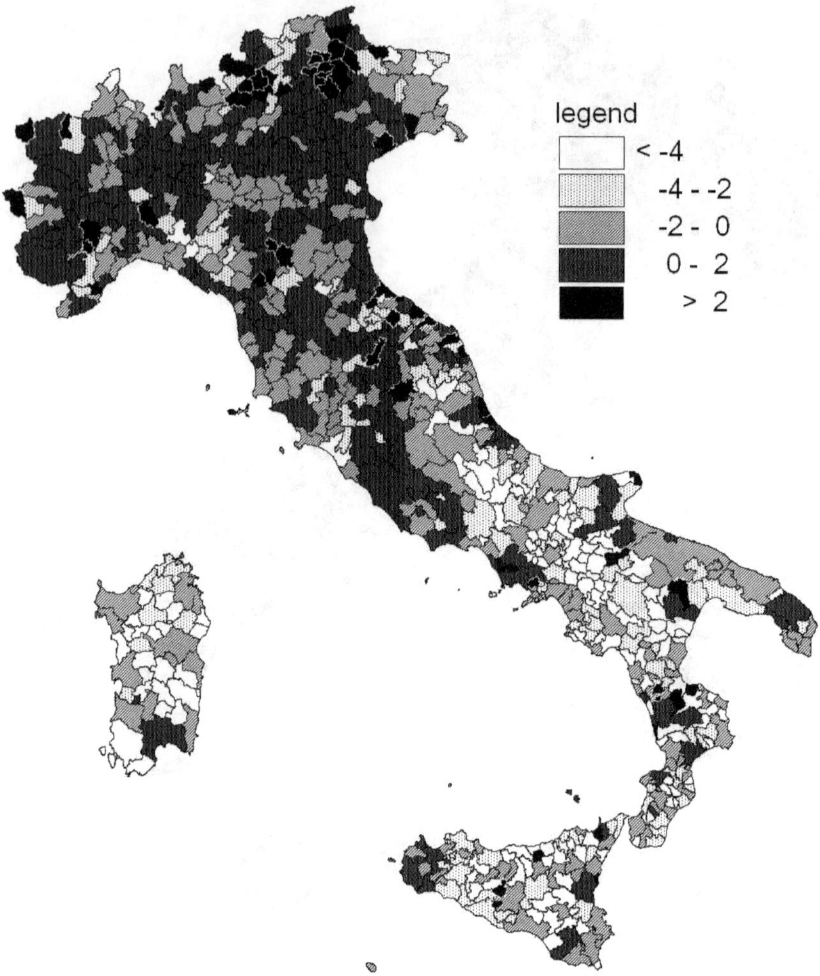

Figure 7.3 Employment dynamics in services in the LLS in Italy, 1991–96 (% annual average growth rate).

activities (14 per cent annual average growth rate), followed by professional and entrepreneurial services (5 per cent). Nevertheless, employment fell in some service sectors: motor vehicles trade, retail (which is the most important sector in terms of total number of employees), post and telecommunications and renting of machinery and personal goods. The worst-performing sectors came from the manufacturing sector, primarily other transport equipment (down 6 per cent), radio, television and communication equipment (down 5.9 per cent) and basic metals (down 4.5 per cent). Only a few manufacturing sectors showed a positive performance: rubber and plastic (up 2 per cent), instruments (up 2 per cent) and machinery (up 0.6 per cent).

Finally, if we analyse the issue of spatial dependence, we obtain conflicting

Table 7.1 Employment growth in macroregions

Macro-region[a]	*Employees ('000)*		*Annual average variation*		
	1991	*1996*	*Total*	*Manufacturing*[b]	*Services*
North-west	4,658	4,546	–0.48	–1.75	0.89
North-east	3,209	3,263	0.33	–0.69	0.65
Centre-north	1,606	1,587	–0.24	–1.04	0.33
Centre-south	1,373	1,344	–0.42	–1.89	–0.19
South	1,691	1,594	–1.18	–2.24	–0.83
Islands	894	810	–1.98	–3.14	–1.73
Italy	13,431	13,144	–0.43	–1.47	0.17

Notes

a North-west: Lombardia, Piemonte, Val d'Aosta, Liguria; north-east: Trentino, Friuli, Veneto, Emilia; centre-north: Tuscany, Umbria, Marche; centre-south: Lazio, Abruzzo, Molise; south: Campania, Puglia, Basilicata, Calabria; islands: Sicily, Sardinia.

b Excluding the building sector.

results (Table 7.4). At the global and macro-sectors level there is evidence of spatial autocorrelation, as already suggested by visual inspection of the maps in Figures 7.1 to 7.3. The Moran index for the whole country and for the manufacturing and services sectors indicates that the dynamics of employment in an LLS are influenced by the performance of nearby areas. Moreover, spatial dependence can be detected in the building industry. However, when employment growth is disaggregated by sector, the occurrence of spatial dependence is more differentiated. In fact, there appears to be a positive and significant spatial dependence in fourteen sectors out of thirty-four.[10] In general, spatial association is stronger in the services sector (eight out of thirteen service sectors show spatial dependence) rather than in manufacturing (six out of twenty sectors show spatial dependence).

The estimation framework

The reduced form that is estimated is based on the idea that employment dynamics is affected by three groups of potential externalities differentiated with respect to their level of specificity: externalities that are unique to a particular local industry, those that are characteristic at the local level and those that are specific for a particular industry.

We, therefore, agree with recent reports (Dekle 2002, Cingano and Schivardi 2003) that employment growth regressions are able to provide interesting information on the reduced form relation between local conditions and employment but not, in any clear-cut way, between local conditions and productivity growth. This is because of possible variation in four factors relevant to the latter: local capital stock, demand elasticity, the effects of agglomeration on labour supply and the degree of substitutability among factors. We believe that in our sample only the first hypothesis can realistically be tested on our sample as it is clear that local externalities affect labour supply and therefore create identification problems. Moreover, it seems rather unlikely that the combination of high demand

Table 7.2 Employment growth in selected areas

LLS	*Region*	*Employees ('000)* 1991	*1996*	*Annual average variation*	*Sectoral performance*	
Top 10 LLS					*Best sector*	*Second best sector*
Melfi	Basilicata	6.0	13.4	16.0	Metals	Car industry
Canazei	Trentino Alto Adige	2.1	3.7	11.1	Furniture etc.	Hotel and restaurants
Pinzolo	Trentino Alto Adige	1.9	3.3	10.4	Rubber and plastic	Wearing apparel
Moena	Trentino Alto Adige	1.0	1.5	8.6	Computer services	Paper
Badia	Trentino Alto Adige	3.3	5.0	8.6	Chemicals	Electronic equipment
Peio	Trentino Alto Adige	1.4	2.1	7.9	Non-metallic minerals	Property
Predazzo	Trentino Alto Adige	1.4	1.9	5.8	Leather and footwear	Electronic equipment
Malé	Trentino Alto Adige	2.0	2.6	5.5	Precision equipment	Printing and publishing
Aversa	Campania	17.6	22.9	5.3	Metals	R&D
Agordo	Veneto	6.1	7.9	5.1	Property	Auxiliary transport services
Worst 10 LLS					*Worst sector*	*Second worst sector*
Sant'Agato di Esaro	Calabria	1.0	0.5	–13.9	Non-metallic minerals	Electronic equipment
Pescopagano	Basilicata	1.2	0.6	–13.3	Rubber and plastic	Textiles
Salandra	Basilicata	0.8	0.4	–12.4	Printing and publishing	Precision equipment
Samugheo	Sardinia	1.1	0.6	–11.1	Electronic equipment	Renting of personal goods
San Giorgo Lucano	Basilicata	0.8	0.5	–10.5	Auxiliary transport services	Renting of personal goods
Palagonia	Sicily	3.0	1.8	–10.1	Wearing apparel	Renting of personal goods
Maierato	Calabria	0.6	0.4	–9.2	Wearing apparel	Rubber and plastic
Candela	Puglia	0.7	0.4	–9.1	Chemicals	Construction
Montecalvo Irpino	Campania	0.8	0.5	–9.1	Wood	Gas and oil
Verzino	Calabria	0.7	0.4	–9.1	Textiles	Printing and publishing

Table 7.3 Employment growth in manufacturing and services sectors

Sector	Employees ('000) 1991	Employees ('000) 1996	Annual average variation	Quota (%) (1996)
1 Food, beverages and tobacco	474	447	–1.2	3.4
2 Textiles	404	345	–3.1	2.6
3 Wearing apparel	419	346	–3.8	2.6
4 Leather and footwear	244	231	–1.1	1.8
5 Wood products, except furniture	186	170	–1.8	1.3
6 Paper	89	85	–0.7	0.6
7 Printing and publishing	195	175	–2.2	1.3
8 Coke and refined petroleum products	29	24	–3.7	0.2
9 Chemicals and chemical products	237	209	–2.5	1.6
10 Rubber and plastic	179	198	2.0	1.5
11 Non-metallic mineral products	276	251	–1.9	1.9
12 Basic metals	170	136	–4.5	1.0
13 Fabricated metal products	615	622	0.2	4.7
14 Machinery	539	554	0.6	4.2
15 Office, computing and electrical machinery	233	224	–0.8	1.7
16 Radio, television and communication equipment	139	103	–5.9	0.8
17 Medical, precision and medical instruments	117	129	2.0	1.0
18 Motor vehicles, trailers and semi-trailers	214	186	–2.8	1.4
19 Other transport equipment	136	101	–6.0	0.8
20 Furniture, recycling and other	315	318	0.2	2.4
Manufacturing (subtotal)	5,210	4,856	–1.4	36.9
21 Building	1,332	1,342	0.1	10.2
22 Motor vehicles trade and repair	491	446	–1.9	3.4
23 Wholesale trade	901	986	1.8	7.5
24 Retail trade	1,909	1,585	–3.7	12.1
25 Hotel and restaurant	727	727	0.0	5.5
26 Transport services	584	594	0.3	4.5
27 Auxiliary transport and travel agencies	186	200	1.5	1.5
28 Post and telecommunications	348	290	–3.6	2.2
29 Financial intermediation and insurance	569	561	–0.3	4.3
30 Real estate activities	83	168	14.0	1.3
31 Renting of machinery and personal goods	20	18	–2.2	0.1
32 Computer and related activities	181	203	2.3	1.5
33 Research and development	16	20	4.0	0.1
34 Other professional and entrepreneurial services	874	1152	5.5	8.8
Services (subtotal)	6,888	6,947	0.2	63.1
Total	*13,431*	*13,144*	*–0.4*	*100.0*

Table 7.4 Moran test on spatial autocorrelation of employment growth among LLS

	Sectors	*Standardized Z-values*	*Probability level*
1	*Food, beverages and tobacco*	*3.3*	*0.0*
2	Textiles	–0.1	0.9
3	*Wearing apparel*	*1.7*	*0.0*
4	Leather and footwear	–0.3	0.7
5	*Wood products, except furniture*	*2.7*	*0.0*
6	*Paper*	*2.8*	*0.0*
7	Printing and publishing	–0.6	0.6
8	Coke and refined petroleum products	0.2	0.8
9	Chemicals and chemical products	0.7	0.5
10	*Rubber and plastic*	*0.9*	*0.0*
11	Non-metallic mineral products	1.5	0.1
12	Basic metals	–0.7	0.4
13	Fabricated metal products	0.5	0.6
14	Machinery	–0.1	0.8
15	Office, computing and electrical machinery	–0.7	0.4
16	Radio, television and communication equipment	1.0	0.3
17	Medical, precision and medical instruments	–0.3	0.7
18	Motor vehicles, trailers and semi trailers	–0.2	0.8
19	Other transport equipment	1.1	0.3
20	*Furniture, recycling and other*	*–2.8*	*0.0*
	Manufacturing (subtotal)	3.7	0.0
21	*Building*	*5.0*	*0.0*
22	*Motor vehicles trade and repair*	*3.0*	*0.0*
23	*Wholesale trade*	*1.8*	*0.0*
24	*Retail trade*	*9.7*	*0.0*
25	*Hotel and restaurant*	*12.4*	*0.0*
26	*Transport services*	*2.1*	*0.0*
27	Auxiliary transport and travel agencies	1.0	0.2
28	Post and telecommunications	0.8	0.4
29	*Financial intermediation and insurance*	*3.7*	*0.0*
30	*Real estate activities*	*1.9*	*0.0*
31	Renting of machinery and personal goods	–0.8	0.4
32	Computer and related activities	0.1	0.9
33	Research and development	0.1	0.9
34	*Other professional and entrepreneurial services*	*5.6*	*0.0*
	Services (subtotal)	17.9	0.0
	Total	*11.6*	*0.0*

Notes

Normal approximation. Sectors with significant spatial autocorrelation are in italics.

elasticity and low factor substitutability occurred in Italy in the early 1990s, a period characterised by diffused reorganisation and restructuring at several levels of the production chain and, most importantly, by stagnating demand.

We therefore categorise factors affecting employment dynamics at the local industrial level into three major groups: (i) local industry level, (ii) local level and (iii) industry level. Let us discuss the various phenomena which are going to be considered as potential determinants of the performance of local industrial employment.

At the local industry level one finds the most debated factors, that is specialisation or Marshall externalities (SE), diversity or Jacobs externalities (DE) and scale effects and/or the degree of competition (SC).

In general, the specialisation or Marshallian externalities capture the advantages gained by firms producing similar products within a bounded geographical location. Marshall externalities are measured by means of an index of relative production specialisation. This variable measures static pecuniary and localisation externalities such as the availability of suitable supplies of labour and primary and intermediate goods (Ellison and Glaeser 1999), the provision of specific goods and services (Bartelsman *et al.* 1994) and the availability of specific infrastructures and networks. Moreover, this specialisation index should also take into account dynamic spillovers arising from the intra-industry flows of localised knowledge that occur among similar firms located in the same area (Henderson *et al.* 1995). Marshall externalities are usually contrasted with diversity externalities in production activities (also known in the literature as Jacobs or urbanisation externalities; Jacobs, 1969). In this work they are measured by the inverse of the Herfindal index applied to employment in all sectors except the one considered. Such externalities are expected to have a positive influence on local growth based on the hypothesis that a firm located in a particular area will benefit from the presence in the same area of a wide range of other firms operating in different sectors since it can enjoy fruitful inter-industry exchanges and cross-fertilisation.

Finally, among local and sector-specific variables, an index of competition or of scale economies is usually included to assess the so-called Porter effect (Porter 1990). Such an index is the average dimension of plants and, in fact, has been used in previous studies to measure two distinct effects: (i) the number of firms per worker (the inverse of SC) is interpreted by Glaeser *et al.* (1992) as a direct measure of the degree of local competition; (ii) the number of employees per firm can be seen as a proxy for economies of scale that may affect labour productivity (O'hUallachàin and Satterthwaite 1992). In principle, it would be better to distinguish between the two effects defining two different indicators and to include both of them in the estimated equation (as is done in Combes 2000a). Unfortunately, the lack of data on employment of individual firms does not allow the construction of a concentration ratio, which would be a more appropriate indicator of local competition. In contrast to previous contributions, we do not attribute a priori either of the two effects to such an indicator, leaving its interpretation ambiguous.

Employment changes at the local industrial level may be attributable to some features that characterise the whole LLS. Local factors may refer to a large set of socioeconomic phenomena that influence the performance of firms in the area. We have classified them as follows: network externalities (NE), human capital (HK), social capital (SK) and labour supply (LS).

The first class of network externalities (NE1) is intended to take into account the influence of the size of the economic system, as measured by the population density (resident population per km^2 in each LLS) where a firm is located (Ciccone and Hall 1996). In practice, one would expect this to have a positive effect on local growth as a higher population density implies higher local demand and the availability of a wider supply of local public services. The closeness of buyers may have both a static and a dynamic effect, the latter being related to the fact that this may facilitate early perception of market needs. At the same time, the increasing size of the local economy may imply diseconomies of scale setting in when congestion effects prevail, giving rise to pollution and greater competition in the factor markets, resulting in higher factor costs.

We have also included a second proxy for network externalities (NE2) that focuses on the supply side, taking into account the presence of small firms within the local economy. The idea is that, when the proportion of small plants is large, firms may have to find ways of compensating for working outside their optimal production scale by cooperating and integrating with other firms at the local level. This stimulates the creation of local externalities. The opposite happens with large firms which are more vertically integrated and therefore are less involved in local networks.

The role of human capital in facilitating innovation activities and information spillovers, and therefore growth, is examined by means of a proxy to measure the availability in the local area of labour forces with a high level of education (share of population with a university education).[11] A large well-educated workforce represents an advantage to firms, thus fostering local growth.

Another important local element that may encourage innovation activities and smooth the process of knowledge diffusion is social capital. However, it is not an easy task to find suitable indicators for such a complex and intangible phenomenon (Helliwell and Putnam 1995). To measure the degree of trust in the local society we include an index of the propensity to cooperate among firms based on the number of inter-firm agreements and participations in consortia surveyed by the industrial census at the provincial level. The idea is that a higher degree of propensity to cooperate among firms in a certain area helps local growth since it facilitates knowledge diffusion, decreases transaction costs and enables firms to take advantage of local externalities.[12]

Finally, we accept the idea that externalities may affect the labour supply (Cingano and Schivardi 2003) and therefore we have tried to account for this possible effect by including an indicator of its size. Such an indicator is given by the participation rate (labour force divided by the total population aged 15–65). Other potential local externalities may be those related to natural endowments and other geographical factors. They should, however, have more of a static than a dynamic effect. We have nevertheless tried to take these into account by means of local fixed effects in the panel regression. However, they proved to have too a strong collinearity with the other local indicators and have therefore been removed from the basic regressions.

The rate of employment growth in a local industry may also be affected by factors that are unique to each production sector although they are common to all areas. These factors can capture, for instance, technological progress and opportunities within each industry at the national level. In our econometric estimation they are proxied by the sectoral fixed effects in the panel regressions.

The econometric results

The econometric analysis is based on a simple equation, as is usual in the literature (Glaeser *et al.* 1992), where the growth rate at the local industry level is represented by labour dynamics, because of the lack of data on output at the local industry level, and is affected by the three components of the technology growth rate described in the previous section:

$$\log(L_{ijt}+1/L_{ijt}) = \chi_1\,SE_{ijt} + \chi_2\,SC_{ijt} + \chi_3\,DE_{ijt} + \beta_1\,NE1_{it} + \beta_2\,NE2_{it} + \beta_3\,HK_{it} + \beta_4\,SK_{it} + \beta_5\,LS_{it} + FE_j$$

Econometric strategy

In contrast to previous studies, in this work we attempt to simultaneously consider various factors that we believe affect local economic growth thanks to the broad perspective suggested by our theoretical framework. In fact, in the search for the best specification we do not apply the usual general to specific approach, which consists of a sequence of deletions of variables that are found to be not statistically significant. Rather, we carry out an analysis of parameter stability with respect to different subsections of our main sample. In other words, we apply the same general specification to subsamples identified with respect to geographical and sectoral features to establish if there is any difference in the value, sign and significance of the estimated coefficients.

The main differences with respect to our previous work on Italy (Usai and Paci 2003) are: (i) we include the entire market economy (manufacture plus services); and (ii) sectors are considered at a higher level of aggregation (two-digit instead of three-digit) in order to increase the probability of finding non-zero observations in the local industry. Indeed, one of the crucial points in the analysis of highly specialised sectors in small areas is that we often deal with too small a number of firms (or even none) and this makes the econometric analysis more problematic. Thus, in order to test the robustness of our findings, we have tried to control for the potential causes of distortion. More specifically, in some estimations we have excluded (i) all local industry observations with a zero number of firms both in the initial and in the final year and (ii) the outlier observations with a residual higher than three times the standard deviation.

To take into account the risk of variables omission with respect to the industry dimension, we include sectoral fixed effects. We have also tried to control for local fixed effects, but it emerges that they generate problems of multicollinearity, given the simultaneous presence of several explanatory variables specific to each area. It is important to note that all our regressors are exogenous to the local industry employment growth rate since they refer to the beginning of the period considered. All variables are in log and are normalised by the value they take at the national level.

Aggregate regressions

Let us start with the analysis of aggregate estimations based on a dataset with two dimensions: geographical and sectoral. Five different panels have been defined: Italy, with 784 LLS and thirty-four sectors; the centre-north (453 LLS, thirty-four sectors); the south (331 LLS, thirty-four sectors); manufacturing (784 LLS, twenty sectors); and services (784 LLS, thirty sectors). The estimation results are reported in Table 7.5.[13]

The first interesting result is the absence of specialisation externalities: the coefficient of SE is negative and highly significant in all subsets considered (north, south, manufacturing, services). This outcome confirms previous studies for the USA (Glaeser *et al.* 1992), France (Combes 2000a) and Italy (Cainelli and Leoncini 1999, Forni and Paba 2000, Cunat and Peri 2001, Usai and Paci 2003). The absence of Marshallian externalities at the LLS level can be partly explained by the fact that our analysis covers a short time period characterised by an economic crisis that may have induced a substantial degree of reorganisation in those local productive systems that were highly specialised and therefore more costly to modify and transform. Moreover, we may also note that most highly specialised local production systems in Italy operate in traditional and mature sectors and that the negative relationship between initial specialisation and employment growth can be linked to a product cycle mechanism.

Average firm size (SC) is always found to be negatively related to local growth, suggesting the absence of economies of scale in employment growth mechanisms. This result is strengthened by the positive sign of network externalities represented by the presence of small firms (NE2). Diversity externalities (DE) appear to be positively related to local growth of the economy as a whole, but remain positive only for manufacturing once the sample is divided by area and by sector.

As far as local specific determinants are concerned, the size of the local system, measured by population density (NE1), shows contrasting results. It appears to be negatively linked to employment dynamics in the north and in manufacturing, but positively related in the south and for the service sector. In other words, this result suggests that in the centre-north (where most manufacturing activity is located) some congestion effects are already at work, whereas a positive agglomeration effect is still present in the southern regions.

The indicators measuring the different qualities of capital (human, social) show interesting composite results. First, university education (HK) emerges as a relevant and positive determinant of local growth (Lodde 2000, Di Liberto 2001).

Table 7.5 Econometric results

Variables		*Italy (with outliers)*	*Italy*	*North–centre*	*South*	*Manufacturing*	*Services*
Local and industry-specific variables							
SE	Specialisation externalities	–8.74[a]	–7.14[a]	–4.76[a]	–12.2[a]	–6.17[a]	–7.77[a]
SC	Scale effect – competition	–0.53[a]	–0.3[b]	–0.50[a]	–0.52[b]	–0.46[a]	–1.51[a]
DE	Diversity externalities	0.75[b]	0.66[b]	–0.43	0.24	4.62[a]	0.07
Local specific variables							
NE1	Population density	–0.08[b]	–1.88	–5.74[b]	8.59[b]	–10.10[b]	0.74
NE2	Small firms	0.29[a]	0.26	0.72[a]	0.84[b]	–0.24	0.38[c]
HK	Human capital	2.01[a]	1.40[a]	0.96[a]	2.42[a]	–1.09[b]	2.80[a]
SK	Social capital	0.19[a]	0.15[a]	0.13[a]	–0.29	0.17	0.14[b]
LS	Labour supply	1.11[a]	1.16[a]	0.89[a]	0.20	1.67[a]	1.16[a]
	No. of observations	23,326	22,293	12,674	9,617	11,551	9,321
	Adjusted R^2	0.07	0.09	0.07	0.15	0.04	0.13
	SE of regression	32.0	22.0	17.8	24.1	21.8	11.3

Notes

Dependent variable: employment growth in the local industry. Annual average 1991–96 (log).

Estimation method: generalised least squares (cross-section weights) with industry fixed effects; White robust standard error.

Level of significance: a=1%, b=5%, c=10%.

We have excluded local industry with zero employees in both 1991 and 1996 and outlier observations with a residual larger than three standard deviations.

However, this relationship becomes more complex when considering a more detailed sectoral analysis. University education negatively influences employment growth in manufacturing, but has a positive effect in the service sector. Second, the importance of social capital is suggested by the coefficient of the variable that measures cooperation among firms (SK), which is positive, as expected, in all regressions except for the south and manufacturing. Finally, the presence of a large labour supply (proxied by the participation rate) exerts a positive influence on employment dynamics.

All these results reinforce the idea that – especially during the negative phase of the business cycle, such as was the case during the period under consideration – a production system based on a diversified network of small flexible firms, which are willing to cooperate and characterised by a well-educated labour force, is a crucial asset in promoting local employment growth.

Sectoral regressions

In this section we turn our attention to the analysis of employment growth in each sector based on a cross-section estimation of the equation above. In this case we are also able to address directly the problem of spatial association. As we have remarked before, employment growth in a region may be influenced by employment dynamics in the nearby areas, introducing a possible bias into regressions that do not take this possibility into account. In order to deal with this problem we have applied the following estimation procedures: (i) ordinary least squares (OLS) estimation with SpaceStat to assess the presence of spatial autocorrelation based on the Lagrange multiplier (LM) tests; (ii) if there is no autocorrelation, and the least squares estimates are efficient and consistent, we have used the OLS–White robust standard errors estimations, which allow us to correct for the heteroscedasticity; (iii) if spatial autocorrelation is detected, we need to correct this by including a spatial lag-dependent variable. In such a case it is necessary to use maximum likelihood (ML) estimation instead of least squares, introducing spatial lag-dependent variables up to the contiguity level necessary to correct for the presence of spatial autocorrelation.

The results of sectoral regressions are reported in Table 7.6. We detected spatial autocorrelation in ten out of thirty-four sectors, and therefore a ML estimation was performed with the inclusion of first- and second-order contiguity spatial lag-dependent variables. These were always positive and significant. As a result of this procedure, spatial autocorrelation was controlled for in all sectors. The sectoral results show that the impact of local characteristics differs significantly in the manufacturing and service sectors.

Some observations deserve emphasis. First, the coefficients for specialisation externalities appear to be mostly negative and statistically significant in both the service and manufacturing sectors. In only one case did specialisation result in increased employment over the period, the tourism sector. Tourism is a growing industry across Italy, and especially in the north-east, where it turned out there were strong agglomeration and specialisation externalities; this was also true of contiguous areas. Second, the magnitude of such negative effects appears to be greater in the service sectors. This may cause employment composition to converge among regions (Rombaldoni and Zazzaro 1997). However, this finding seems to conflict with evidence from the USA, where the service sector seems to be becoming more concentrated with time as a result of decreasing transport costs. Further analysis, possibly over a longer time span, is needed to determine whether this is just a temporary phenomenon related to the period under examination.

Diversity externalities have a positive and significant influence on employment dynamics in less than half of our sectors, in ten manufacturing and five service sectors to be exact. There are also four sectors in which diversity plays a negative role. In the case of this indicator, we believe that more evidence needs to be collected in order to distinguish between those effects that are truly cross-fertilisation spillovers (and therefore more dynamic in nature) and those which are due to input–output relationships (and therefore with more static consequences).[14]

The variable that measures both scale internal economies and competition effects, as expected, varies greatly across sectors. A positive correlation is found mostly in the manufacturing sectors (basic metals, printing, petroleum, rubber, etc.), indicating, most probably given the selection of industries, economies of scale at work rather than the counter-effects of competition. Interestingly, a positive role is also found for some service sectors, notably in retail trade, where a process of strong concentration has been taking place over the last decade. The other service sector that displays a positive sign is R&D. Furthermore, it is worth noting that for four service sectors (motor vehicles trade and repairs, hotels and restaurants, real estate activities and other business services) either diseconomies of scale are affecting employment growth or, more likely, local competition effects are at work. Finally, for construction the coefficient is negative and significant.

Of the other determinants, we can see that human capital, that is the availability of employees with a university degree, turns out to be especially important in the service sectors. Similar results are found for social capital, the effect of which is mostly positive and significant mainly in the service sectors. As for the size of the economy, results are ambiguous. In five sectors (three in manufacturing and two in services) there are positive and significant effects, whereas in three others (two in manufacturing and one in services) the effect is negative. The indicator concerning labour supply proved to be mostly positive, especially in the service sectors.

Concluding comments

This chapter has attempted to measure local economic performance in the context of an ongoing process of structural change that is transforming the economies from manufacturing to service ones. It is argued that such a process has important implications for the analysis of the geography of economic activities in that the forces of agglomeration are different in the two sectors. The main contribution of this chapter is, therefore, the analysis of local short-term economic performance, as expressed by employment dynamics, in both the service and the manufacturing

Table 7.6 Summary of OLS[a] results for the thirty-four sectors

	Sector	*Estimation method*	*No. of observations*	*SC*[b]	*SE*	*DE*	*NE1*	*NE2*	*HK*	*SK*	*LS*	*Spatial lag first order*	*Spatial lag second order*
1	Food, beverages and tobacco	ML	784	n	*N*	p	n	p	p	p	p	*P*	
2	Textiles	OLS-W	730	n	n	*P*	*P*	p	n	n	p		
3	Wearing apparel	OLS-W	774	p	p	*P*	*P*	p	p	n	p		
4	Leather and footwear	OLS-W	596	*N*	n	*N*	p	p	n	p	p		
5	Wood products, except furniture	OLS-W	784	*P*	n	*P*	*N*	n	n	*P*	*P*		
6	Paper	ML	476	p	*N*	p	n	*N*	n	n	n	*P*	
7	Printing and publishing	OLS-W	729	*P*	*N*	*P*	p	p	*P*	p	n		
8	Coke and refined petroleum products	OLS-W	366	*P*	*N*	*N*	p	p	*P*	p	*P*		
9	Chemicals and chemical products	OLS-W	574	p	*N*	*P*	p	n	p	n	n		
10	Rubber and plastic	OLS-W	619	*P*	*N*	p	n	n	*N*	*P*	p		
11	Non-metallic mineral products	OLS-W	779	p	*N*	p	*N*	p	n	p	*P*		
12	Basic metals	OLS-W	454	*P*	*N*	n	n	p	n	p	p		
13	Fabricated metal products	OLS-W	784	n	*N*	*P*	n	n	*N*	n	*P*		
14	Machinery	OLS-W	732	p	*N*	*P*	n	p	n	p	p		
15	Office, computing and electrical machinery	OLS-W	664	n	*N*	*P*	*P*	n	*N*	n	p		
16	Radio, television and communication equipment	OLS-W	668	p	*N*	p	p	n	*P*	p	p		
17	Medical, precision and medical instruments	OLS-W	735	*P*	*N*	*P*	n	n	p	p	n		

18	Motor vehicles, trailers and semi-trailers	OLS-W	370	p	*N*	n	n	p	p	n	n		
19	Other transport equipment	OLS-W	431	p	*N*	n	p	p	p	p	p		
20	Furniture, recycling and other	ML	771	p	*N*	*P*	p	*N*	n	n	p	*P*	
21	Building	ML	784	*N*	*N*	n	n	*P*	p	p	n	*P*	p
22	Motor vehicles trade and repair	ML	784	*N*	*N*	n	*N*	p	*P*	p	*P*	p	
23	Wholesale trade	ML	784	p	*N*	*P*	*P*	*P*	*P*	n	p	*P*	
24	Retail trade	ML	784	*P*	*N*	p	n	*P*	*P*	n	*P*	*P*	*P*
25	Hotel and restaurant	ML	784	*N*	*P*	*P*	n	n	*P*	p	*P*	*P*	
26	Transport services	OLS-W	784	p	*N*	*N*	p	p	*P*	p	*P*		
27	Auxiliary transport and travel agencies	OLS-W	737	*P*	*N*	p	*P*	p	*P*	n	p		
28	Post and telecommunications	OLS-W	784	n	*N*	p	p	p	p	*P*	p		
29	Financial intermediation and insurance	ML	784	p	*N*	*P*	p	*N*	*P*	p	p	*P*	
30	Real estate activities	OLS-W	696	*N*	*N*	*P*	n	*N*	*P*	*P*	p		
31	Renting of machinery and personal goods	OLS-W	679	p	*N*	*N*	p	p	*P*	*P*	*P*		
32	Computer and related activities	OLS-W	753	n	*N*	*P*	n	n	*P*	*P*	*P*		
33	Research and development	OLS-W	585	*P*	*N*	n	n	n	*P*	p	*N*		
34	Other professional and entrepreneurial services	ML	784	*N*	*N*	n	p	p	*P*	p	p	*P*	

Notes

a ML, maximum likelihood; OLS-W, ordinary least squares–White robust standard errors. p = positive coefficient; *P* = positive, statistically (up to 10 per cent) significant coefficient; n = negative coefficient; *N* = positive, statistically (up to 10 per cent) significant coefficient.

b SC, scale-effect competition; SE, specialisation externalities; DE, diversity externalities; NE1, population density; NE2, small firms; HK, human capital; SK, social capital; LS, labour supply.

sectors. Thanks to a large set of variables and data, we have been able to explain some of the differences in the economic performance of sectors by assessing the role of several potential determinants of local economic dynamics.

Our results confirm that the picture of agglomeration forces operating at very small geographical units is multifaceted. Overall, we find that specialisation has negative effects, possibly because of the specific critical period we are analysing, but also as a result of a process of restructuring that replaced labour with other factors.

Average firm size is always negatively related to local growth, suggesting the absence of economies of scale in employment growth mechanisms (or the effects of pro-competitive effects). This result is confirmed by the positive sign of the indicator for the presence of small firms in the local area. Finally, as in previous work, diversity externalities appear to be positively related to local growth for the whole economy, and maintain their positive influence in manufacturing, but not services. Human and social capital also prove to be important for employment growth. All these results reinforce the idea that – especially during the negative phase of a business cycle such as the one considered – a production system based on a diversified network of small flexible firms, willing to cooperate and characterised by well-educated labour forces, is a crucial asset to promote local employment growth.

In the case of sectoral regressions, the picture becomes even more complicated, apart from the role of specialisation, which appears always to be negatively linked to employment dynamics with the notable exception of the tourism sector. Spatial correlation is taken into account, when needed, by the estimation of spatial lag equations.

Some interesting extensions lie ahead. First of all, we would be interested to know to what extent some of the results are dependent on the economic downturn that the economy was experiencing during the period under study. In this regard, it is important that new data from the Italian census will soon be available to enable us to perform such an update. Newly available data at the plant and provincial level will enable us to convert employment data to value added, thus making possible the analysis of real economic performance as measured by productivity.

Acknowledgements

We thank Sonia Deidda, Giuliana Caruso and Barbara Dettori for excellent research assistance. We also thank the participants of the 2002 EARIE conference in Madrid, the 2003 ERSA conference in Jyvaskyla and seminars held at the University of Reading, as well as FIB in Salvador Bahia and the University of Bergamo. We acknowledge the financial support of MIUR (COFIN 2002 no. 2002138187_02).

Notes

1 Most analyses have, in fact, concentrated on the manufacturing sectors only. The main notable exceptions being those of Combes (2000a) for France, who considers forty-two service sectors, and, more recently, Almeida (2001) for Portugal, who analyses

thirty-two sectors. Dekle (2002) also considers the service sectors, but at a very aggregated level.

2 The analysis of differences across areas, but in manufacturing only, is mainly pursued in Usai and Paci (2003).

3 In the USA in particular, most studies (Glaeser *et al.* 1992, Henderson *et al.* 1995) have relied on the city as the geographic unit of analysis, so they have necessarily to consider them as economic islands.

4 Marshall (1990 [1890]) identified three causes: (i) specialised labour forces and the generation of new ideas, arising from face-to-face communications and human capital accumulation, (ii) the availability of specialised inputs and infrastructure and (iii) economies of mass production. In Marshall's view, firms tend to collocate with their buyers and suppliers, which creates positive externalities arising from transportation, communication and coordination efficiencies.

5 In fact, Glaeser *et al.* (1992) also included Porter's arguments in contrast to Jacobs's and Marshall's ones. According to Porter (1990), urban areas which are very specialised may boost growth as a result of competitive effects.

6 However, in Combes (2000a) the significance levels of results are not given for sector by sector regressions.

7 As a matter of fact, this was also the case in Glaeser *et al.* (1992). But in this case, the specialisation coefficient is already negative and the elimination of the bias would just possibly reinforce that result.

8 Most importantly, Cingano and Schivardi (2003) show that within the same sample, if one uses employment growth as the dependent variable, specialisation effects became negative.

9 See also Baldwin and Martin (2004) for the effects of tradability, transaction costs and capital mobility on the growth dynamics within a centre–periphery model.

10 The unexpected presence of negative and significant spatial dependence in furniture and recycling may be interpreted as a purely statistical result because this is the 'residual' sector in the classification of manufacturing activities and therefore it is highly heterogeneous.

11 We have also tried another proxy – the share of population who complete only primary education – which measures low-level education and therefore should negatively affect local growth.

12 We have also tested a second indicator to capture the characteristics of the social environment: an index of the existence of organised crime at the provincial level, based on the hypothesis that a high level of crime is detrimental to local development as it increases firms' costs and reduces expected revenues.

13 In the panel estimations it is not feasible to deal with the problem of spatial association due to technical storage limits imposed by SpaceStat on such large datasets. Spatial association is dealt with in the sectoral estimations, where we find that most results are, nevertheless, robust with respect to the presence of spatial autocorrelation.

14 See the interesting methodology developed by Forni and Paba (2002) on this aspect.

References

Almeida, R. (2001) 'Local characteristics and growth in Portuguese regions', mimeo, Universitat Pompeu Fabra.

Arrow, K.J. (1962) 'The economic implications of learning by doing', *Review of Economic Studies*, 29: 155–73.

Baldwin, R.E. and Martin, P. (2004) 'Agglomeration and regional growth', in Henderson, J.V. and Thisse J.F. (eds.) *Handbook of Urban and Regional Economics*, Amsterdam: North-Holland.

Bartelsman E., Caballero, R. and Lyons, R. (1994) 'Customer- and supplier-driven externalities', *American Economic Review*, 84: 1075–84.

Brusco, S. (1982) 'The Emilian model: productive decentralisation and social integration', *Cambridge Journal of Economics*, 6: 167–84.

Cainelli, G. and Leoncini, R. (1999) 'Externalities and long-term local industrial development: some empirical evidence for Italy', *Revue d'Economie Industrielle*, 90: 25–39.

Ciccone, A. and Hall, R. (1996) 'Productivity and the density of economic activity', *American Economic Review*, 86: 54–70.

Cingano, F. and Schivardi, F. (2003) 'Identifying the sources of local productivity growth', mimeo, Bank of Italy Research Department.

Combes, P. (2000a) 'Economic structure and local growth: France, 1984–1993', *Journal of Urban Economics*, 47: 329–55.

Combes, P. (2000b) 'Marshall–Arrow–Romer externalities and city growth', CERAS Working Paper 99/06.

Combes, P. and Overman, H. (2004) 'The spatial distribution of economic activities in the European Union', in Henderson, J.V. and Thisse, J.F. (eds.) *Handbook of Urban and Regional Economics*, Amsterdam: North-Holland.

Cunat, A. and Peri, G. (2001) 'Job creation: geography, technology and infrastructures', *Giornale degli Economisti*, 61: 23–54.

Dekle, R. (2002) 'Industrial concentration and regional growth: evidence from the prefectures', *Review of Economics and Statistics*, 84: 310–15.

De Lucio, J.J, Herce, J.A. and Goicolea, A. (2002) 'The effects of externalities on productivity growth in Spanish industry', *Regional Science and Urban Economics*, 32: 241–58.

Desmet, K. and Fafchamps, M. (2003) 'What are falling transport costs doing to spatial concentration across US counties?', CEPR Discussion Paper 3853.

Di Liberto, A. (2001) 'Stock di capitale umano e crescita delle regioni italiane. Un approccio panel', *Politica Economica*, 17: 159–84.

Duranton, G. and Puga, D. (2001) 'Nursery cities: urban diversity, process innovation, and the life-cycle of products', *American Economic Review*, 91: 1454–75.

Ellison, G. and Glaeser, E. (1999) 'The geographic concentration of industry: does natural advantage explain agglomeration?', *American Economic Review Papers and Proceedings*, 89: 301–16.

Forni, M. and Paba, S. (2000) 'The sources of local growth: evidence from Italy', *Giornale degli Economisti e Annali di Economia*, 59: 1–49.

Forni, M. and Paba, S. (2002) 'Spillovers and the growth of local industries', *Journal of Industrial Economics*, 50: 151–71.

Glaeser, E.L., Kallal, H.D., Sheinkman, J.A. and Sheifler, A. (1992) 'Growth in cities', *Journal of Political Economics*, 100: 1126–52.

Helliwell, J. and Putnam, R. (1995) 'Economic growth and social capital in Italy', *Eastern Economic Journal*, 21: 295–307.

Henderson, V. (2003) 'Marshall's scale economies', *Journal of Urban Economics*, 53: 1–28.

Henderson V., Kunkoro, A. and Turner, M. (1995) 'Industrial development in cities', *Journal of Political Economics*, 103: 1067–90.

Jacobs, J. (1969) *The Economy of Cities*, London: Jonathan Cape.

Krugman, P. (1991) *Economic Geography and Trade*, Cambridge, MA: MIT Press.

Krugman, P. and Venables, A. (1995) 'Globalisation and the inequality of nations', *Quarterly Journal of Economics*, 110: 857–80.

Lodde, S. (2000) 'Education and growth: some disaggregate evidence from the Italian regions', *Rivista Internazionale di Scienze Economiche e Commerciali*, 47: 267–93.

Marshall, A. (1990 [1890]) *Principles of Economics*, Basingstoke: Macmillan.

O'hUallachàin, B. and Satterthwaite, M. (1992) 'Sectoral growth patterns at the metropolitan level: an evaluation of economic development incentives', *Journal of Urban Economics*, 31: 25–58.

Piore, M. and Sabel, C. (1984) *The Second Industrial Divide: Possibilities for Prosperity*, New York: Basic Books.

Porter, M. (1990) *The Competitive Advantage of Nations*, New York: Free Press.

Rombaldoni, R. and Zazzaro, A. (1997) 'Localizzazione delle imprese manifatturiere e specializzazione regionale in Italia: 1970–1990', *Rassegna lavori ISCO*, 14: 151–81.

Romer, P. (1986) 'Increasing returns and long-run growth', *Journal of Political Economy*, 94: 1002–37.

Sforzi, F. (ed.) (1997) *I Sistemi Locali del Lavoro 1991, Argomenti no. 10*, Rome: ISTAT.

Usai, S. and Paci, R. (2003) 'Externalities and local economic growth in manufacturing industries', in Fingleton B. (ed.) *European Regional Growth*, Berlin: Springer-Verlag.

van Soest, D.P., Gerking, S.D., and van Oort, F.G. (2002) 'Knowledge externalities, agglomeration economies and employment growth in Dutch cities', Center Discussion Paper 2002-41, Tilburg University.

8 Accessibility and regional growth in Europe

The role of ICT policies

Roberta Capello and Alessia Spairani

Introduction

Powerful economic processes of internationalisation and globalisation have occurred over the last fifteen years. Particularly in Europe, national boundaries are no longer barriers to economic activity and commerce, thanks to the institutional integration of European states into the EU and to advances in transport and communication networks. This means that European regions compete in a global, or at least continental, market. In this context, the concept of accessibility is increasingly important as a determinant of local economic competitiveness. Accessibility indicates the extent to which it is possible to overcome spatial distance at low cost and gather strategic information before competitors. In a worldwide economy, accessibility reinforces its role as a strategic factor in regional competitiveness. In operational terms, accessibility is generated through the existence of physical transport networks, which reduce distance in space. However, with the rapid development of new technologies and the birth of a new form of production organisation, a new type of accessibility must be considered. This is not physical, but 'virtual' accessibility deriving from information and communication technologies (ICTs). In this chapter, we focus on this new concept of accessibility, and we will assess its impact on regional growth and competitiveness.

The chapter is structured as follows. In the next section we present a review of the role played by accessibility in spatial economic theory. The third section contains our empirical analysis of the impact of accessibility on regional growth. It describes our accessibility indicators, presents a descriptive analysis of the current situation of endowment and use of ICTs relating to the economic development of the regions, and contains an econometric estimation of the impact on regional growth of ICT accessibility. Alternative policy options and their forecast results are presented in the fourth section, while the final section highlights the differences in the impacts of accessibility on regional growth due to the existence of different preconditions favouring ICT exploitation. The last section contains some concluding remarks.

Accessibility in spatial economic theory

The concept of accessibility is one of the basic elements of spatial economic theory. The concept encompasses the advantages for economic activity of reduced geographical distance, measured in terms of reduced transport costs. In spatial economics, accessibility means the possibility of overcoming spatial distance and the spatial barriers for the exchange of goods and information; accessibility means access to sources of inputs with low transport costs; it means the ability to gather strategic information before competitors. In general terms, accessibility means reduced transport costs when space is included in the explanation of market forces. In fact, the existence of transport costs – and therefore of different levels of accessibility in space – is significant for spatial economic theory, since it is the factor that discriminates space and justifies its treatment in economic theory. If transport costs were zero, accessibility to input or output markets, to specific central locations or to the 'business centre' would not be a relevant and discriminating factor among territories.

In location theory, accessibility is the principle governing the location choices of firms and individuals, and therefore the organisation of activities in space. In a logic of a monocentric city and continuous space, Von Thünen's and Alonso's models elegantly explain the way in which accessibility governs location choices for both firms and individuals, and the consequent spatial distribution of urban space among possible alternative destinations (Von Thünen 1826, Alonso 1964). Moreover, in location theory, accessibility explains the regularities in the differences of price and demand in a spatial market; therefore, accessibility explains the behaviour of consumers in a spatial market, their choice between alternative producers and the identification of 'market areas' (Lösch 1954). Finally, in some theories location is the result of a balanced choice between accessibility to input and to output markets, which guarantees minimum total transport costs (Weber 1929).

In regional development theories, characterised by a microeconomic and behavioural approach, the importance of transport costs (and therefore accessibility) is theorised in the concept of 'agglomeration economies' or 'proximity economies'. The microeconomic local endogenous development theories merge with local location theory, since they identify reduced transport costs and higher accessibility to input and output markets as the economic rationale for firms' clustering. Local growth is, in these theories, based on the concepts of 'agglomeration economies' or 'proximity economies' which embed the advantages stemming from reduced geographical distance.[1] Accessibility to relevant input markets, to specific information, to specialised knowledge and to relevant services is recognised and highlighted as reflecting the advantages of clustering, and as sources of economic competitiveness. A high level of competitiveness attracts new activities, whose presence increases agglomeration advantages, giving birth to a cumulative and self-reinforcing mechanism of local development.

In regional growth theories characterised by a macroeconomic approach, accessibility still plays a role in defining economic growth. Central locations offer accessibility to qualified inputs, to a diversified and large output market and to a large labour market, all elements enhancing the chances of economic growth. A region's level of accessibility becomes a key factor in attracting activities, in increasing the development potential of the area and thus in entering a virtuous cycle of regional development. Following this reasoning, the models of 'economic potentials' look at accessibility as a necessary condition for regional growth (Giersch 1949, Friedmann 1966). According to the centrality–peripherality approach, accessibility is the main element explaining the differing economic performance and growth potential of central regions with respect to peripheral ones (Clark *et al.* 1969, Keeble *et al.* 1988).

Another set of less abstract and more operational theories interprets local public investment in accessibility as a strategic promoter of local growth. When devoted to transport infrastructures, public investment is also expected to affect economic growth because it acts on the accessibility of the area.[2] Following this approach, our chapter focuses on a more modern kind of accessibility, a sort of 'virtual' accessibility, based on information and communication technology (ICT) networks. These networks become strategic resources underpinning the competitiveness of firms and territories. These technologies allow information and knowledge to be achieved in real time and with no geographical constraints.

In this chapter, our interest lies in the empirical analysis of the role of accessibility in regional development, with accessibility being measured in our work as 'virtual accessibility'. A vast literature was produced during the 1980s on the impact of ICTs on regional development (Goddard 1985, Goddard and Thwaites 1986, Gillespie and Williams 1988, Gillespie *et al.* 1989, Capello 1994). These studies made an important finding relating to differences in the way ICT networks and services were adopted and used: in order to generate economic growth, these new communications networks need to be used intensively and in a strategic way. The introduction of ICT networks is not in itself a guarantee of economic development. This important result is present in our empirical analysis. We, in fact, build two accessibility indicators, one capturing only adoption, the other also measuring the use of ICTs.

Our study differs in two respects from the existing literature on ICTs and regional development. First, it encompasses all European regions together, and is therefore not confined to the study of particular areas or regions, which inevitably provides partial evidence. So far, hardly any studies have focused on all the regions of fifteen-country Europe at the same time, given the difficulties in finding territorially disaggregated data on ICT diffusion. Second, and most importantly, our evidence provides *ex ante* assessment of future accessibility effects on regional growth, by evaluating the future regional per capita growth in gross domestic product (GDP) generated by European ICT implementation policies. In particular, our chapter presents a measurement of the impact of European ICT policies on regional development, giving emphasis to alternative policy options that can be put in place, and on the costs of the alternative options in terms of loss of efficiency and cohesion.[3]

Four main aims drive our analysis, namely: (i) the creation of adequate accessibility indicators to cover both ICT endowment and ICT intensity of use; (ii) the assessment of the impact of accessibility (in terms of both endowment and use) on regional growth; (iii) the extension of the results of the assessment model into the future, through a scenario-building methodology with alternative accessibility policy options; (iv) the identification of different regional impacts of accessibility policies due to different territorial preconditions in different regions, such as learning capacity in their use, the endowment level of ICTs (which defines the marginal efficiency of the networks) and the intensity of ICT use (which defines network congestion levels).

Accessibility and regional growth: empirical evidence

The accessibility indicators

The first difficulty in analysing the role of accessibility in regional growth concerns the availability of ICT data at a territorially disaggregated level. The main data source available at present is a survey commissioned by the European Commission from EOS Gallup in 1999 and updated by INRA in 2002. Both surveys were based on over 44,000 household interviews in 130 regions of the fifteen member states (EOS Gallup 1999, INRA 2003). It is by far the largest survey at a European level that has been undertaken in the sector. Data are available at NUTS-2 level, covering only the traditional fifteen EU member states. A second critical issue is the definition of indicators. As a measure of physical endowment, several indicators are available at NUTS-2 level:[4] the number of internet connections, the number of cable and satellite TVs, and fixed telephony penetration, each expressed as the percentage of households equipped with these technologies. Each indicator reflects a different level of technological endowment, from traditional telephone networks to advanced networks, such as internet connections and cable and satellite TV.

As far as ICT use is concerned, a more innovative indicator of accessibility, also taking into account the use made of ICTs, is built on a gravitational model, adapted from Newton's universal gravitational law. In our model the population is used as mass, and the share of households using internet as an e-commerce vehicle is used as the inverse of the spatial friction:

$$U_{\mathrm{ICT}_{rt}} = \sum_{s} \frac{P_{st}}{d_{st}^{g_{rt}}} \tag{8.1}$$

where:

$U_{\mathrm{ICT}rt}$ = ICT use in region r in year t;
r, s = regions;
P_{st} = population of region s in year t;
d_{sr} = distance in km between region s and region r $\forall\ s \neq r$ (if $s=r$, d_{sr} is assumed to be = 1, because division by zero is not allowed);

g_{rt} = spatial friction between r and s measured by the inverse of c;
c_{rt} = $1/g$ = percentage of households using the internet as an e-commerce vehicle.

This index can be read as the number of people interested in e-commerce that can be reached through an internet connection. It is a sort of potential use, since it indicates the potential market for a firm adopting and using ICTs in a strategic way.

A descriptive analysis

Once the appropriate indicators for ICTs have been constructed, we can investigate the relationship between ICTs and economic growth. This relationship can be initially sketched using some descriptive maps. Below, we use an econometric model to analyse the relationship in greater detail. Our main source of economic data is the Eurostat Regio databank (Eurostat 2000). The data cover many different areas: GDP, employment, patents, human resources in high-tech sectors, population. Moreover, data are in most cases available in at least five-year time series.

The map of per capita GDP levels in 1999 clearly shows significant disparities in the EU between advanced regions and less developed regions (Figure 8.1). The highest levels of per capita GDP are in the central regions of the EU, particularly northern Italy, Austria and southern Germany. Peaks can also be found in the metropolitan regions of Paris and London, and in northern Europe, where the low population density pushes up the per capita GDP. The poorer regions are the more peripheral ones, such as Portugal and Greece.

Current regional disparities in ICT endowment, known as the digital divide, are very evident from the maps based on data extracted from the EOS Gallup survey (Figures 8.2, 8.3 and 8.4).[5]

The first map (Figure 8.2) shows that the percentage of households with a fixed telephone is quite high everywhere, as expected from the pervasive presence of the telephone in everyday life. However, we can see the values are lower in more peripheral countries with a lower GDP (Portugal, Spain, Ireland). A comparison of Figures 8.1 and 8.2 shows that the fixed telephony index is generally a good proxy for the level of wealth of regions. Home internet access is less widespread than fixed telephones, resulting in a greater digital divide (Figure 8.3). This is to be expected, since the internet is a new technology and, compared with the fixed telephone, is considered less essential. Thus, the correlation with GDP is higher than for fixed telephones, except in Sweden, Norway, Denmark and Finland, where a low population density favours new communication technologies more than traditional ones. The most developed area in terms of internet connections is undoubtedly Scandinavia, followed by the rich areas of central Europe. In developed regions with a low population density (such as Finland and other Scandinavian countries), mobile and internet technologies have developed faster and have more thoroughly penetrated the fixed telephone market area.

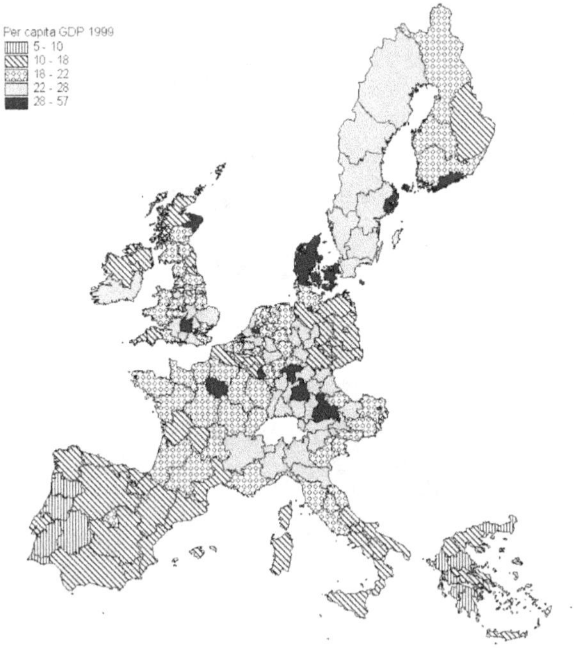

Figure 8.1 Per capita GDP, 1999 ('000 euros in PPS). Source: EOS Gallup (1999).

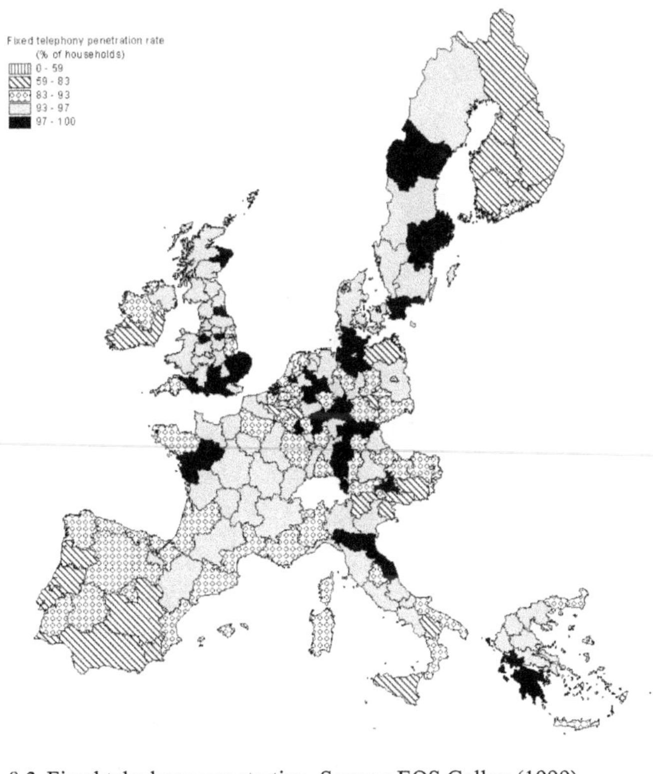

Figure 8.2 Fixed telephony penetration. Source: EOS Gallup (1999).

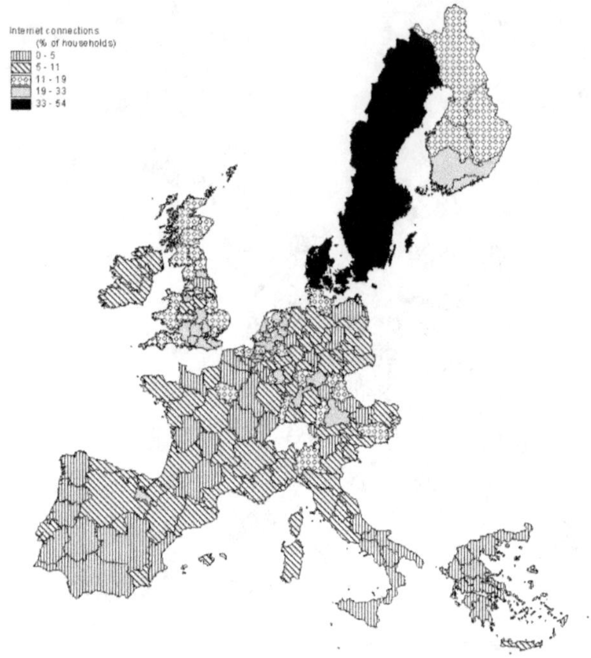

Figure 8.3 Internet connections. Source: EOS Gallup (1999).

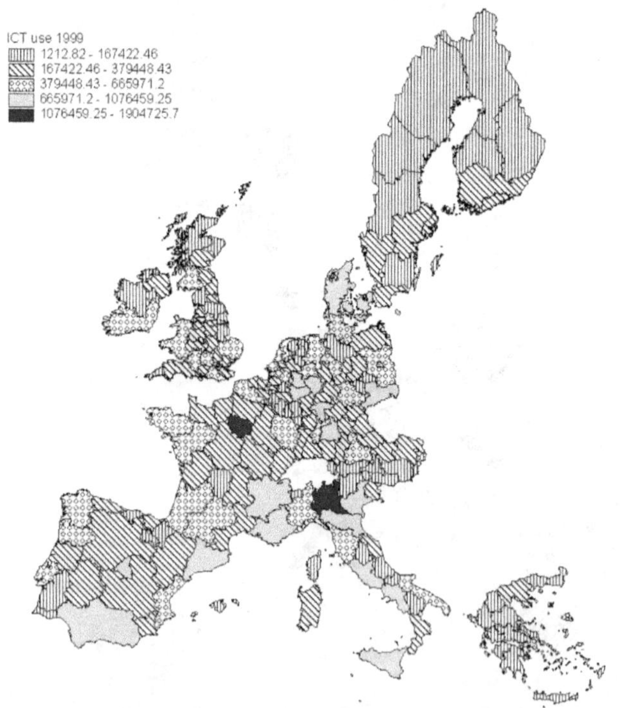

Figure 8.4 'Virtual' accessibility (number of people interested in e-commerce who can be reached through an internet connection). Source: Authors' elaborations on data from EOS Gallup (1999).

Our indicator of 'virtual accessibility', based on population and internet use, highlights the strong position of geographically central and highly populated regions, as expected, with some exceptions: southern Spain and Italy show high virtual accessibility due to their higher than average internet use (Figure 8.4).

By comparing the map of per capita GDP (Figure 8.1) with those of ICT endowment and use, we can see that the regions with highest ICT endowment and use are the richest regions: 'virtual' accessibility and per capita GDP levels are in some way related. It is interesting to see how alternative ICT policies, fostering accessibility in different geographical areas, affect GDP growth. This relationship can be best explained through an interpretative model, presented in the next section.

An interpretative analysis

The purpose of this section is to build an interpretative model to analyse the impact of ICT endowment and use on economic growth. From the methodological point of view, we estimate a production function to measure the role that ICTs play in regional performance, as first suggested by Aschauer and replicated in other studies (Biehl 1986, Aschauer 1989). The estimated model is the following:

$$\text{Lgdp99p} = f(\text{Luse, Lfixtel, Lcabsta, Ltotemp, Lhitech}) \qquad (8.2)$$

where:

L indicates conversion to a natural logarithm (ln);
gdp99p = per capita GDP in 1999;
use = ICT use in 1999;
fixtel = percentage of households with a fixed telephone in 1999;
intcon = percentage of households with an internet connection in 1999;
cabsat = percentage of households with a cable or satellite TV in 1999;
totemp = total employment in 1999;
hitech = high-tech employment in 1999.

From a conceptual point of view, the framework of analysis is based on the idea that ICT infrastructures and services are production factors which, together with the traditional labour and capital factors, account for the GDP level. Thus, a change in ICT investments produces a change in ICT endowment which enters the quasi-production function and estimates changes in the per capita or absolute GDP growth rate. The results are presented in Table 8.1 (columns 1 and 2). Interestingly, all the ICT variables are significant and have the expected positive sign. The fit of the model is quite good, with an R^2 index around 0.67.

However, when working with territorial data, a problem of spatial dependence between the observations may arise.[6] Statistical tests to detect the presence of spatial dependence were run, and showed the presence of both spatial lag and spatial error.[7] Table 8.1 (columns 3 and 4) contains the results of the model corrected for

Table 8.1 Model results

	Normal model		Spatial lag model	
	Coefficient value	t-value	Coefficient value adjusted for spatial dependence	Z-test value
Constant	–3.386	(3.38)**	–3.552	(–4.07)**
Luse	0.042	(2.38)**	0.051	(3.31)**
Lfixtel	0.733	(4.09)**	0.574	(3.61)**
Lintcon	0.049	(2.45)**	0.037	(2.07)*
Lcabsat	0.107	(5.30)**	0.061	(3.13)**
Lhitech2	0.061	(1.96)*	0.004	(0.12)
Ltotemp			0.457	(3.65)**
ρ			0.437	(5.14)**
R^2	0.67			

Notes
Number of observations = 185. Dependent variable: Lgdp99p.
*Significant at $P < 0.05$.
**Significant at $P < 0.01$.

Table 8.2 Calibration of the spatial lag model (dependent variable Lgdp99p)

Indicators	Estimated coefficients	Calibrated coefficients	Differences
Constant	–3.552	–3.552	0.000
Luse	0.051	0.055	0.004
Lfixtel	0.574	0.650	0.076
Lintcon	0.037	0.037	0.000
Lcabsat	0.061	0.070	0.009
Lhitech2	0.004	0.005	0.001
Ltotemp	0.457	0.640	0.183
ρ	0.437	0.300	–0.137

spatial dependence. Finally, in order to obtain a better fit with real data, the model was calibrated as shown in Table 8.2.

A dummy variable is built in order to analyse regional disparities. This dummy splits regions between lagging and non-lagging, following the criteria expressed by the European Commission for the definition of Objective 1 NUTS-2 regions for the period 2000–2006.[8]

Alternative ICT policy options

Building different policy alternatives

Based on some hypotheses on the distribution of EU financial resources among regions and among possible policy actions (network endowment, support to service use, investments in skills and people in the ICT sector), the model presented in the previous section is able to provide an estimate of future GDP growth and of its spatial distribution.

The magnitude of future EU investments in ICTs over the next twenty years is estimated as follows. ICT investments at the national level between 1990 and 2000 in the fifteen EU member states, at 2000 prices, reached around 50 billion euros per year[9] (Table 8.3). Given the financial efforts made by the EU in those years, which were equal to 4 per cent of the total investments made by national governments, and given the entry of the new accession countries, we assume that the EU financial commitment in this field over the next twenty years will amount to 2 per cent of total investments made by the fifteen EU member states, reaching a level of around 1 billion euros per year. This amount, multiplied by twenty, provides a twenty-year investment scenario.[10]

Once the financial expenditure on ICT policies has been calculated, alternative policy options are built according to the Europe 2002 Action Plan of the Community, which envisages three main normative actions (European Commission 2000): (i) investment in a cheaper, faster and more secure internet, i.e. a focus on ICT infrastructure; (ii) investment in people and skills, i.e. an adoption support policy; (iii) investment in stimulating internet service development (e-government, e-commerce, intelligent transport systems), i.e. an ICT policy oriented towards service promotion.

These intervention policies are rather different in nature since they act on different features. The first action aims at enhancing ICT endowment: ICTs are in fact expected to act on accessibility, allowing territorial peripherality to be overcome, and generating the popular perception of a 'death of distance' (Castells and Hall 1994). In remote areas in particular, ICTs are generally perceived as providing the opportunity to overcome geographical disadvantages, to be connected in real time to the 'core'. The second and third actions are directed at supporting strategic use through the creative and organisational transformation of firms' internal operations, where strategic and intensive ICT use results in greater competitiveness.

Table 8.3 European country investments in ICTs

Country	*Average annual investments in ICTs, 1990–2000 (in euros at 2000 prices)*
Austria	1,563,787,293
Belgium	1,157,658,681
Denmark	742,494,404
Finland	792,154,994
France	6,442,682,384
Germany	13,287,718,072
Greece	793,073,081
Ireland	397,119,895
Italy	7,699,435,038
Luxembourg	89,723,676
Portugal	1,275,765,608
Spain	3,949,101,599
Sweden	1,208,488,436
The Netherlands	2,161,829,687
United Kingdom	8,776,795,290
Total	*50,337,828,138*

Different impacts on regional performance are therefore expected from the three policy actions:

1 The first policy action generates an increase in ICT endowment, but not necessarily in real use of ICTs. This policy can be applied to lagging areas to fill in the infrastructural gap, and to non-lagging areas to overcome the bottlenecks that characterise these areas. In our model, this policy corresponds to an increase in internet connections.
2 The second policy action is a medium-term policy, since it helps in the medium term to spread the necessary skills and knowledge for innovative and strategic ICT use to all areas. In our model, this policy influences the high-tech employment share.
3 The third policy action is a long-term policy; it aims to develop advanced ICT services (and their employment) in the economy, influencing the long-term efficiency of the whole productive system. In our model, this policy corresponds to an increase in ICT use.

The increased financial commitment made in the ICT field is translated into an increase in physical ICT endowment or ICT use or high-tech employment, by estimating the elasticity of internet connections, of accessibility and of high-tech employment to financial investment, and therefore its marginal efficiency.[11] Capital invested in ICTs can been calculated by cumulating the investments over the period 1990–2000 at 2000 prices. The results of the three regressions are presented in Table 8.4; as regressions are run on the logarithms of the variables, the results obtained are the elasticity of, respectively, accessibility, internet connections and high-tech employment to investments, and are therefore comparable. Even at a first look, it is evident that investments in internet connections prove to be much more efficient; a 1 per cent increase in financial resources devoted to internet connections provides an increase in internet connections of 0.96 per cent, whereas the same investment generates an increase of only 0.22 per cent and 0.26 per in high-tech employment and accessibility respectively. The substantial differences in the marginal efficiency of investments between the different policy actions show that the impact of ICT policies on territorial distribution significantly depends on the choice of alternative policy actions.

Given a certain level of financial resources devoted to ICTs (Table 8.3), three alternatives can be envisaged on the basis of the policy actions chosen and the spatial distribution of financial resources, with a time reference of twenty years (Table 8.5). The results are compared against a do-nothing scenario, in which per capita GDP growth is equal to zero. In order to highlight ICT policy impacts, our model considers ICT policies to be the only factor affecting GDP growth.

The indiscriminate ICT policy option envisages widespread diffusion of ICT infrastructures and services throughout Europe, with implementation of all three European ICT policy actions in all countries and regions of the EU, whatever their economic performance and ICT endowment level. Funds are subdivided among regions according to their population share, and then directed in equal parts to the three policy actions.

Table 8.4 Elasticity of accessibility, internet access and high-tech employment to financial investments

	Dependent variable		
Independent variable	*Accessibility (ln) (1999)*	*Internet access at home (ln) (2002) (% of households)*	*High-tech employment (ln) (1999) (%)*
Invested capital 1990–2000	0.26	0.98	0.22
(ln)	(2.3)*	(12.7)**	(2.13)*

Notes
t-Values are given in brackets.
*Significant at $P<0.05$.
**Significant at $P<0.01$.

Table 8.5 Distribution of investments by region and ICT policy according to the different scenarios

ICT policy options	*Regional distribution*	*ICT policy actions*
A: indiscriminate policy option	All regions receive equal investment distributed according to regional population	Among all regions 33% use, 33% internet, 33% high-tech employment
B: efficiency policy option	Lagging regions receive 20% of total investments. Investment is distributed according to the lagging region's share of the population	Lagging regions: 90% use, 10% internet
	Non-lagging regions receive 80% of total investments. Investment is distributed according to the non-lagging region's share of the population	Non-lagging regions: 10% use, 90% internet
C: cohesion policy option	Lagging regions receive100% of total investment. Investment is distributed according to the lagging region's share of the population	Lagging regions : 33% use, 33% internet, 33% high-tech employment

The efficiency ICT policy option envisages implementation of ICT policy actions according to the marginal efficiency of investments (Table 8.4). In this case, 80 per cent of financial investment in ICTs is directed to the more efficient non-lagging regions, with the remaining 20 per cent going to the lagging regions. Moreover, 90 per cent of financial resources within each subgroup of regions are devoted to the policy action with the highest marginal efficiency of investment. Therefore, once investments are weighted by population, they are divided within each subgroup of regions as follows:

1 In Objective 1 areas, 90 per cent of European regional ICT resources are directed at increasing ICT use, while the remainder is invested in increasing infrastructure development.

2 In advanced areas, 90 per cent of European regional ICT resources are invested in infrastructure development, while the remaining 10 per cent is invested in ICT use.

The third policy, cohesion policy option, envisages that increased accessibility is directed at lagging regions, as has been the case in the past with the STAR and Telematique projects run by the EU. In this case, all the resources are devoted to Objective 1 regions, one-third for each policy action.

Future GDP growth

The growth in per capita GDP differs substantially in the three cases. In Table 8.6 the growth rates for the whole sample and for the two subsamples of lagging and non-lagging regions are presented.

Results at the regional level are plotted in Figures 8.5, 8.6 and 8.7. The do-nothing alternative is zero, i.e. if no ICT investment is made, GDP growth is equal to zero. In the indiscriminate scenario (A), the GDP growth rate is 0.033 per cent; in this scenario the effect appears to be higher in lagging regions (+0.12 per cent) than in non-lagging ones (+0.016 per cent). Figure 8.5 shows that the GDP growth rate is broadly evenly distributed in most regions, with some peaks (positive or negative) that in most cases can probably be explained by statistical effects. Most regions show per capita GDP growth rates between 0.012 per cent and 0.03 per cent. Thus, as expected, this scenario affects all regions more or less in the same way.

In the efficiency scenario (B), as expected, the growth rate in per capita GDP turns out to be stronger than in scenario A. Figure 8.6 is directly comparable with Figure 8.5. The difference is a stronger GDP growth rate in some non-lagging regions, like the regions belonging to the so-called Blue Banana (The Netherlands, Belgium, Luxembourg, and French regions near the Reno River) and to the Sunbelt (southern regions of France and Spain and northern Italy). The efficiency scenario produces the highest per capita GDP growth rate, as expected (+0.037 per cent), most of which is in advanced regions (+0.04 per cent), leaving to lagging regions only 0.012 per cent of the increase.

In scenario C, all financial resources are devoted to lagging regions, with the result that growth rates in these regions are higher under this scenario than in the other two scenarios. The concentration of investments means that not only

Table 8.6 Per capita GDP growth rate in the three policy options

	GDP growth rate over twenty years (%)		
Policy options	*Lagging regions*	*Non-lagging regions*	*Total*
0: do nothing	0.000	0.000	0.000
A: indiscriminate	0.120	0.016	0.033
B: efficiency	0.012	0.040	0.037
C: cohesion	0.140	0.000	0.023

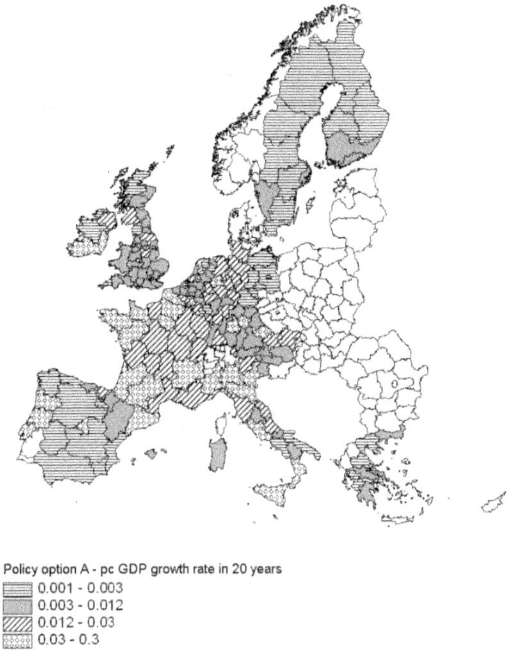

Figure 8.5 Policy option A: per capita GDP growth rate in twenty years.

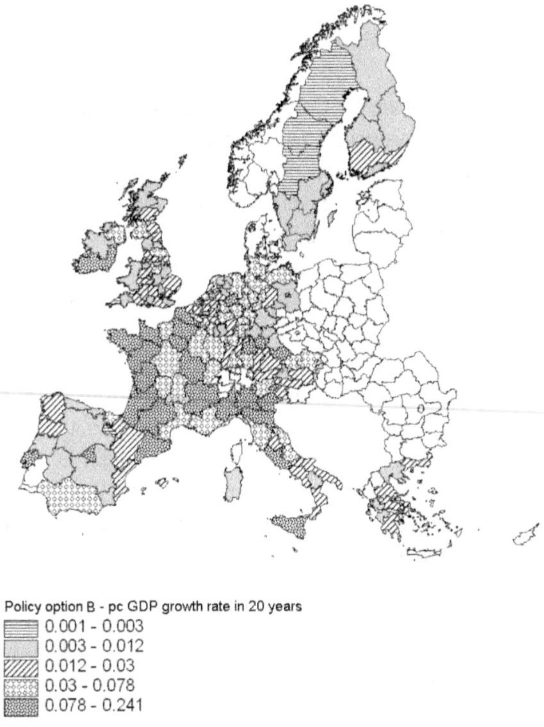

Figure 8.6 Policy option B: per capita GDP growth rate in twenty years.

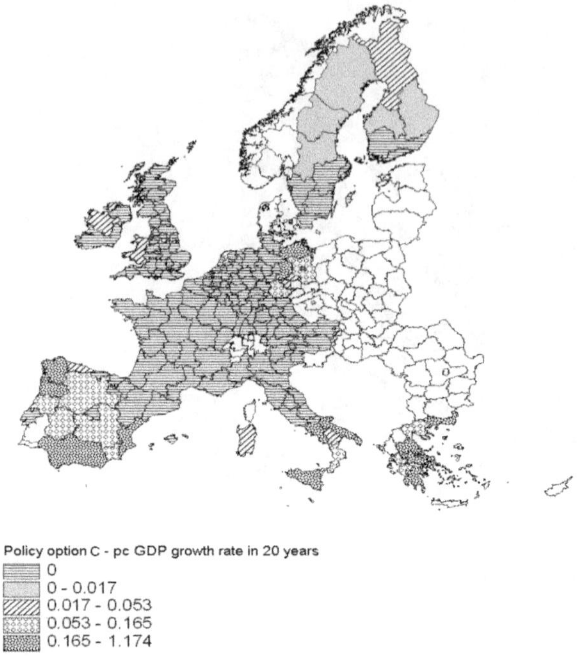

Figure 8.7 Policy option C: per capita GDP growth rate in twenty years.

GDP, but also accessibility and internet connections, increase in Objective 1 areas (Figure 8.7).

Thus, from the point of view of efficiency (i.e. of economic growth), scenario B is obviously the most appropriate, as scenarios A and C result in lower economic growth. In the case of the cohesion policy, the negative effect on growth rate is relatively large, the increase in per capita GDP being only 0.023 per cent compared with 0.037 per cent for the efficiency policy. The indiscriminate policy also leads to lower efficiency gains, although, as expected, the effect is less severe than with the cohesion policy: with the indiscriminate policy per capita GDP increases by 0.033 per cent compared with 0.037 per cent under the efficiency policy.

The second main result of the forecasting model concerns the aim of achieving cohesion. Differences in income growth between regions from the three different policy alternatives are presented in Figures 8.8 to 8.10. Policy A results in some peaks, mainly as a result of statistical effects, such as arises from the low population density in the Scandinavian countries or the low level of GDP in some countries. However, in general, very few regions present consistent differences from the EU mean (northern Italy, some regions of France and Portugal) (Figure 8.8).

In option B, the highest relative regional growth rates are in two French north–south corridors, in northern Italy and in southern Ireland, although Germany, central Italy, Belgium and the Netherlands also show relatively high per capita growth rates (Figure 8.9).

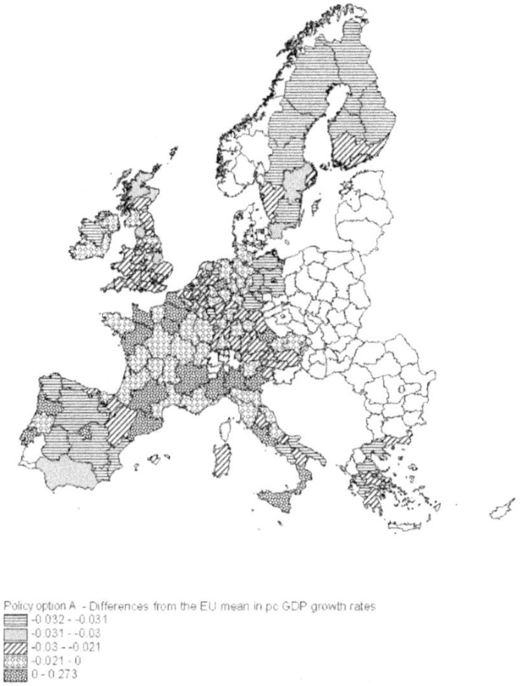

Figure 8.8 Policy option A: differences from the EU mean in per capita GDP growth rates.

Figure 8.9 Policy option B: differences from the EU mean in per capita GDP growth rates.

Alternative C results in the highest relative per capita GDP growth rate in lagging regions such as parts of southern Italy, Greece and Spain (Figure 8.10).

A way of quantifying changes in regional disparities is through Gini's concentration index and its graphic representation through the Lorenz curve. The Gini coefficients for the different scenarios are presented in Table 8.7.

As regards GDP distribution, option A results in a coefficient similar to the current situation, as expected, whereas option B increases regional disparities and option C decreases them. The magnitude of the effects is very small because of the very small change in per capita GDP that we are forecasting. These results can be represented by a Lorenz curve. As a result of the very small difference in the Gini coefficients, the curves produced by the different scenarios are very close to each other. The differences are more clearly seen in the zoomed area. Interestingly, the efficiency option does not substantially increase regional disparities compared with the present situation, while the current regional imbalance would be greatly improved by choosing the cohesion alternative.

The same results are presented in Figure 8.11. Option C, satisfying its cohesion objective, reduces regional disparities by creating a more equal distribution. The curves obtained under alternatives A and B are quite similar; as we can see in the magnified area, the efficiency scenario results in a lower Lorenz curve, a sign that disparities in income distribution are increasing. If this is true at the general level, it would be interesting to examine whether the capacity to take advantage

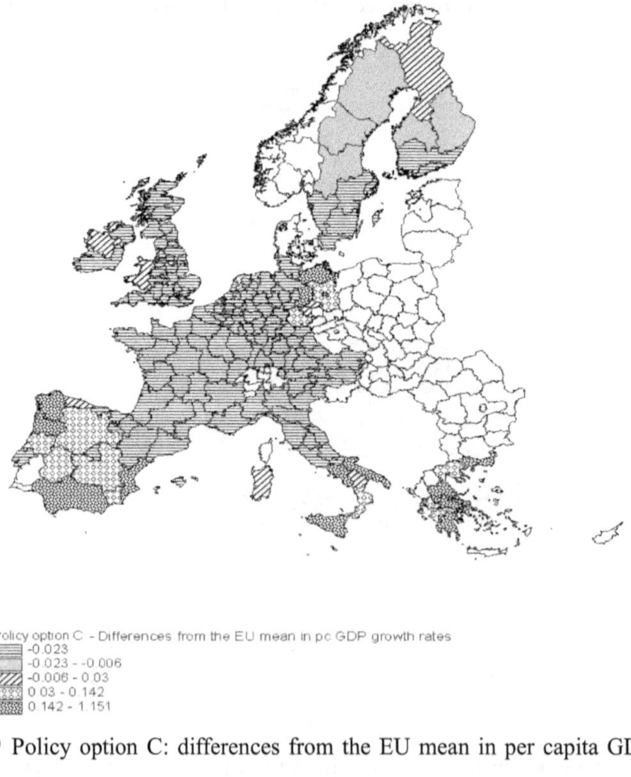

Figure 8.10 Policy option C: differences from the EU mean in per capita GDP growth rates.

Table 8.7 Gini coefficients

Policy alternatives	*Per capita GDP*	*Accessibility*	*Internet*
Current situation	0.37170	0.3992	0.22558
Option A	0.37170	0.4383	0.24562
Option B	0.37173	0.4382	0.24379
Option C	0.37161	0.4381	0.22354
Equal distribution	0.00000	0.00000	0.00000

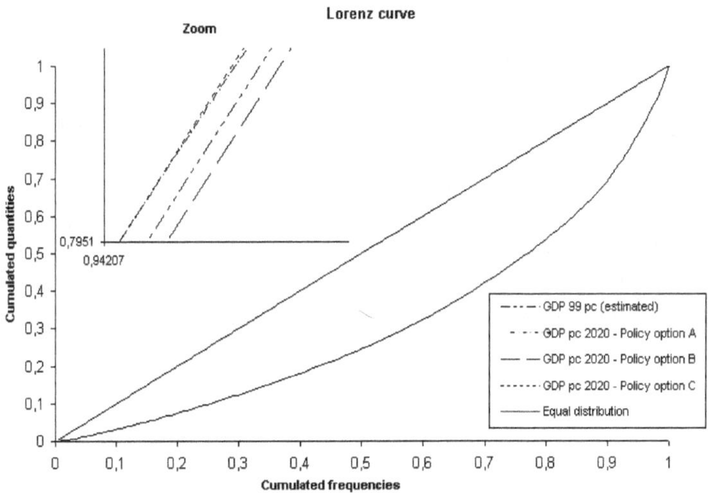

Figure 8.11 Per capita GDP distribution in the three policy options.

of the growth opportunities provided by ICT policies is the same in each region. As we will see in the next section, this is not the case. Our analysis highlights the importance of choosing appropriate policy options in the ICT field.

Preconditions for ICT policy exploitation

From the maps presented above it is quite evident that advanced regions react differently to ICT investment policies. Some are better able to grasp the opportunities offered by these exogenous policies, whereas others are more inclined to react only if policies are directly concerned with particular local needs. The same holds for backward regions, among which the response capacity to ICT policy opportunities differs substantially, irrespective of the policy choice made (Figures 8.8, 8.9 and 8.10).

A way to isolate common behaviours to ICT policies is by running a cluster analysis, a statistical technique able to group observations (in our case the regions) according to their similarities in the values of some selected variables (in our case, GDP growth and the growth rate of internet connections). Our cluster analysis identified four different clusters, mapped in Figure 8.12. The subdivision of regions among clusters is rather interesting. Nearly 50 per cent of both lagging and advanced regions do not react in a decisive way to ICT policies (cluster 3). The reasons are probably different in lagging and advanced regions; in the former the reasons may be found in the limited level of knowledge and learning capacity in exploiting ICT networks. In the case of advanced regions, the reasons may be related to the already high endowment of ICTs, which limit the effects of additional investments on the performance of these regions.

Another large group of lagging regions (37 per cent) reacts only to the cohesion policy scenarios, while a very limited number of backward regions (7.5 per cent) are able to grasp growth opportunities offered by an efficiency policy scenario; interestingly, no lagging region gains greatly from an indiscriminate ICT policy (Table 8.8). On the other hand, advanced regions react either to the efficiency policy only (31.9 per cent) or to indiscriminate and efficiency policies (18.1 per cent) (Table 8.8).

Figure 8.12 shows which regions belong to each of the four clusters. Advanced regions that react to both indiscriminate and efficiency policies are found in northern Italy and the western part of France. Regions reacting to efficiency policies are principally the German regions (where the country effect is sufficiently strong that efficiency policies are useful even in the eastern regions), some French regions

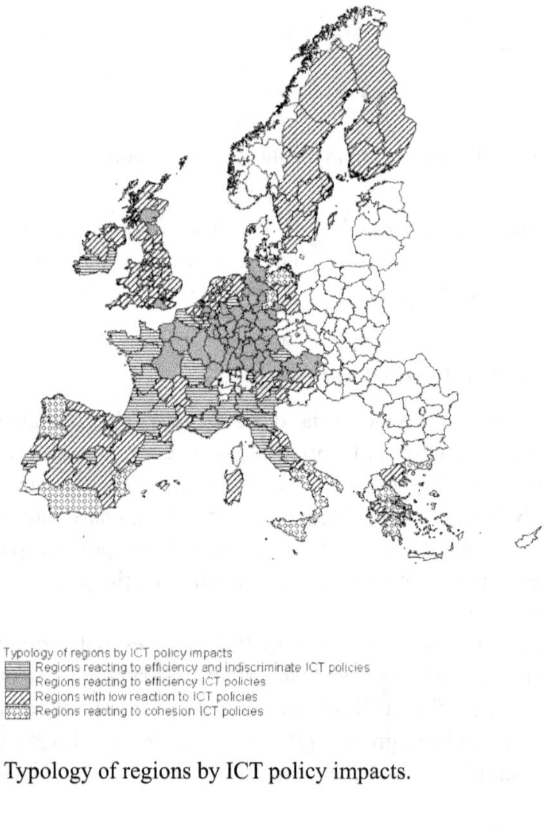

Figure 8.12 Typology of regions by ICT policy impacts.

Table 8.8 Regions by type of impact of ICT policies: cluster analysis results

Indicators	*Cluster 1: regions reacting to efficiency and indiscriminate ICT policies*	*Cluster 2: regions reacting to efficiency ICT policies*	*Cluster 3: regions with low reactions to ICT policies*	*Cluster 4: regions reacting to cohesion ICT policies*	*Mean*
Number of cases	26	49	94	15	184
Scenario A indicators					
Per capita GDP ('000 euros)	13.37	44.95	13.80	13.72	22.19
Per capita GDP growth rate (%)	0.035	0.014	0.007	0.09	0.016
Scenario B indicators					
Per capita GDP ('000 euros)	13.38	44.96	13.80	13.72	22.19
Per capita GDP growth rate (%)	0.095	0.038	0.016	0.022	0.035
Scenario C indicators					
Per capita GDP ('000 euros)	13.37	44.94	13.80	13.76	22.19
Per capita GDP growth rate (%)	0.000	0.004	0.013	0.28	0.029
Proportion of lagging regions (%)	0.0	7.5	55	37.5	21.7
Proportion of non-lagging regions (%)	18.1	31.9	50	0.0	78.3

and some Scottish ones. Regions reacting to cohesion policies only are most of the Greek regions, part of Spain and southern Italy. Regions that do not react strongly to any ICT policy are those in the UK, the Scandinavian countries and the central regions of Spain.

Concluding remarks

The concept of accessibility is increasingly important in the context of a globalising economy. Accessibility can be defined as the ability to overcome spatial distance at low transport cost, as well as to gather strategic information before competitors. Consequently, accessibility becomes a strategic factor for the competitiveness of regions. Traditionally, accessibility is operationally related to mobility, and therefore to physical transport networks. However, in this chapter, we focused on a new concept of accessibility, deriving from ICTs. Our aim was to assess the impact of ICT accessibility on regional growth and competitiveness.

The importance of accessibility through ICT and not only through physical networks for economic growth is clearly evident. In particular, ICT accessibility policies show very different impacts (from the point of view of cohesion and efficiency) when projected twenty years into the future. European economic growth as well as economic cohesion will also significantly depend on the political decisions that are made regarding ICTs – decisions on ICT actions and the regional distribution of financial resources. Once applied, ICT policies should also take into account the different local preconditions relating to the level of ICT use, the level of ICT endowment and the learning processes required to use these technologies. All these elements affect the impact of ICT policies in fostering regional development and cannot be ignored when policy actions are planned.

Notes

1 On local economic development, see, among others, Ciciotti and Wettmann (1981), Garofoli (1981), Johannisson and Spilling (1983), Becattini (1990), Stöhr (1990), Courlet and Pecqueur (1992) and Ganne (1992). See Vásquez-Barquero (2002) for a general presentation of these theories.

2 For studies concerning the role of infrastructure on regional development, see Perroux (1955), Keeble *et al.* (1982), Biehl (1986), Aschauer (1989), Barro (1990), Bruinsma *et al.* (1992), Vickerman (1991), Fabiani and Pellegrini (1997) and Ferri and Mattesini (1997).

3 The analysis presented here and developed over the fifteen member states of the EU, at regional (NUTS-2) level, is part of the ESPON 2.1.1 project (Territorial Impact of EU Transport and Ten Policies) coordinated by Johannes Bröcker of the University of Kiel. The research unit of the Polytechnic of Milan was coordinated by Roberta Capello.

4 EOS Gallup (1999) included a larger number of ICT endowments than INRA (2003). Our interpretative model was run on 1999 data. Since it interprets a structural relationship, the 1999 data are acceptable.

5 The digital divide remains the same when the analysis is based on the more up-to-date data of the INRA report. We prefer to present the 1999 data here, as this is what is used in the interpretative model presented in the following section.

6 For more details concerning spatial dependence problems, see Anselin (1988, 1992), Anselin and Hudak (1992) and Anselin *et al.* (1996).

7 We applied Moran's *I*, the Lagrange multiplier and the robust Lagrange multiplier. These tests assume higher and significant values when there is positive spatial autocorrelation in the dependent variable (lag) or in the errors. For calculating the spatial autocorrelation tests and the spatial lag model, we used STATA 7 with the extensions for spatial analysis (Pisati 2001). The results are presented in the following table:

Test	*Statistic*	*d.f.*	P-*value*
Spatial error			
Moran's *I*	7.621	1	0.000
Lagrange multiplier	40.385	1	0.000
Robust Lagrange multiplier	2.695	1	0.101
Spatial lag			
Lagrange multiplier	51.264	1	0.000
Robust Lagrange multiplier	13.574	1	0.000

8 European Commission (1999). The Objective 1 regions should meet one of the following requirements: (a) GDP <75 per cent of EU average; (b) most remote regions (DOM-TOM, Azores, Madeira, Canaries); (c) very low population density (old Objective 6 areas – in particular the Scandinavian regions).

9 ITU data on national investments (ITU 2003).

10 It seems quite a reasonable hypothesis when compared with the results of other studies such as Technopolis *et al.* (2002).

11 Table 8.5 shows the elasticity of internet connections, accessibility and high-tech employment to financial investments; once the elasticity is calculated, the marginal efficiency of investments is easily obtained by multiplying the elasticity value for the ratio of each dependent variable (internet connections, accessibility and high-tech employment) to the independent one (invested capital).

References

Alonso, W. (1964) *Location and Land Use: Towards a General Theory of Land Rent*, Cambridge, MA: Harvard University Press.

Anselin, L. (1988) *Spatial Econometrics: Methods and Models*, Dordrecht: Kluwer Academic.

Anselin, L. (1992) *SpaceStat Tutorial. A Workbook for Using SpaceStat in the Analysis of Spatial Data*, Morgantown, WV: Regional Research Institute, West Virginia University.

Anselin, L. and Hudak, S. (1992) 'Spatial econometrics in practice. A review of software options', *Regional Science and Urban Economics*, 22: 509–36.

Anselin, L., Bera, A.K., Florax, R. and Yoon, M.J. (1996) 'Simple diagnostic tests for spatial dependence', *Regional Science and Urban Economics*, 26: 77–104.

Aschauer, D. (1989) 'Is public expenditure productive?', *Journal of Monetary Economics*, 23: 177–200.

Barro, R.J. (1990, 'Government spending in a simple model of endogenous growth', *Journal of Political Economy*, 98: S103–25.

Becattini, G. (1990) 'The Marshallian industrial district as a socio-economic notion', in Pyke, F., Becattini, G. and Sengenberger, W. (eds.) *Industrial Districts and Interfirm Cooperation in Italy*, Geneva: International Institute of Labour Studies.

Biehl, D. (1986) *The Contribution of Infrastructure to Regional Development*, Brussels: Regional Policy Division, European Community.

Bruinsma, F., Nijkamp, P. and Rietveld, P. (1992) 'Regional economic transformation and social overhead investments', *Tijdschrift voor Economische en Social Geografie*, 83: 3–13.

Capello, R. (1994) *Spatial Economic Analysis of Telecommunications Network Externalities*, Aldershot: Avebury.

Castells, M. and Hall, P. (1994) *Technopoles of the World: The Making of the 21st Century Industrial Complexes*, London: Routledge.

Ciciotti, E. and Wettmann, R. (1981) 'The mobilisation of indigenous potential', Internal Documentation on Regional Policy, no. 10, Brussels: Commission of the European Community.

Clark, C., Wilson, F. and Bradley, J. (1969) 'Industrial location and economic potential in Western Europe', *Regional Studies*, 3: 197–212.

Courlet, C. and Pecqueur, B. (1992) 'Les systèmes industriels localisés en France: un nouvel model de développement', in Benko, G. and Lipietz, A. (eds.) *Les régions qui gagnent*, Paris: Presses Universitaires de France.

EOS Gallup (1999) *Residential Survey*, Brussels: DG Information Society of the European Commission (available online at www.europa.eu.int/ISPO/infosoc/telecompolicy/en/EOStudy/Resid/accueil.htm>).

European Commission (1999) 'Commission decision of 1 July 1999 drawing up the list of regions covered by Objective 1 of the Structural Funds for the period 2000 to 2006 (1999/502/CE)', *Official Journal of the European Communities*. Brussels: European Commission.

European Commission (2000) *eEurope Action Plan 2002 – An Information Society for All*, Feira Council.

Eurostat (2000) *NewCronos Database*, Theme 21 Regio, CD-ROM.

Fabiani, S. and Pellegrini, G. (1997) *Education, Infrastructure, Geography and Growth: An Empirical Analysis of the Development of Italian Provinces*, Rome: Banca d'Italia, Temi di Discussione, no. 323.

Ferri, G. and Mattesini, F. (1997) *Finance, Human Capital and Infrastructure: an Empirical Investigation of Post-War Italian Growth*, Rome: Banca d'Italia, Temi di Discussione, no. 321.

Friedmann, J. (1966) *Regional Development Policy: a Case Study of Venezuela*, Cambridge, MA: MIT Press.

Ganne, B. (1992) 'Place et évolution des systèmes industriels locaux en France: économie politique d'une transformation', in Benko, G. and Lipietz, A. (eds.) *Les régions qui gagnent*, Paris: Presses Universitaires de France.

Garofoli, G. (1981) 'Lo sviluppo delle aree periferiche nell'economia italiana degli anni settanta', *L'Industria*, 5: 391–404.

Giersch, H. (1949) 'Economic union between nations and the location of industries', *Review of Economic Studies*, 17: 87–97.

Gillespie, A. and Williams, H. (1988) 'Telecommunications and the reconstruction of regional comparative advantage', *Environment and Planning A*, 20: 1311–21.

Gillespie, A., Goddard, J., Hepworth, M. and Williams, H. (1989) 'Information and communications technology and regional development: an information economy perspective', *Science, Technology and Industry Review*, 5: 86–111.

Goddard, J. (1985) 'Effetti delle nuove tecnologie dell'informazione sulla struttura urbana', in IReR Progetto Milano (ed.) *Tecnologie e Sviluppo Urbano*, Milan: Angeli.

Goddard, J. and Thwaites, A. (1986) 'New technology and regional development policy', in Nijkamp, P. (ed.) *Technological Change, Employment and Spatial Dynamics*, Berlin: Springer Verlag.

Johannisson, B. and Spilling, O. (1983) *Strategies for Local and Regional Self-Development*, Oslo: NordREFO.

Keeble, D., Owens, P.L., and Thompson, C. (1982) 'Regional accessibility and economic potential in the European Community', *Regional Studies*, 16: 419–32.

Keeble, D., Offord, J. and Walker, S. (1988) *Peripheral Regions in a Community of Twelve Member States*, Luxembourg: Office for Official Publications of the European Communities.

INRA (2003) *Telecoms Services Indicators* (available online at www.europa.eu.int/information_society/topics/ecomm/useful_information/library/studies_ext_consult/index_en.htm).

ITU (2003) *World Telecommunications Indicators*, Geneva: International Telecommunications Union.

Lösch, A. (1954) *The Economics of Location*, New Haven, CT: Yale University Press.

Perroux, F. (1955) 'Note sur la notion de pôle de croissance', *Economie Appliquée*, 7: 307–20.

Pisati, M. (2001) 'Tools for spatial data analysis', *Stata Technical Bulletin*, 60: 21–37.

Technopolis Ltd, IRISI (Europe), Tsipouri L. and Eris@ (2002) *Final report for the Thematic Evaluation of the Information Society*, for the DG Regional Policy of the European Commission.

Stöhr, W. (1990) 'On the theory and practice of local development in Europe', in Stöhr W. (ed.) *Global Challenge and Local Responses*, London: Mansell Publisher.

Vásquez-Barquero, A. (2002) *Endogenous Development*, London: Routledge.

Vickerman, R. (1991) 'Infrastructure and regional development: introduction', in Vickerman R. (ed.) *Infrastructure and Regional Development*, London: Pion.

Von Thünen, J.H. (1826) *Der Isolierte Staat in Beziehung auf Landwirtschaft und Nationalökonomie*, Hamburg: Puthes.

Weber, A. (1929) *Alfred Weber's Theory of the Location of Industries*, Chicago: University of Chicago Press, translated from original (1909) *Über der Standort der Industrien*, Tübingen: Verlag Mohr.

9 Regional inequalities and EU enlargement

The macrospatial dimension

Marinella Terrasi

Kennst du das Land, wo die Zitronen blühn,
Im dunklen Laub die Goldorangen glühn,
Ein sanfter Wind vom blauen Himmel weht
Die Myrte still und hoch der Lorbeer steht?[1]
(J. W. Goethe, Mignon, 1783)

Introduction

Since Krugman's contributions (Krugman 1991a,b) a new approach to spatial economics has been developed. This 'new economic geography' aims at integrating trade with geography, having finally discovered that 'space matters' in international as well as in regional economics.

One of the most commonly used experimental fields for these theoretical developments has been European integration. European integration appears for many reasons to be the ideal context to which the predictions of the new theories could be applied. First, the integration process has come about in consecutive phases, which can be identified either as an enlargement of the space of integration or as an intensification of its degree. This makes it possible to verify the effects of the reduction in transport cost that plays such an important role in the models of the new economic geography.

Second, in each phase of European integration a well-defined centre and well-defined periphery have emerged, which again are essential ingredients to the new economic geography approach. If we go as far back as 1961, we can read in the documents of the 'Conférence sur les économies régionales' that 'L'espace économique communitaire est doméné par une dichotomie très caractéristique: sous l'angle du développement économique s'opposent une Europe périphérique et une Europe centrale' (CEE 1961: 164). Subsequently, the identification of central and peripheral regions has been of constant interest to the European Commission and has fuelled a long list of applied studies (Clark *et al.* 1969, Keeble *et al.* 1982, 1988, Copus 1999, Schürmann and Talaat 2000).

But perhaps the main reason why European integration has become such an important case of study for the new economic geography research is the adoption of a spatial cohesion objective in the European constitutive Treaties and the resulting emergence of a European regional policy, which has gradually become one of the most important items in the EU budget (Boldrin and Canova 2003). It is clear that, from the point of view of cohesion, Krugman's approach has important consequences. If it is true that economic integration can feed spatial divergence between centre and periphery, regional policy becomes an essential instrument in creating cohesion and must be supported by the identification of the appropriate centre/periphery spatial structure.

Today we have just passed over the threshold of a new phase of European integration: the entry of ten new members into the EU, which has increased its area by 23 per cent and its population by 20 per cent. But what matters the most is the 'unprecedented widening of economic disparities within the Union and the geographical shift in the pattern of disparities' that the new enlargement will bring with it (European Commission 2003: 2).

In this chapter some new empirical evidence will be offered about the change in the EU regional inequality problem resulting from the admission of eight acceding countries (excluding Malta and Cyprus, which do not play an important role in the problem of European regional inequalities) and some hypotheses will be advanced about its future evolution in light of the experience of past enlargements. The chapter is organized as follows: in the next section the main results obtained by the new economic geography are reviewed and their relevance for the European case are discussed. In the third the evolution of European regional disparities is analysed in terms of different variables, such as gross value added (GVA), gross domestic product (GDP), labour productivity and rate of employment, during consecutive phases of the integration process, starting from 1950 and ending with 1997. The Theil coefficient and its various decompositions are the principal tools of analysis adopted. In the fourth the changing environment of the regional inequality problem after the new enlargement will be presented, while the fifth section focuses on the determinants of regional productivity inequalities. Finally, some general conclusions are drawn that are relevant for the formulation of future European regional policy.

The spatial effects of economic integration

Traditional economic theory has analysed the effects of economic integration in terms of different endowments of resources and comparative advantages. According to this view, integration is beneficial to all the participants of the economic game because although the strongest players may have an absolute advantage, there is still room for the weakest ones to produce what they are relatively better endowed for. In international trade, equilibrium is met through the mobility of goods, while in inter-regional trade the mobility of production factors plays the most important equilibrating role.

In this economic model, space is present only for its original heterogeneity, which is exogenously determined. There is no room for transport costs or for the costs of migration, and no advantages result from the agglomeration of firms, because economies of scale and external economies are ruled out. The predictions of the dominating model, i.e. the diffusion of economic activities and equilibrium in productivity levels and input rewards, rarely come true in reality, but according to Krugman (1991a,b) economic theory was not provided with the right tools for modelling the much more complex world that emerges when mobility meets a cost and production is carried out in conditions of increasing returns.

In fact, some non-mainstream economists such as Perroux (1955), Myrdal (1957), Hirschman (1958) and Kaldor (1970) have claimed that increasing returns and agglomeration economies are important determinants of trade and growth, but their arguments were not supported by an adequate analytical framework. It was only in the 1990s, when the toolbox of the economists had been enriched with models of the 'new industrial organization', the 'new trade theory' and the 'new growth theory' (Krugman 1998), that the costs of overcoming distance and increasing returns could be explicitly introduced in modelling international and inter-regional trade. It is at this point that a new genre of research emerged, namely the 'new economic geography'.

Even though different versions of the new economic geography model have been proposed and they are undergoing continuous evolution because of the short period of time that has elapsed since its first appearance, some interesting results, relevant to the European integration process, have already been achieved. In this approach an essential role is played by transport cost, which must be considered a very general category embracing not only the pure cost of transferring goods from one place to the other, but also trade taxes, costs of frontier formalities and different product standards, difficulty of communication and cultural differences (Krugman and Venables 1990). The reduction in transport cost that is associated with economic integration does not determine, however, a lone result because of the presence of increasing returns. In the simplest model with two regions and two sectors, which are manufacturing (operating under conditions of increasing returns and monopolistic competition) and agriculture (operating under conditions of constant returns to scale and perfect competition), different results are associated with different levels of transport costs. When transport costs are high, diffusion of manufacturing prevails, determined by the costs of transferring goods. When the level of transport costs is middling, concentration of manufacturing emerges as a result of the agglomeration economies that dominate transport costs. Finally, at low levels of transport costs diffusion again prevails owing to the congestion in the agglomeration centre, which results in the prices of production factors being higher than in the peripheral regions. This process is fuelled by a cumulative mechanism that runs between the home market of final products and/or intermediate inputs and the location choices of firms, so that firms move towards the centre because they find a larger market, but in this way they contribute to making the home market even larger. In these conditions the spatial effect of integration remains open-ended, depending essentially on the size of the reduction in transport cost and on the differential of input prices in central and peripheral locations.

The new economic geography model, according to this essential version, seems particularly suited to providing a sound theoretical framework in which to analyse the evolution of the centre/periphery dichotomy that characterizes the European case. Along these lines the essential task is to establish whether or not the reduction in transport cost has been large enough to determine the diffusion of footloose activities. Of course, the essential model may be enriched in many directions. One of the most interesting for the European case is that of the multiregional structure of the integrating economies. In this case, the results depend not only on the parameters but also on the geometry of the economy (Krugman 1998) and the model provides a justification for the 'market potential' function so frequently used in location studies (Harris 1954). At the end of the process, depending on the initial conditions, various centres of agglomeration may emerge and a third type of region may be identified between the centre and the periphery, the intermediate one, which may end up winning the game at the expense of both the central and peripheral regions.

The new economic geography model represents the theoretical framework in which the present chapter was conceived. Although the model has been formulated as a location model rather than as a growth/development model, it is possible to establish a link between the two approaches (Baldwin and Martin 2003) and interpret along those lines the evolution of regional income disparities at the European level, which constitutes the principal objective of the chapter. The analysis starts with the first phase of European integration in the late 1950s and follows the evolution of regional disparities in three consecutive phases, the entry of the UK, Ireland and Denmark in the 1970s, then Greece, Spain and Portugal in the 1980s and, finally, some central and eastern European countries (CEEC). The admission of Austria, Finland, Sweden and eastern Germany in the 1990s is not separately analysed because of their limited contribution to the level of European regional disparities (Terrasi 2002). In each phase, regional disparities are examined not only in the aggregate but also component by component. The comparison between two of these components, the disparities between countries and those between groups of regions, represents one of the focal points of the analysis. As Krugman and Venables (1990: 59) write 'Increasingly it makes sense to think of economic Europe as consisting not of a collection of internally homogeneous countries, but of a collection of regions, of varying degrees of peripherality from a centre located somewhere around Brussels'.

Regional inequalities during consecutive phases of European integration: 1960–97

Before starting the historical excursus of European regional inequalities, another important point must be clarified. In the new economic geography model, production technology and the phase of economic development of the integrating economies also play a part in determining the concentration of economic activities. In the simple model of two regions and two sectors originally proposed by Krugman (1991a), production technology is represented by a fixed cost in the production function, while the phase of development determines the shares of mobile (manufacturing) and immobile (agriculture) economic activities in the aggregate economy. Therefore, it is important to consider that during the long period of time that has elapsed since the beginning of the European integration process not only the space and the degree of integration, but also the technological paradigm and the relative position of the different sectors in the aggregate economy, have changed. In other words, structural change must also be considered as an important factor in the evolution of European regional disparities (Paci and Pigliaru 1997, 1999).

The beginning

To analyse regional disparities back in the 1950s, when the first six countries (EU-6) decided to move towards a common market, there is only one suitable source of information: the database collected by Molle and his associates on population, GDP in US dollars and employment in sixty-one regions of the European Community (Molle *et al.* 1980).

The Theil index[2] was calculated from these data by using an alternative decomposition: between-country/within-country versus between-macroregion/within-macroregion components. The macroregions were derived from the map of the economic potential that appears in the study by Clark *et al.* (1969) for EU-6 in 1960–64. On the basis of the values of economic potential, three macroregions were identified: central, intermediate and peripheral. The central macroregion embraces the three Benelux countries, four German regions and seven French regions. The periphery consists of twelve Italian regions and four French regions, while the remaining regions are considered intermediate. In 1970 the centre had a population share of 40 per cent, while both the periphery and the intermediate regions had a population share of 30 per cent. In Appendix 9.1 the elementary regions pertaining to each macroregion can be found, while in Table 9.1 the results of the calculations are reported for the only three years available: 1950, 1960, 1970.

Table 9.1 shows that (i) European regional disparities start to decrease between 1950 and 1960, but the decrease intensified between 1960 and 1970 in connection with the integration process; (ii) the disparities between countries and within countries absorb a similar share of total inequality, with the between-countries share increasing from 1960 to 1970; (iii) both between-country and within-country disparities decrease, mostly between 1960 and 1970, with disparities within countries decreasing more that those between countries; (iv) in 1970 the three macro-areas reach the same share of total disparity as the six countries, but their share substantially grows from 1950 to 1970; (v) both between-macro-area and within-macro-area disparities decrease, with within-macro-area disparities decreasing more than the between-macro-area disparities.

Table 9.2 provides some more interesting information about the components of regional disparities. Here we find the disaggregation of total and between-group inequality in labour productivity and employment rate inequalities.

Table 9.2 shows that productivity accounts for a much greater share of total inequality than does the employment rate, but, whereas the productivity share

Table 9.1 EU-6, Theil coefficient: total, between- and within-group, 1950–70

Year	*Total*	*Between-country*	*Within-country*	*Between-country/ total (%)*	*Between-macroregion*	*Within-macroregion*	*Between macroregion/ total (%)*
1950	0.0735	0.0387	0.0348	52.65	0.0327	0.0407	44.49
1960	0.0623	0.0323	0.0300	51.85	0.0321	0.0302	51.52
1970	0.0447	0.0246	0.0201	55.03	0.0246	0.0200	55.03

Source: processed by Molle *et al.* (1980).

Table 9.2 EU-6, Theil coefficient: productivity and employment rate components, 1950–70

Year	*Productivity*	*Employment rate*	*Productivity/total (%)*	*Productivity: between-country/ total (%)*	*Employment: between-country/ total (%)*	*Productivity: between-macroregion/ total (%)*	*Employment: between-macroregion/ total (%)*
1950	0.0660	0.0074	89.80	49.25	3.26	42.99	1.50
1960	0.0503	0.0116	80.74	40.77	10.91	46.87	4.65
1970	0.0346	0.0100	77.40	44.52	10.51	46.76	8.38

Source: processed by Molle *et al.* (1980).

decreases, the employment rate share increases. The same mechanism can be recognized at the country and at the macroregion levels, with the between-group employment rate shares growing. This result shows that in the catching-up process of the weakest regions, productivity plays the most important role, but at the same time there is evidence of difficulty in employing the labour force released from the low-productivity activities.

In terms of the new economic geography reasoning, we could argue that the reduction in the transport cost associated with the low cost of labour in peripheral locations is enough to determine a process of diffusion both at the country and at the macroregion level and that this process comes about through diffusion within countries as well as within macro-areas. At the same time, it should be noted that in the initial period of European integration a delimitation based on the centre/intermediate/periphery categories is useful in interpreting the process of spatial adjustment.

The first enlargement: the entry of the UK, Ireland and Denmark

Starting in 1975, regional disparities can be analysed using the Regio database collected by Eurostat for different levels of territorial units, called NUTS-1, -2 and -3 (Eurostat 1999). The following analysis is based on GVA in 1985 euros and population and employment data obtained from the Cambridge Econometrics dataset, which is a revised version of the Regio database (Cambridge Econometrics and Ereco 2001).

Tables 9.3 and 9.4 present values for the various Theil coefficients for the nine countries and seventy-six regions of the enlarged Economic Community (EU-9). Of course, the new data are not homogeneous with Molle's, and for this reason it is not possible to compare the values of the Theil indexes in Tables 9.3 and 9.4 with those calculated for EU-6 in Tables 9.1 and 9.2. Neither are the regions and macroregions comparable with those of the previous tables. Regions are now mostly NUTS-2, but in some cases NUTS-1 are adopted (Terrasi 2002). As for the macroregions, a more recent study on the economic potential at the European regional level has been used (Keeble *et al.* 1988). On this basis, four macroregions have been identified – central, intermediate, northern peripheral and southern peripheral – which in 1975 accounted for, respectively, 41, 43, 7 and 8 per cent of the total population. It seems appropriate to identify two separate peripheral macroregions, in order to take into account their different historical and cultural roots (Terrasi 2003). The precise delimitation of each macroregion can be found in Appendix 9.1.

Table 9.3 reports the three-year average of total, between- and within-group Theil coefficients for the lengthy period 1975–97. Although in the mid-1980s regional disparity again changed as a result of further enlargement, it is of interest first to examine what occurred at the EU-9 level during the entirety of this period before moving on to examine regional disparities in the new enlarged community.

Table 9.3 EU-9, Theil coefficient: total, between- and within-group, 1975–97

Period	*Total*	*Between-country*	*Within-country*	*Between-country/ total (%)*	*Between-macroregion*	*Within-macroregion*	*Between macroregion/ total (%)*
1975–77	0.0243	0.0087	0.0156	35.80	0.0134	0.0109	55.14
1980–82	0.0258	0.0091	0.0167	35.27	0.0118	0.0140	45.74
1985–87	0.0251	0.0080	0.0171	31.87	0.0115	0.0136	45.82
1991–93	0.0265	0.0086	0.0179	32.45	0.0114	0.0152	43.02
1995–97	0.0256	0.0051	0.0205	19.92	0.0115	0.0141	44.92

Source: processed by Cambridge Econometrics and Ereco (2001).

Table 9.4 EU-9, Theil coefficient: productivity and employment rate components, 1975–97

Period	*Productivity*	*Employment rate*	*Productivity/total (%)*	*Productivity: between-country/ total (%)*	*Employment: between-country/ total (%)*	*Productivity: between-macroregion/ total (%)*	*Employment: between-macroregion/ total (%)*
1975–77	0.0166	0.0076	68.31	22.82	12.94	44.86	9.88
1980–82	0.0177	0.0080	68.60	23.42	11.67	33.72	12.01
1985–87	0.0158	0.0093	62.95	16.77	15.22	32.27	13.55
1991–93	0.0173	0.0092	65.28	18.14	14.16	29.43	13.21
1995–97	0.0151	0.0105	58.98	3.16	16.80	26.17	18.36

Source: processed by Cambridge Econometrics and Ereco (2001).

According to Table 9.3, between-country disparity in the last three years accounts for a much lower share of total disparity than before, reaching a value of about 20 per cent. In contrast, between-macroregion disparity still accounts for a considerable share of total disparity (45–55 per cent).

Regarding the contributions of productivity and employment rate to total inequality, Table 9.4 shows that productivity was the predominant factor contributing to inequality throughout the study period although its share fell over time. This trend was a result of a fall in productivity inequality share at both the between-country and between-macroregion levels. In contrast, the proportion of total inequality contributed by employment inequality increased over the period as a result of increases both between countries and between macroregions, but especially the latter.

For the first period, 1975–84, which in fact corresponds to the first enlargement, a regression equation has been estimated, in which the various Theil coefficients are the dependent variables and time is the independent one. The results are reported in Table 9.5. It seems quite clear that divergence at the between-country level and convergence at the between-macroregion level have prevailed. At the same time, there is a process of divergence both within countries and within macro-areas. Generally, the analysis produces better results at the macro-area than at the country level.

How do these results match with the predictions of the new geography models? Surely, they are in line with the prediction that the centre/periphery dimension will prevail over the national one as integration goes on. The enlargement of the European space to include three northern countries makes it possible for the centre/periphery structure to emerge more clearly. But with respect to the preceding period, the diffusion among the macro-areas is accompanied by concentration within the macro-areas. This, again, is in accordance with the prediction of the new geography theory that the spatial structure is subject to a process of endogenous transformation due to integration, from which winners and losers will emerge.

It must also be taken into account that the period 1975–84 was one of structural change, in which the general economic situation was subject to a substantial turnabout and a new technological revolution was being prepared. This may have reinforced the role of the economies of agglomeration within the different macro-areas.

The second enlargement: the entry of Greece, Spain and Portugal

Starting in 1985, we find European regional inequalities in a completely different setting. Not only do three Mediterranean countries at a much lower level of development, Greece, Spain and Portugal, join the group, but the degree of integration intensifies with the adoption of the Single Market Programme.

Using the same database as above, Table 9.6 shows the usual Theil coefficients calculated for the resulting twelve countries (EU-12) and 101 regions from 1985 to 1997. The Theil indexes calculated for EU-9 at the beginning of the period are also reported in order to make the comparison with EU-12 easier. Four macro-

Table 9.5 EU-9, results of the regression equation IT=$a+bt+u$, 1975–85

Dependent variable	*Country*			*Macro-area*		
	b *sign*	*Student's* t[a]	R^2	b *sign*	*Student's* t[a]	R^2
IT_{total}	+	3.06**	0.54	+	3.06**	0.54
$IT_{between-}$	+	3.50**	0.60	–	–5.69***	0.80
$IT_{within-}$	+	1.75**	0.28	+	7.05***	0.86
$IT_{between-, productivity}$	+	2.72*	0.48	–	–6.79***	0.85
$IT_{between-, employment}$	–	–1.28	0.17	+	2.52*	0.44
$IT_{within-, productivity}$	+	1.7	0.28	+	5.80***	0.81
$IT_{within, employment}$	+	6.65***	0.84	–	–0.23	0.01

Note

a Significant at *0.05, **0.01, ***0.005.

regions are again identified through the economic potential calculated in Keeble *et al.* (1988). In 1985, 33 per cent of the total population lived in the central macroregion, compared with 36 per cent in the intermediate regions, 6 per cent in the northern periphery and 25 per cent in the southern periphery. As before the precise delimitation can be found in Appendix 9.1.

From Table 9.6 it is easy to evaluate the large increase in regional disparity that the new enlargement brought. It is evident that the between-country inequality accounted for a much larger share of the total, even though towards the end of the period the between-macroregion share reached a similar size.

The results of the productivity/employment rate decomposition are reported in Table 9.7 and confirm once more the role of productivity disparity.

The temporal behaviour of the various inequality coefficients can best be appreciated by looking at Table 9.8, in which the results of the same simple regression equation estimated above are reported. Regional convergence clearly emerges at the total, between-country and between-macro-area levels, while divergence dominates the within-country scene. At the within-macro-area level no clear tendency can be identified.

It seems reasonable to comment on these results along the following lines. Unlike before, the new enlargement involved some countries at a much lower level of development than the European average, which had to undertake a process of substantial structural change. In these conditions, national factors were more important than spatial ones in determining convergence. Nevertheless, there is clear evidence that the European centre/periphery structure is still relevant. The behaviour of both total and between-group inequality supports the hypothesis that the reduction in transport cost favoured a process of diffusion, but this was achieved at the expense of within-country disparity, whose productivity and employment rate components increase. Again, there is evidence that the process of integration feeds the endogenous change of the spatial structure at the country level.

Table 9.6 EU-9, EU-12, Theil coefficient: total, between- and within-group, 1985–97

Period	*Total*	*Between-country*	*Within-country*	*Between-country/ total (%)*	*Between-macroregion*	*Within-macroregion*	*Between macroregion/ total (%)*
EU-9							
1985–87	0.0251	0.0080	0.0171	31.87	0.0115	0.0136	45.82
EU-12							
1985–87	0.0681	0.0501	0.0180	73.57	0.0442	0.0240	64.90
1991–93	0.0638	0.0458	0.0180	71.79	0.0395	0.0243	61.91
1995–97	0.0610	0.0409	0.0201	67.05	0.0381	0.0229	62.46

Source: processed by Cambridge Econometrics and Ereco (2001).

Table 9.7 EU-12, Theil coefficient: productivity and employment rate components, 1985–97

Period	*Productivity*	*Employment rate*	*Productivity /total (%)*	*Productivity: between-country/ total (%)*	*Employment: between-country/ total (%)*	*Productivity: between-macroregion/ total (%)*	*Employment: between-macroregion/ total (%)*
EU-9							
1985–87	0.0158	0.0093	62.95	16.77	15.22	32.27	13.55
EU-12							
1985–87	0.0550	0.0131	80.76	62.79	11.30	55.80	27.02
1991–93	0.0524	0.0114	82.13	62.62	9.15	53.92	7.99
1995–97	0.0490	0.0120	80.33	57.87	9.18	54.59	7.87

Source: processed by Cambridge Econometrics and Ereco (2001).

Table 9.8 EU-12, results of the regression equation IT=$a+bt+u$, 1985–97

Dependent variable	*Country*			*Macro-area*		
	b *sign*	*Student's* t[a]	R^2	*b sign*	*Student's* t[a]	R^2
IT_{total}	–	–14.65***	0.95	–	–14.65***	0.95
$IT_{between-}$	–	–11.77***	0.93	–	–13.27***	0.94
$IT_{within-}$	+	3.55***	0.53	–	–1.73	0.21
$IT_{between-, productivity}$	–	–7.8***	0.85	–	–10.87***	0.91
$IT_{between-, employment}$	–	–8.72***	0.87	–	–6.25***	0.78
$IT_{within-, productivity}$	+	2.51*	0.36	–	–1.33	0.14
$IT_{within, employment}$	+	4.53***	0.65	+	0.75	0.01

Note
a Significant at *0.05, **0.01, ***0.005.

The change in regional inequalities after the new enlargement

Ten new members joined the EU in 2004, but for the purpose of analysing the change in regional inequalities, eight of them are particularly important: the Czech Republic, Estonia, Hungary, Lithuania, Latvia, Poland, Slovenia and Slovakia (EU-8). Thus, Cyprus and Malta are left out of the following analysis.

Basing the analysis of regional disparity on a homogeneous set of data becomes more difficult when the eight new entrants are added to the fifteen countries of the old EU (EU-15). Fortunately, Eurostat has recently made available a new stock of data, suitable to this purpose, in its Regio database. These data make it possible to analyse regional inequalities in terms of three variables: GVA, GDP in euros and GDP in purchasing power standards (PPS). Comparing regional GDP in PPS seems to be the best way to evaluate the relative welfare position of the regions pertaining to EU-23.[3] But at the same time GDP and GVA in euros are useful in evaluating the competitiveness of different regions in the international markets. Moreover, the new Regio dataset shows GVA in euros disaggregated in eight sectors, which is very useful information when the productivity components of regional disparity are considered. For this reason, in Tables 9.9 and 9.10 the usual Theil coefficients are reported for all three variables: GVA, GDP in PPS and GDP in euros.

The regional delimitation adopted is NUTS 1999 (Eurostat 1999) for EU-15, which makes it possible to identify 124 elementary regions corresponding generally to NUTS-2 and sometimes to NUTS-1 levels. For the acceding countries the statistical delimitation of Eurostat (2003) has been adopted, which gives a total of thirty-nine elementary regions. The macroregional dimension is still maintained, and for its identification a more recent study on the economic potential in the enlarged EU has been used (Schürmann and Talaat 2000). Five macroregions have been identified: central, northern, intermediate, southern peripheral and acceding countries. In 1999, which is the year selected for the analysis, the five macroregions accounted for, respectively, 29, 20, 17, 17 and 17 per cent of the total population. The precise delimitation can be found in Appendix 9.1.

Table 9.9 EU-8, EU-15, EU-23, Theil coefficient: total, between- and within-group; GVA, GDP PPS and GDP euros, 1999

GVA, GDP PPS, GDP euros	*Total*	*Between-country*	*Within-country*	*Between-country/ total (%)*	*Between-macroregion*	*Within-macroregion*	*Between-macroregion/ total (%)*
EU-8							
GVA	0.0585	0.0274	0.0311	46.84			
GDP PPS	0.1421	0.0304	0.1117	21.39			
GDP euros	0.0571	0.0260	0.0311	45.53			
EU-15							
GVA	0.0452	0.0210	0.0242	46.46	0.0239	0.0213	52.88
GDP PPS	0.0304	0.0059	0.0245	19.41	0.0092	0.0212	30.26
GDP euros	0.0461	0.0218	0.0243	47.29	0.0258	0.0203	55.97
EU-23							
GVA	0.1801	0.1548	0.0253	85.95	0.1527	0.0274	84.79
GDP PPS	0.0930	0.0541	0.0389	58.17	0.0518	0.0412	55.70
GDP euros	0.1784	0.1530	0.0254	85.76	0.1520	0.0264	85.20

Source: processed by Eurostat Regio (2003).

Table 9.10 EU-8, EU-15, EU-23, Theil coefficient: productivity and employment rate components, GVA, 1999

EU	*Productivity*	*Employment rate*	*Productivity/total (%)*	*Productivity: between-country/ total (%)*	*Employment: between-country/ total (%)*	*Productivity: between-macroregion/total (%)*	*Employment: between-macroregion/total (%)*
EU-8	0.0508	0.0077	86.84	42.90	3.93		
EU-15	0.0336	0.0113	74.83	36.75	9.80	46.10	7.13
EU-23	0.1688	0.0111	93.83	83.55	2.44	83.21	1.67

Source: processed by Eurostat Regio (2003).

The indexes of disparity for the year 1999 in EU-8, EU-15 and EU-23 are reported in Table 9.9. It can be seen that, for EU-8, the total index of disparity is higher in PPS than in euros. This behaviour can be explained by the difference in price levels among acceding countries, indicating that the poorer countries have a higher price level. The opposite happens for the EU-15 where the index in PPS is lower than in euros, denoting that in these cases the poorer countries have a lower price index. Regarding the comparison in PPS, it must be pointed out that PPS is determined for a standard basket of goods and services, 'selected to represent the whole range of goods and services, and to be representative of consumption patterns in various countries' (Eurostat 2003: 46). This seems quite arbitrary when countries are very different in terms of average income. Moreover, 'no conversion rates at regional levels are available', so, for example, 'the same conversion factor is used for northern and southern Italy or for western and eastern Germany' (Eurostat 2003: 46). For all these reasons the comparison in terms of GVA and GDP in euros must be considered more significant (Mele 2002).

The essence of the problem of regional disparity after the most recent enlargement is shown in Table 9.9 by the change in the total Theil coefficient, which increases almost fourfold in terms of GVA and GDP in euros, and threefold in terms of GDP in PPS. This is a much greater increase than occurred following the entry of Greece, Spain and Portugal in 1985–87, when the index in terms of GVA increased 2.7 times compared with that of the EU-9 (Table 9.6).

The share of disparity accounted for by between- and within-group inequality also changed substantially, the between-country share jumping from 47.29 to 85.76 and the between-macroregion share from 55.97 to 85.20. Therefore, even though the country share increased considerably, the macroregional dimension remains a relevant component of the regional inequality problem. In comparison with the entry of Greece, Spain and Portugal, when the between-country and between-macroregion shares were respectively 73.57 and 64.90 per cent (Table 9.6), the weight of the two components increased.

Table 9.10 shows the results obtained for the disaggregation of total inequality into its productivity and employment rate components. Productivity accounts for practically the whole inequality, rising to 94 compared with 75 per cent for the EU-15. The shares of the productivity index accounted for by between-country and between-macroregion components are 83.55 and 83.21 per cent respectively. In Table 9.7 the corresponding shares after the entry of Greece, Spain and Portugal were 80 per cent for total productivity and 58 and 55 per cent for between-country and between-macroregion components.

All the above results indicate that, as other studies have already pointed out (Martín *et al.* 2001, Boldrin and Canova 2003), there are many similarities between the enlargement of the mid-1980s and the recent enlargement, but at the same time the change appears to be greater in the latter case and supports the hypothesis that its spatial effects may be even stronger. What might be the expected results of these effects? According to the new economic geography model, the relevant point concerns the size of the reduction in transport cost compared with the economies of agglomeration and the price of factor inputs. Many data support the hypothesis that diffusion at the country and at the macroregion level will again prevail.

As explained beforehand, transport cost must be understood in an extensive way, embracing cultural and communication obstacles in addition to pure mobility costs. In the case of the new entrants, it has already been proposed that, as Europe regains its full dimension, old historical and cultural links can be fully rediscovered and renewed (Terrasi 2003). The best example of this recomposition of 'old acquaintances' is the Scandinavian–Baltic region, which is going to become a highly integrated and dynamic area of the new EU (Peschel 1992, 1998). In the same way, another strong, integrated region may emerge around Austria, and it is worth noting that Slovenia in 2000 had already reached a per capita GDP in PPS of 67 per cent of the EU-15 average, which is the same as Greece and slightly below Portugal's 70 per cent (Stapel 2002).

At the same time the experience of past enlargements suggests that a growth of within-country and within-macroregion disparities must be expected. Not only is there clear evidence of a trade-off between convergence at the macro scale and divergence at the micro scale during past European integration processes, but the size of the share of between-group inequality in the case of the new enlargement makes it easy to predict that the trade-off will be particularly high.

A final point must be made regarding the southern peripheral regions of the EU-15. Although their problems appear at present to be less serious than those of the new entrants, they still exist and may become even worse if the convergence process of these regions is interrupted by the recent enlargement. In fact, according to the predictions of the new economic geography, the change in the geometry of the European space could substantially alter the conditions regarding their potential for attraction and convergence.

The determinants of regional productivity inequalities

Up to this point the analysis of European regional inequalities has been carried out through a concise index of measurement with the aim of showing that the macroregional dimension plays a comparable role to the country one. At the same time it has been shown that European regional disparities are mostly due to differences in productivity, although the employment rate becomes increasingly important during the process of integration.

The final objective of this chapter is to delve deeply into the productivity component of regional disparity and the macroregional dimension itself. For this purpose, a disaggregated analysis of productivity inequalities will be developed by making use of the sectoral data of GVA given in the new Regio dataset. However, in so doing, the UK regions have been eliminated since they are not present in the database, so the analysis continues for EU-14 rather than EU-15 and for EU-22 rather than EU-23. Eight sectors in total are considered in the Regio dataset, but two of them, 'mining and quarrying' and 'electricity, gas and water supply', have been aggregated for the purpose of the following analysis, leaving a total of seven sectors. The complete classification used is given in Appendix 9.3.

In order to understand what underlies productivity differences between regions, it is usually considered important to identify the role played by two different kinds of factors: (i) the industry mix of regions, where high- and low-productivity sectors are present with different weights and (ii) the different endowment of competitive factors that causes both high- and low-productivity sectors to be present with lower productivity in some regions and with higher productivity in others. Thus, while the first factor captures the contribution of the production structure of the regions, the second one shows their general competitiveness.

From the contribution of Lederbur and Moomaw (1983) until Esteban's recent one (2000), shift-and-share analysis was considered a powerful tool in separating the above-mentioned effects. Esteban (2000) applied this method to different sets of European regional data and was able to conclude that 'region-specific productivity differentials account for virtually all interregional differences in aggregate productivity per worker' (Esteban 2000: 362).

This study parts with Esteban's contribution as regards both the dataset used and the kind of decomposition of regional productivity adopted. It has already been pointed out that a new Regio dataset is used, and for the method of decomposition we have reformulated the original decomposition suggested by Lederbur and Moomaw (1983) in order to isolate the role played by the macroregions and have come up with the following formula:

$$x_r - \bar{x} = \sum_i p_r^i \left(x_m^i - \bar{x}_m\right) + \sum_i p_r^i \left(x_r^i - x_m^i\right) + \sum_i p_m^i \left(x^i - \bar{x}\right) + \sum_i p_m^i \left(x_m^i - x^i\right) \tag{9.1}$$

where x_r, $\bar{x}$ and $\bar{x}_m$ are total labour productivities in region *r*, in Europe and in macroregion *m;* x^i_m, x^i and x^i_r are labour productivities of sector *i* in macroregion *m*, in Europe and in region *r*; and p^i_m and p^i_r are the shares of total employment in sector *i* in macroregion *m* and region *r.* According to equation (9.1), in each region the difference in productivity compared with the European average can be decomposed into four parts: the structural component (α) of the difference in productivity between the region and the macro-area; the competitive component (δ) of the difference in productivity between the region and the macro-area; the structural component of the productivity difference between the macro-area and the European average (γ); and the competitive component (π) of the productivity difference between the macro-area and the European average. In order to fully appreciate the contribution of the four components, α, δ, γ, π, introduced in equation (9.1) to the total variance of productivity between the regions considered, we have also come up with the following formula:

$$\begin{aligned} \mathrm{var}(x_r) = {} & \mathrm{var}(\alpha) + \mathrm{var}(\delta) + \mathrm{var}(\gamma) + \mathrm{var}(\pi) + \\ & 2[\mathrm{cov}(\alpha,\delta) + \mathrm{cov}(\alpha,\gamma) + \mathrm{cov}(\alpha,\pi) + \\ & \mathrm{cov}(\delta,\gamma) + \mathrm{cov}(\delta,\pi) + \mathrm{cov}(\gamma,\pi)] \end{aligned} \tag{9.2}$$

where var = variance and cov = covariance.

In this way it is possible to evaluate the share of the variance of each component in the total variance of regional productivity. A high share for the variance of the structural component γ and/or of the competitive component π will indicate that the delimitation adopted is able to capture substantial productivity differences between macro-areas.

Equations (9.1) and (9.2) were applied to two groups of regions: EU-14 and EU-22 in 1999. In this way it was possible to evaluate the contribution of each component before and after the new enlargement. The results of the analysis are reported in Tables 9.11 and 9.12.

In Table 9.11 the structural (γ) and the differential components (π) for the macro-areas are reported. The first column of the table shows that in the EU-14 the central regions have the highest level of productivity, but the northern and the intermediate regions also lie well above the European average. The region that is left behind is the southern peripheral region, with 70 per cent of the European average. The next two columns of Table 9.11 show that the competitive component accounts for the majority of the difference, while the last column, in which the structural component has been eliminated, clearly demonstrates the weakness of the southern regions and the strength of the northern ones. It seems reasonable to conclude that at the EU-14 level there is only one real economic periphery: the south. The second part of Table 9.11 shows the effect of enlargement to EU-22. The competitive component remains dominant, but productivity in the southern regions now compares favourably with that of the acceding countries, which is approximately 30 per cent of the European average net of the structural component.

The greater significance of the macrospatial dimension after the new enlargement is evident in Table 9.12, where the share of the total variance covered by π amounts to 32 per cent for EU-14 and to 67 per cent for EU-22. Column 2 of the same table shows that at the EU-14 level a high share of the variance is accounted for by inequalities within the central and the southern peripheral regions. These results shed much light on the likely effects of the most recent European enlargement and lead to a fundamental question: will it be possible to reconcile the needs of the old economic periphery and the new economic periphery that emerges from the new phase of the integration process?

Conclusions

The previous analysis reveals that enlargement has both positive and negative effects on European regional inequalities, and provides an awareness of the enormous change to be expected in the next few years. On the positive side, there has been a general tendency towards diffusion and convergence, except during the period 1975–84, which was characterized by great economic instability and structural change. On the negative side, convergence on a macro-territorial scale is often accompanied by divergence on a micro scale, either within countries or within large regions. Thus, we cannot agree with Boldrin and Canova's (2001: 211) conclusion that '... neither convergence nor divergence is taking place within

Table 9.11 EU-14, EU-22, disaggregation of productivity differences from the European average by macroregion, 1999

		Components		
Macroregions	*Productivity (%)*	*Structural* (γ)	*Competitive* (π)	*Productivity standardized by industrial structure*
EU-14				
Central	110.31	4.07	6.24	106.24
Intermediate	104.97	–0.49	5.46	105.46
Northern	107.10	–2.63	9.72	109.72
Southern peripheral	70.43	–6.55	–23.02	76.98
Average	*100.00*	*0.00*	*0.00*	*100.00*
Standard deviation between macroregions	*15.74*	*4.05*	*12.17*	*12.17*
Total standard deviation	*21.84*			
EU-22				
Central	129.42	6.70	22.72	122.72
Intermediate	123.15	1.37	21.77	121.77
Northern	125.64	–0.61	26.26	126.26
Southern peripheral	82.62	–5.82	–11.55	88.45
Acceding countries	22.88	–8.76	–68.36	31.64
Average	*100.00*	*0.00*	*0.00*	*100.00*
Standard deviation between macroregions	*40.17*	*5.98*	*34.85*	*34.85*
Total standard deviation	*42.66*			

Source: processed by Eurostat Regio (2003).

Table 9.12 EU-14, EU-22, shares of total productivity variance by component and macroregion, 1999

Macroregion	*Var.(α)/var. tot. (%)*	*Var.(δ)/var. tot. (%)*	*Var.(γ)/var. tot. (%)*	*Var.(π)/var. tot. (%)*
EU-14				
Central	2.73	19.73		
Intermediate	0.79	5.47		
Northern	0.47	1.66		
Southern peripheral	1.00	8.94		
Total	*4.99*	*35.80*	*3.74*	*32.18*
EU-22				
Central	0.80	5.70		
Intermediate	0.24	1.63		
Northern	0.15	0.49		
Southern peripheral	0.29	2.63		
Acceding countries	0.08	0.37		
Total	*1.56*	*10.82*	*2.01*	*67.43*

Source: processed by Eurostat Regio (2003).

EU. Exception made for a couple of miracles and a few disasters, more regions are growing at a fairly uniform rate irrespective of their initial conditions'. Although these authors insist on the importance of territorial delimitation when analysing regional convergence, they seem to underestimate the centre/periphery dimension that is present in the European space.

However, the most interesting question is the extent to which past experience can be used to predict the effects of the recent enlargement. The exceptionally large increase in regional inequalities that has resulted from the entry of the acceding countries, and particularly the increase in inequality attributable to between-country differences, suggests that a big trade-off will take place between the macro- and the micro-territorial scales. According to the new economic geography model, if, as is likely, concentration at the micro scale prevails, an endogenous process of transformation of the spatial structure will start, and will fuel future regional disparities. Some of the 'disasters' to which Boldrin and Canova refer, such as southern Italy, could be interpreted exactly as the results of this process (Faini 1983). The main message here is to put a limit to this process of concentration at the micro scale and to sustain the formation of alternative poles of development in the disadvantaged regions (Braunerhjelm *et al.* 2000).

Another crucial point regards the possibility that the old European periphery, i.e. the southern regions, will bear most of the burden of the recent enlargement. Their weakness appears to be substantially reduced compared with the new peripheral regions, but their competitiveness factors may be strongly affected by the new entrants. There is a danger that the shift of the European centre to the east and the revival of historical and cultural links between some old and new members will isolate the southern peripheral regions. The present phase of international development, in which globalization and knowledge-intensive technologies prevail, could further favour the new entrants because of their higher educational attainment in comparison with southern regions.

All this suggests that European regional policy should not be dismissed, as Boldrin and Canova (2003) seem to propose, but rather should be completely reformulated, as the same authors maintain, in accordance with the new environment in which regional inequalities will develop in the future.

Since the first reform of structural funds, European regional policy has been guided by some general strategies that have been considered valid for all types of regions, with the consequence that regions that were not able to adapt to these strategies, often the weakest ones, have been cut off from the policy. In addition, a pedantic account of the level of development of different regions has determined their eligibility for different objectives, which frankly appears incorrect in statistical terms, due to the difficulty of evaluating the precise level of development, and unsatisfactory in political terms because of the absence of a broad-minded spatial strategy. Finally, the goal of promoting participation from the bottom up, according to the principle of subsidiarity, has on the one hand contributed to dispersing financial intervention and, on the other hand, often reinforced the national government as the only available interlocutor between Europe and the periphery.

What could be suggested on the basis of these remarks is that European regional policy should be reformulated by explicitly taking into account the macrospatial structure that is present in the European space and by envisaging differentiated strategies for different macroregions. In particular, the old and new problems of the southern regions should not be underestimated. These regions appear particularly weak in terms of the so-called C-factors, i.e. competence, culture, communication and creativity (Peschel 1998). At the same time they have not been able, so far, to achieve a cooperative approach to their development problems and have behaved mostly according to a competitive zero-sum game. An explicit strategy for the southern regions that takes into account these characteristics is to be preferred to the continuation of the one-for-all strategy. After all, what we are calling for is a European regional policy aimed at exploiting resources specific to the different kinds of regions, which may become either the strength or the weakness of the new Europe.

Appendix 9.1: Delimitation of macroregions

Table 9A.1 EU-6

Macroregion	*Regions*
Central	1601, 1602, 1603, 19, 1501, 1502, 1503, 1504, 112, 1132, 1133, 1141, 1411, 1412, 1413, 1417, 142, 1431, 1432
Intermediate	1111, 1112, 1113, 1114, 1131, 1142, 115, 1414, 1415, 1416, 1433, 1441, 1442, 1443, 1451, 1452, 1453, 1461, 1462, 1471, 1472, 1473, 1311, 1312, 1313, 1314, 1321, 1322, 1323, 1324
Peripheral	1451, 1452, 1471, 1473, 1331, 1332, 1333, 1334, 1341, 1342, 1343, 1344, 1345, 1346, 1347, 1348

Source: processed from Molle *et al.* (1980).

Table 9A.2 EU-9

Macroregion	*NUTS-1/2 regions*
Central	BE1, BE2, BE3, NL3, NL4, DE1, DE3, DE5, DE6, DE7, DE9, DEA, DEB, DEC, FR1, FR3, FR42, UK5, UK7
Intermediate	DK01, DK02, DK03, DE2, DEF, FR21, FR22, FR23, FR24, FR25, FR26, FR41, FR43, FR51, FR52, FR71, FR72, FR82, IT11, IT12, IT13, IT2, IT31, IT32, IT4, IT51, IT52, IT53, IT6, LU, NL1, NL2, UK1, UK2, UK3, UK4, UK6, UK8, UK9
Northern peripheral	IE, UKA, UKB, FR53, FR61, FR62, FR63, FR81
Southern peripheral	FR83, IT33, IT71, IT72, IT8, IT91, IT92, IT93, ITA, ITB

Source: processed from Keeble *et al.* (1988).

Table 9A.3 EU-12

Macroregion	*NUTS-1/2 regions*
Central	BE1, BE2, BE3, NL3, NL4, DE1, DE3, DE5, DE6, DE7, DE9, DEA, DEB, DEC, FR1, FR3, FR42, UK5, UK7
Intermediate	DK01, DK02, DK03, DE2, DEF, FR21, FR22, FR23, FR24, FR25, FR26, FR41, FR43, FR51, FR52, FR71, FR72, FR82, IT11, IT12, IT13, IT2, IT31, IT32, IT4, IT51, IT52, IT53, IT6, LU, NL1, NL2, UK1, UK2, UK3, UK4, UK6, UK8, UK9
Northern peripheral	IE, UKA, UKB, FR53, FR61, FR62, FR63, FR81
Southern peripheral	FR83, IT33, IT71, IT72, IT8, IT91, IT92, IT93, ITA, ITB, GR1, GR2, GR3, GR4, ES11, ES12, ES13, ES21, ES22, ES23, ES24, ES3, ES41, ES42, ES43, ES51, ES52, ES53, ES61, ES62, PT11, PT12, PT13, PT14, PT15

Source: processed from Keeble *et al.* (1988).

Table 9A.4 EU-23

Macroregion	*NUTS-1/2 regions*
Central	BE1, BE2, BE3, DE1, DE2, DE3, DE4, DE5, DE6, DE7, DE9, DEA, DEB, DEC, DED, DEE. DEG, FR1, FR21, FR22, FR24, FR26, FR3, FR41, FR42, FR43, LU, NL1-NL11, NL2, NL3, NL4
Intermediate	FR23, FR25, FR51, FR52, FR53, FR61, FR62, FR63, FR71, FR72, FR81, FR82, IT11, IT12, IT13, IT2, IT31, IT32, IT33, IT4, IT51, IT52, IT53, IT6, IT71, IT72, AT1, AT2, AT3
Northern	FI13, FI14, FI15, FI16, FI17, FI2, SE01, SE02, SE04, SE06, SE07, SE08, SE09, SE0A, DK, DE8, DEF, UKC, UKD, UKE, UKF, UKG, UKH, UKI, UKJ, UKK, UKL, UKM2+UKM3, UKM1+UKM4, UKN, IE01, IE02
Southern peripheral	FR83, IT8, IT91, IT92, IT93, ITA, ITB, GR1, GR2, GR3, GR4, ES11, ES12, ES13, ES21, ES22, ES23, ES24, ES3, ES41, ES42, ES43, ES51, ES52, ES53, ES61, ES62, PT11, PT12, PT13, PT14, PT15
Acceding countries	CZ01, CZ02, CZ03, CZ04, CZ05, CZ06, CZ07, CZ08, EE, HU01, HU02, HU03, HO04, HU05, HU06, HU07, LT, LV, PL01, PL02, PL03, PL04, PL05, PL06, PL07, PL08, PL09, PL0A, PL0B, PL0C, PL0D, PL0E, PL0F, PL0G, SI, SK01, SK02, SK03, SK04

Source: processed from Schürmann and Talaat (2000).

Appendix 9.2: Theil index

Calculation of Theil index

The Theil index was calculated according to the following formula:

$$T = \sum_r y_r \log(y_r / x_r)$$

where T is total inequality among regions and y_r and x_r are regional shares of European population and GVA (or GDP) respectively. A dual form also exists, in which the roles of population share and GVA shares are interchanged, but in our case it seems more appropriate to weight the contribution of each region to inequality by its demographic rather than by its economic strength.

Decomposition of Theil index into between-group and within-group components

The following formulas were calculated:

$$T = T_{\text{bc}} + T_{\text{wc}}$$

$$T_{\text{bc}} = \sum_c Y_c \log(Y_c / X_c)$$

$$T_{\text{wc}} = \sum_c Y_c \left[\sum_r \left(\frac{y_r}{Y_c} \right) \log \left(\frac{y_r / Y_c}{x_r / X_c} \right) \right]$$

where T is total inequality, T_{bc} is between-group inequality, T_{wc} is within-group inequality, y_r and x_r are regional shares of European population and GVA (or GDP) respectively, and Y_c and X_c are the same shares for groups of regions.

Decomposition of Theil index into productivity and employment rate components

The following formulas apply:

$$T = T_{\text{pr}} + T_{\text{emp}}$$

$$T_{\text{pr}} = \sum_r y_r \log(n_r / x_r)$$

$$T_{\text{emp}} = \sum_r y_r \log(y_r / n_r)$$

where T is total inequality, T_{pr} is the share of total inequality due to regional differences in labour productivity, T_{emp} is the share due to regional differences in employment rate (i.e. ratio of employed to resident population) and y_r, n_r and x_r are the shares of European population, employment and GVA (or GDP) of region r.

Appendix 9.3: Sector definitions

1 Agriculture, hunting, forestry and fishing.
2 Mining and quarrying; electricity, gas and water supply.
3 Manufacturing.
4 Construction.
5 Wholesale and retail trade, repair of motor vehicles, motorcycles and personal and household goods; hotels and restaurants; transport, storage and communication.
6 Financial intermediation; real estate, renting and business activities.
7 Public administration and defence, compulsory social security; education; health and social work; other community, social and personal service activities; private households with employed persons.

Notes

1 Do you know the land where lemon trees bloom, in the darkness of the lives the golden oranges burn, a light wind blows from the blue sky, the myrtle stands still and the laurel high?
2 The Theil index is considered the most suitable measurement of spatial inequality (Walsh and O'Kelly 1979, Terrasi 2002, Brülhart and Traeger 2003). The various formulas used in this chapter can be found in Appendix 9.2.
3 In the preceding cases taken into consideration, the evaluation of GDP in PPS was considered less relevant, both because countries have gradually become an integrated monetary area and because PPS are estimated by Eurostat for countries but not for regions, which are actually the areas in which the differences in purchasing power are most relevant.

References

Baldwin, R. and Martin, P. (2003) 'Agglomeration and regional growth', *CEPR Discussion Paper Series* no. 3960, London: CEPR.

Boldrin, M. and Canova, F. (2001) 'Inequality and convergence: reconsidering European regional policies', *Economic Policy*, 32: 207–53.

Boldrin, M. and Canova, F. (2003) 'Regional policies and EU enlargement', in Funck, B. and Pizzati, L. (eds.) *European Integration, Regional Policy, and Growth*, Washington, DC: The World Bank.

Braunerhjelm, P., Faini, R., Norman, V., Ruane, F. and Seabright, P. (2000) *Integration and the Regions of Europe: How the Right Policies Can Prevent Polarization*, London: CEPR.

Brühlhart, M. and Traeger, R. (2003) 'An account of geographic concentration patterns in Europe', paper presented at the 43rd ERSA European Congress, Jyväskylä, August 2003.

Cambridge Econometrics and Ereco (2001) *European Regional Data*, Cambridge: Cambridge Econometrics.

CEE (1961) *Documents de la conférence sur les économies régionales*, Vol. II, Brussels: Services des Publications des Communautés Européennes.

Clark, C., Wilson, F. and Bradley, J. (1969) 'Industrial location and economic potential in Western Europe', *Regional Studies*, 3: 197–212.

Copus, A. (1999) 'A new peripherality index for the NUTS III regions of the European Union', ERDF/FEDER Study 98/00/27/130, European Commission, Directorate General XVI.A.4.

Esteban, J. (2000) 'Regional convergence in Europe and the industry mix: a shift-share analysis', *Regional Science and Urban Economics*, 30: 352–64.

European Commission (2003) *Second Progress Report on Economic and Social Cohesion*, COM (2003) 34 final.

Eurostat (1999) *Regions: Nomenclature of Territorial Units for Statistics*, Luxembourg: Office for the Official Publications of the European Communities.

Eurostat (2003) *Regions: Statistical Yearbook 2003*, Luxembourg: Office for the Official Publications of the European Communities.

Faini, R. (1983) 'Cumulative process of deindustrialization in an open region: the case of Southern Italy, 1951–1973', *Journal of Development Economics*, 12: 277–301.

Harris, C.D. (1954) 'The market as a factor in the localization of production', *Annals of the Association of American Geographers*, 44: 315–48.

Hirschman, A. (1958) *The Strategy of Economic Development*, New Haven, CT: Yale University Press.

Kaldor, N. (1970) 'The case for regional policy', *Scottish Journal of Political Economy*, 18: 337–48.

Keeble, D., Owens, P.L. and Thompson, C. (1982) 'Regional accessibility and economic potential in the European Community', *Regional Studies*, 16: 419–31.

Keeble, D., Offord, J. and Walker, S. (1988) *Peripheral Regions in a Community of Twelve Member States*, Luxembourg: Office for the Official Publications of the European Communities.

Krugman, P. (1991a) *Geography and Trade*, Cambridge, MA: MIT Press.

Krugman, P. (1991b) 'Increasing returns and economic geography', *Journal of Political Economy*, 99: 483–99.

Krugman, P. (1998) 'What's new about the new economic geography?', *Oxford Review of Economic Policy*, 14: 7–17.

Krugman, P. and Venables, A.J. (1990) 'Integration and competitiveness of peripheral industry', in Bliss, C. and Braga de Macedo, J. (eds.) *Unity with Diversity in the European Community*, Cambridge: Cambridge University Press.

Lederbur, L.C. and Moomaw, R.L. (1983) 'A shift-share analysis of regional labor productivity in manufacturing', *Growth and Change*, 14: 2–9.

Martín, C., Velázquez, F.J. and Funck, B. (2001) 'European integration and income convergence: lessons for Central and Eastern European Countries', *World Bank Technical Papers* no. 514, Washington, DC: World Bank.

Mele, G. (2002) 'Not only EU enlargement: the need of changing the community regional policy', *Rivista di Politica Economica*, 2002: 283–320.

Molle, W., van Holst, B. and Smit, H. (1980) *Regional Disparity and Economic Development in the European Community*, Westmead: Saxon House.

Myrdal, G. (1957) *Economic Theory and Underdeveloped Regions*, London: Macmillan.

Paci, R. and Pigliaru, F. (1997) 'Structural change and convergence: an Italian regional perspective', *Structural Change and Economic Dynamics*, 8: 297–318.

Paci, R. and Pigliaru, F. (1999) 'European regional growth: do sectors matter?', in Adams, J. and Pigliaru, F. (eds.) *Economic Growth and Change, National and Regional Patterns of Convergence and Divergence*, Cheltenham: Edward Elgar.

Perroux, F. (1955) 'Note sur la notion de pôle de croissance', *Economie Appliquée*, 8D: 307–20.

Peschel, K. (1992) 'European integration and regional development in Northern Europe', *Regional Studies,* 26: 387–97.

Peschel, K. (1998) 'Perspectives of regional development around the Baltic Sea', *The Annals of Regional Science*, 32: 299–320.

Schürmann, C. and Talaat, A. (2000) *Towards a European Peripherality Index*, Dortmund: University of Dortmund, Institut für Raumplanung.

Stapel, S. (2002) 'Purchasing power parities and related economic indicators for EU, acceding and candidate countries', *Statistics in Focus*, Theme 2–56, Eurostat.

Terrasi, M. (2002) 'National and spatial factors in EU regional convergence', in Cuadrado-Roura, J.R. and Parellada, M. (eds.) *Regional Convergence in the European Union*, Berlin: Springer-Verlag.

Terrasi, M. (2003) 'Le componenti territoriali dello sviluppo nell'Unione Europea alle soglie del nuovo allargamento', in CAPPEDEM-IDIM, Université de Corse, *Le développement intégré en Méditerranée*, Corte: Éditions Alain Piazzola.

Walsh, J.A. and O'Kelly, M.E. (1979) 'An information theoretic approach to measurement of spatial inequality', *Economic and Sociological Review*, 4: 267–86.

Index

For Product Safety Concerns and Information please contact our EU representative GPSR@taylorandfrancis.com
Taylor & Francis Verlag GmbH, Kaufingerstraße 24, 80331 München, Germany

www.ingramcontent.com/pod-product-compliance
Lightning Source LLC
LaVergne TN
LVHW011122300926
849160LV00008B/471

* 9 7 8 0 4 1 5 6 4 6 4 8 2 *